Praise for *Will There Be Faith?*

"Can we, will we, see to it that Christian faith flourishes? Thomas Groome answers with a resounding yes! Alert to the challenges and the gifts of this moment in the life of the Church and the wider world, Groome offers a persuasive vision of how to pass on the Christian faith in a way that informs, forms, and transforms persons, communities, and societies."

—Roger Cardinal Mahony, Archbishop Emeritus of
Los Angeles

"In showing how to bring life to faith and faith to life, Groome presents a learned and practical synthesis of the basic elements of Christian religious education for today and the future. He skillfully combines biblical learning, solid theology, concern for justice, official Catholic documentation, social-science insights, and delightful wit and wisdom to develop a powerful vision of holistic religious education."

—Daniel J. Harrington, SJ, professor of New Testament,
Boston College School of Theology and Ministry

"Quintessential Thomas Groome, this new book is a plainspoken, story-saturated, practical guide to Groome's 'life to Faith to life' approach to Christian religious education. In these pages, Groome shares insights he has developed over thirty-five years, distilled into the most fundamental elements. He engages with biblical narratives, educational theory, and Roman Catholic teaching to anchor his ideas, and he presents them in his own, most engaging, lecture style—spinning stories and weaving words. The book will be valuable to teachers, parents, and learners who seek to be faithful disciples in a world filled with distractions."

—Mary Elizabeth Moore, dean, Boston University School of
Theology, and author of *Teaching as a Sacramental Act*

"Groome, one of the country's leading Catholic theologians and writers, has a unique ability to make the complicated seem simple; the abstract seem concrete; and the difficult seem easy. His terrific new book is an absolutely superb resource for all parents, teachers, and community leaders who seek to pass on the Catholic faith. In chapters that are by turns provocative, inviting, challenging, inspiring, and, above all, real, Groome helps all of us understand how best to teach the lessons taught by the great Teacher, Jesus of Nazareth."

—James Martin, SJ, author of *The Jesuit Guide to (Almost) Everything*

"Never before in Western civilization has religious identity seemed so fragile and yet, for many of us, so necessary. For four decades Groome has been a wise and perceptive guide in helping parents, religious educators, and church leadership cultivate and hand on a religious faith that can sustain today's followers of Jesus. His latest book, *Will There Be Faith?*, is the culmination of a lifetime of experience, reflection, and scholarship. In this work, Groome offers a remarkably balanced and hopeful account of the lifelong process of handing on the faith in parishes, intentional Christian communities, schools, and Christian households. He is one of the American Catholic church's greatest treasures."

—Richard R. Gaillardetz, McCarthy Professor of Catholic Systematic Theology, Boston College

"Thomas Groome is clearly the leading religious educator today. His new book, *Will There Be Faith?*, may be his most important. I recommend it highly."

—Richard McBrien, professor of theology, University of Notre Dame

WILL THERE BE FAITH?

WILL THERE BE FAITH?

A New Vision for Educating and Growing Disciples

Thomas H. Groome

HarperOne
An Imprint of HarperCollinsPublishers

HarperOne

WILL THERE BE FAITH?: *A New Vision for Educating and Growing Disciples.* Copyright © 2011 by Thomas H. Groome. All rights reserved. Printed in the United States of America. No part of this book may be used or reproduced in any manner whatsoever without written permission except in the case of brief quotations embodied in critical articles and reviews. For information address HarperCollins Publishers, 10 East 53rd Street, New York, NY 10022.

HarperCollins books may be purchased for educational, business, or sales promotional use. For information please write: Special Markets Department, HarperCollins Publishers, 10 East 53rd Street, New York, NY 10022.

HarperCollins website: http://www.harpercollins.com

HarperCollins®, 👑®, and HarperOne™ are trademarks of HarperCollins Publishers

FIRST EDITION

Library of Congress Cataloging-in-Publication Data
    Groome, Thomas H.
        Will there be faith? / Thomas H. Groome. — 1st ed.
            p.   cm.
    ISBN 978–0–06–203728–2
        1. Christian life—Catholic authors. I. Title.
    BX2350.3.G755 2011
    248.4'82—dc22   2010051152

11 12 13 14 15   RRD(H)   10 9 8 7 6 5 4 3 2 1

For Colleen and Teddy,
my "domestic church"

CONTENTS

WILL THERE BE FAITH?

Will There Be Faith?

So Much Depends on How We Share It

Toward the end of Jesus's public ministry, we hear him wonder, "When the Son of Man comes, will he find faith on earth?" (Luke 18:8). Though the origins, meaning, and translation of "Son of Man" are much debated, all four Gospels have it as Jesus's favorite title for himself. Here, Jesus's musings come somewhat as a surprise, just after a teaching about perseverance in prayer and the inspiring story—only in Luke—of the "persistent widow." Jesus's question reads like a throwaway line or a rhetorical rumination to himself. Taking it at face value, however, it looks as if he really was wondering whether his own mission would endure over time. Jesus was asking, "Will there be faith on earth?"

Jesus's question has become all the more pressing in our postmodern times, at least in the Western democracies. Social scientists now generally agree that present cultural conditions do not encourage religious faith, but actively work against it. A straw in the wind is the recent spate of books by the "new" atheists, many making the bestseller lists, which means they are being read widely. These authors focus on the worst possible versions of religion—all too ready at hand—claiming that religion lends societies a sacred legitimation for violence, sexism, racism, homophobia, domestic abuse, environmental destruction, and every other social ill and, on the personal level, that it is the great repressor of sensual pleasure and of human flourishing. They insist that belief in God and practicing religion are simply beneath the intelligence of enlightened people and for safety's sake the world should rid itself of such destructive superstition.

Far more worrisome to me than the "new" atheists (who will wax and wane like the old ones) is how bewildered and often discouraged are the countless good parents and committed religious educators I meet along the way. Too often they feel overwhelmed with the challenge of educating and growing the upcoming generations in Christian faith and more embattled than empowered in their own faith journey. In my travels I've heard, without exaggeration, a thousand personal stories about the roadblocks and deterrents encountered in the struggle to ensure that there will be faith on earth, that is, that faith will be vibrant in people's lives in our time. These are often painful stories.

Typically their narrators are deeply convinced that they can tell the "greatest story ever told" and that Christian faith is wonderful soil in which to plant seeds that will grow into flourishing lives. They firmly believe that Jesus is "the way, and the truth, and the life" (John 14:6) and that there is no better or more fulfilling way to live than as his disciples, following the example he modeled and made possible. They fear that the rich spiritual wisdom Jesus left "for the life of the world" (6:51) may be lost for upcoming generations, if faith on earth declines. Yet for those on the front line the battle at times can seem all uphill.

Now, let's presume that handing on the faith has been a challenge in every era. For example, the proclivity of teenagers to rebel against parental values is likely constitutive of human nature rather than a modern phenomenon. Jesus's parable of the prodigal son infers as much. Note that the second son also had his moment of rebellion; I hope he went into the feast. Social scientists now suggest, however, that our age may be the most challenging yet for faith on earth. And the stories I hear suggest that the difficulties are posed not only by the secular conditions of this postmodern age but, according to some perceptions at least, by the very Church itself. One such story.

On a return trip from some presentations in England, I was bumped to first class and found myself sitting beside a fairly well known young movie star (though embarrassingly not to me) return-ing from a film location. After the initial pleasantries and sharing what we "do," we gradually moved into a deep conversation. She volunteered that she was raised in a traditional Catholic home and still goes to Mass regularly. Now, however, she was very hesitant about raising her two-year-old daughter in the Faith and had de-cided not to have her baptized. I asked why, and the litany began (women priests, respect for gay people, birth control, clergy sex abuse, lack of lay voice, etc.). Eventually I asked, "So how will you raise her instead? What faith will you share with her?" My new friend fell silent.

Throughout the remainder of our conversation—and with some prompting from me, though mostly in the form of questions—it emerged that, in spite of her disagreements with the institution that represents her church on lots of contemporary issues, she still has a deep Catholic faith. She believes in a God who is Love and in love with us; in Jesus, who was God among us to save and liberate us for fullness of life, both here and hereafter; in his gospel, which is the "good news" of God's unconditional love as the very ground of our lives, calling us to live with love and compassion, peace, and justice

in the world; that the Holy Spirit is ever present to prompt and sustain our efforts to live "life to the full" (John 10:10, JB) for ourselves
and for others; and that the Eucharist is indeed the Real Presence
of the Risen Christ as the "bread . . . that gives life to the world"
(6:33). She still experiences receiving Holy Communion as a time
of personal encounter and deep friendship with Jesus. And the list
went on. Indeed, she was totally convinced that the whole collage
of her Catholic Christian faith gives us a great positive perspective
on ourselves and on life in the world, assuring us that our lives are
meaningful and worthwhile, and that we give glory and praise to
God just by being alive in the divine image and likeness. And we
agreed that this can be a powerful antidote to the rat-race myth
about proving ourselves and earning approval.

As our conversation wound down—in Boston—she finally
agreed, "Yeah. I'd hate her to miss out on all that. Send me a copy
of one of your books" (which I will—*this* one). My story, of course,
is not at all to imply that education in Christian faith is simply a no-
brainer. The world in which that young movie star lives epitomizes
many of the challenges posed by our contemporary situation; I'm
sure it's far more difficult to be a good Christian in Hollywood than
in my little neighborhood. But it is easy nowhere now. Which is why
we need a whole new vision and approach that can be effective in
our time and place for educating and growing Christian disciples.

When I say that we a need whole new vision and approach to
religious education if Christian faith is to flourish in our time and
culture, I'm implying that the outcome is not inevitable. People of
faith often assume, if only subconsciously, that God will ensure the
flourishing of faith. From one perspective, this can be itself a valid
act of faith, placing confidence in the promises of the Risen Christ
to be with us always until the end of time (Matt. 28:20) and that the
Holy Spirit continues God's saving work in the world. Indeed, if
Jesus himself had not posed the question first, "Will there be faith

on earth?" my posing it here could sound skeptical or even imperti-
nent. On the other hand, a constant danger for Christians is to presume upon "cheap grace," in other words, to rely on God to fulfill
what is, in fact, our side of the covenant, our own responsibilities.

Meanwhile, history provides many examples cautioning that
we cannot be sanguine about the continued flourishing of faith in
any context. For example, there was a large Christian community
in North Africa in the time of St. Augustine of Hippo (354–430).
It has disappeared. Much of Europe that once had a deep Christian faith now seems to be secularized. Note too the rapid decrease
in church participation in what had been, until recently, deeply
Catholic contexts like Quebec and Ireland. In both places, Mass
attendance has dropped from 80 percent in some parishes to the
low teens. That this happened "almost overnight" is something of
a sociological phenomenon. We know that we can rely on God's
grace to encourage *faith on earth,* but, as I will remind many times
throughout this work, grace always comes to us as a responsibility—
a response-ability.

Will There be Faith?[1] offers a new vision that can enable parents
and teachers to embrace their responsibility for religious education
in our time and, with the help of God's grace, to fulfill it well. It
proposes an approach that is *contemporary, natural, holistic,* and
flexible. I summarize it quite simply as "bringing life to Faith and
Faith to life." It is *contemporary* in that it takes seriously our present sociocultural situation, draws upon its assets (for it has some),
and meets its challenges for educating in faith. It does this while
drawing wisdom from the past two thousand years of the Church's
catechetical ministry, beginning with the way Jesus himself taught.
A *life to Faith to life* approach is also *natural* in that it reflects the
process that goes on in our heads and hearts whenever we learn the
stuff of life that shapes who we are and how we live, what really
matters. And because the approach is natural, any parent or teacher

can readily use it effectively. It is *holistic* too in that just as Christian faith should shape beliefs, relationships, and values, this approach engages people's heads, hearts, and hands. Likewise, it encourages family, parish, and program/school, the three stakeholders in religious education, to work together as a coalition for *faith on earth*.

The *life to Faith to life* approach is *flexible* too. It certainly can be used in the formal setting of a classroom. I've done so for kindergarten up to the doctoral level, and so have thousands of other educators. It is also effective in less formal contexts, such as youth ministry gatherings, adult education classes, parish scripture study and catechumenal programs, retreats, and faith-sharing groups. Parents can readily take this approach to sharing their faith and use it to guide the everyday conversations about the great and small issues of life that constantly arise in a family. People have also found that *life to Faith to life* has potential as a style of preaching, spiritual mentoring, and pastoral counseling, though I don't deal with those here.[2] I will, however, offer numerous examples and suggestions gleaned from my own thirty-five years of both teaching religious educators and doing religious education myself and, more recently, from my belated experience as a parent.

My focus is explicitly Christian and often reflects my Catholic perspective, identity, and context. I know from experience, however, that a *life to Faith to life* approach can appeal to a broad spectrum of mainline Christian communities. Also, over the years, many of my students from the other great world religions have found it effective for educating in their faith. The approach can also be used in non-confessional contexts as long as the intent is that people learn *from* and not merely learn *about* Christian faith or other religions. Last, I try to write in accessible language, keeping notes and technical terms to a minimum.[3] In sum, this book is for any parent or teacher, pastor or layperson involved in or concerned about whether *there will be faith on earth*.

Not Doing So Well—But Tough Times

In addition to anecdotal evidence like my own, there are lots of empirical data that mainline religions in the United States are not doing so well with their religious education.[4] Even among churches that seem to have some success in retaining their youth, the research indicates that their young people's faith often reflects a "moralistic therapeutic deism" rather than authentic Christianity. They embrace a "nice guy" image of a God who comforts and consoles, is called upon only as needed, and makes no real demands on their daily living other than that they "be good, nice, and fair to each other."[5]

For my own Catholic community, all the statistics indicate a significant falling away from the practice of faith. The latest report from the Pew Forum indicates that there are as many as 30 million "former" Catholics in the United States.[6] Though the American Catholic population appears to remain stable, this is only because of immigration from the Southern Hemisphere. The Pew survey also reveals that all mainline Christian denominations are losing their youth and young adults at an alarming rate; however, the one suffering the greatest losses is the Catholic community. Rather than jumping to easy explanations or playing the blame game, however, let us first recognize that these are extraordinarily difficult times for *faith on earth*.

Beyond the virulent "new atheists" already mentioned, there are more subtle social and cultural influences at work that actively discourage faith. The brilliant social philosopher Charles Taylor explains how the Western world once had sociocultural conditions that favored religious belief, even required it. A nonbeliever in a village might bring the wrath of God on everyone, so the village required all its members to believe and practice their faith. Up until about 1800 and for most people, ours was an "enchanted world" in which faith in God and belief in a spiritual realm pervaded daily life. Except among elites, the notion of atheism was unknown. A strong corporate identity among ordinary people disposed all to believe because the community believed. The social conditions greatly favored faith.

Taylor makes a convincing argument, however, that ours is a "secular age" in which the sociocultural conditions now actively *discourage* faith. For a great variety of reasons, we have become "disenchanted" in the sense of not seeing the religious and spiritual as suffusing public or private life or as necessary for keeping evil forces at bay, for legitimating the civil authority, or for human flourishing. Insofar as most people advert to God at all, they do so more in the form of "therapeutic deism," referred to above, in which God is not unlike our childhood Santa Claus. Taylor contends that instead of relying on religious faith as the foundation of life, as it was in premodern times, postmodern society has embraced an "exclusive humanism," exclusive in that it leaves out any reference to God as needed for living humanly. Instead, it encourages self-sufficiency and "expressive individualism" as the fulfillment of our human potential, without any reference to transcendent sources, values, or hopes.[7]

In the face of such sociocultural challenges, there are some strong restorationist sentiments in my Catholic context, in other words, a nostalgia for and an attempt to return to old ways. In religious education, for example, the sentiment is loud (more than large) to "just teach the catechism" or some such doctrinaire presentation of the Faith. Many imagine that returning to the memorized question-and-answer format that dominated Catholic catechesis for some four hundred years[8] will restore people's faith commitment. Neuroscientists have established, however, that memorized data have little lasting effect on people's values or identity over time. Meanwhile, values and identity are the central concerns of faith communities. Although there is a place for memorizing core prayers, texts of scripture, formulas of faith, and moral codes[9] (more on this in Chapter 9), regressing to a question-and-answer catechism—or to any doctrinaire didaction of Christian faith—would leave our next state worse than this one.

Instead, what is urgently needed is a comprehensive approach to religious education that is effective in the context of our time and user-friendly for both teachers and parents. *Will There Be Faith?* attempts to propose as much.

Religious Education as an Enduring Human Need

Regardless of contemporary conditions to the contrary, faith of some kind will always remain a human universal. Everyone needs a center of value around which to craft their lives, a core commitment that lends meaning to the rest. Whatever that mainstay might be, it always requires "a leap"—of faith. It may range from the Ultimate Transcendent, as in the Christian notion of God, to the totally immanent—fame or fortune, power, pleasure, or prestige, even the "self." No matter what it is, everyone has a "god."

Given the spiritual nature of the human person, the universality of faith should not surprise. The two creation myths in the Bible reflect the conviction that humankind is made in God's own image and likeness (Gen. 1:26–27) and that our life arises from the very life breath of God (2:7). Confirming the truth of such texts, since the dawn of history people have reflected a capacity and a desire to reach for something beyond themselves. Whether awed by the created world and impelled to make sense out of life within it or mesmerized by the dynamics of consciousness (e.g., our capacity to think and then to think about our thinking, and then some), people have been prompted to turn to their spirit or soul and respond to their innate yearning for transcendence.

In the effort to realize themselves as spiritual beings, people have developed religions, that is, systems of beliefs, practices, and morals that reflect their imagining of and *response* to the Transcendent; the latter always takes the initiative. Oftentimes, people have created religions from a great leader's spiritual experience that resonated with their own, or simply because they recognized that the religious remains amorphous and illusive unless brought to explicit expression.

All the disenchantment of our age will not obliterate the innate human disposition for the spiritual or the religious. Just as pornography cannot erase the human desire for love and sexual intimacy, even the negative influences of religion will never quench the human capacity to reach for the Transcendent. The great French scholar Blaise Pascal (1623–62) summarized it well: "There is a God-shaped hollow in the human heart that nothing else can fill." This is what impels communities of religion to hand on their faith to the upcoming generations and to encourage their adults to grow in the faithful living of the religion's tenets. Religious education, then, is a vital responsibility for every community of faith, if only for its survival across time. For Christian faith in particular, the last great mandate that the Risen Christ gave to the little remnant community on a hillside in Galilee was that they should "make disciples of all nations . . . teaching them" what he had taught (Matt. 28:16–19). The Christian Church has no greater responsibility than to "teach the Faith" in vital and life-giving ways in every time and place.

Religious Education as a Pressing Social Issue

How and to what end faith communities educate religiously is also a pressing *social* issue. It is more evident than ever that the quality of religion is crucial to the well-being of civil society and the public realm. The Enlightenment and modernity assumed the inevitability of secularization—in the sense of banning religion from influence in the public square. This expectation, however, has been confounded in our time by the force with which religion has returned to center stage as a social issue. Throughout the twentieth century, we assumed that economics was the fault line of political divide for societies drawn between communism and capitalism. Now that assumption seems passé. Rather, as the morning papers attest, the public variable with the most political and social import seems to be religion. And all the great religions have the capacity to promote both life and death, love and hate, peace and war. The pages of history are strewn with their mixed legacy. Again, so much depends on how and to what end we "teach them."

People need to be educated in their own faith traditions in formative and life-flourishing ways *and* to be encouraged toward interreligious understanding and respect. Everyone needs a home within God's family. Yet, as Jesus reminded, "In my Father's house, there are many dwelling places" (John 14:2). So the first responsibility of religious educators is to inform and form people in their own particular tradition, giving them a sense of belonging to a spiritual home. We must ground them in the particular, however, in a way that diligently discourages sectarianism and bitterness toward "others." Let us enable people, instead, to embrace the universality of God's love for all humankind and to respect and appreciate all life-giving religious traditions.

Education for interfaith understanding has become all the more urgent with the religious diversity of postmodern societies due to developments in communication, transportation, and relocation. Traditionally, the great religions remained located in geographic areas, indigenously intertwined with their local cultures. Not anymore! Now the ashram and mosque that were once "over there" are on the same block as the local church and synagogue. America has become "the world's most religiously diverse nation."[10] Even within families, almost 40 percent of married couples in the United States have different religious backgrounds. In the face of such diversity, religious education that maximizes the life-giving potential of people's own traditions and promotes interfaith understanding and respect is imperative, not only for the future of religion, but for the future of the world.

The Approach in Summary

Drawing upon my experience and theoretical work over the past thirty-five years, *Will There Be Faith?* suggests an approach to religious education that can maximize the life-giving potential of Christian faith for persons, communities, and societies. It offers parents and teachers a comprehensive and user-friendly approach that can *inform, form,* and *transform* in Christian faith and identity. With the help of God's grace, this approach can:

- Educate people to know, understand, and embrace with personal conviction Christianity's core beliefs and values (*inform*).

- Grow people's identity through a formative pedagogy and the intentional socialization of Christian family and community (*form*).

• Open people to a lifelong journey of conversion toward holiness and fullness of life for themselves and "for the life of the world" (John 6:51; *transform*).

Will There be Faith? also reflects an approach that honors the concern for interreligious understanding raised above. The pedagogy it proposes can effectively ground people in the *particulars* of Christian faith, but without sectarian bias and in ways that open them to the *universal*—to the universality of God's love and saving intent through all worthy religions.

As noted already, the overarching approach I propose invites people to "bring their lives to their Faith, and their Faith to their lives." Whether crafting a formal teaching/learning event, facilitating a faith-sharing group, or carrying on the conversation of faith in the home, parish, or school/program, such a pedagogy must begin with something of real interest and relevance to participants' lives. It should engage what the great educator Paulo Freire (1921–97) called a "generative theme," that is, something of pressing concern that can actively engage people in the teaching/learning process, because they perceive the theme to be of real interest and meaningful to their lives. After reflection on and conversation about a particular generative theme, participants need to have ready and persuasive access to the scriptures and traditions of Christian faith relevant to the focused theme, raising up the life-flourishing truths and spiritual wisdom of Christianity in meaningful ways, that is, in ways that echo and strike a chord in participants' lives. Then the dynamic needs to move back to life again, inviting people to take and make these truths and spiritual wisdom their own, to appropriate the Faith into their lives in the world, and to make decisions—of head, heart, or hands—in its light.

Effective religious education demands the intentional participation of three key "agents"—the home, the parish, and the school or formal program of instruction. All three stakeholders in faith education must work in coalition. In sum, educating in Christian faith takes a family with a village and a village with a school or program of some kind. These three contexts and the leaders within them (parents, pastoral ministers, teachers) must review every aspect of their shared life for what they are teaching, including the "teachings" that participants will absorb by osmosis, and intentionally craft their communal life to nurture life-giving Christian faith and identity.

The approach I'm proposing requires all three sets of leaders to be clear about:

- *Who* it is they are teaching and those learners' positive potential as persons and disciples of Jesus Christ;

- *The nature* of Christian faith that they want to pass on—how holistic it is (engaging head, heart, and hands), its salvific and liberating possibilities and social responsibilities, its potential to comfort the disturbed and to disturb the comfortable, and its great truths and spiritual wisdom for life;

- *The purpose* of educating in faith—educators' task of enabling people to flourish through Christian commitment, to know their faith in ways that inform, form, and transform their identity, and to commit to the positive difference *for life for all* that Christian faith can effect in society;

- *The context* of Christian religious education—the family, parish, and school/program, and the imperative that the three be intentionally crafted to work together to socialize people into Christian identity and lived faith;

- *How to* go about it—how to develop a consistent pedagogy of religious education that constantly invites people, both learners and teachers (who are also learners), to "bring their lives to their Faith and their Faith to their lives."

My proposals with regard to these great foundational issues will unfold in the above sequence throughout the chapters of *Will There Be Faith?*

The times are most challenging, and we need a new vision and approach for effective religious education in this postmodern age. However, my confidence that there will be faith on earth when the "Human One" (now suggested as a better translation than "Son of Man") returns in glory was renewed by the following experience and still is by the memory of it.

I was walking with my then four-year-old son, Teddy, on a lovely fall afternoon. He was kicking his way ahead of me through the piles of fallen leaves at road's edge, and I was reflecting, as parents do, about what life might hold for my little boy. Suddenly, Teddy stopped both of us in our tracks, and said, "Dad, listen!" I wondered what he heard. I could hear nothing. Gradually I began to realize that Teddy wanted me to hear the rustle of the wind through the trees and the lonely singing of the remnant birds not yet left for warmer climes. We stood together for quite a while, drinking it all in. Then it dawned on me. This was more than a magical moment. It was a sacramental one.

Teddy's attention to the beauty around us reminded me that God "still speaks" in our lives, albeit often in a whispering breeze (see 1 Kings 19:11–13, story of Elijah's encounter with God). He helped me remember that God's grace—the old name for God's effective love—still is and always will be at work, most often through the ordinary things of everyday life. I realized again that we need not worry about God's side of the faith equation. God's covenant partnership with us will remain forever in place and the Risen Christ *will be* "with [us] always to the end of time" (Matt. 28:20, JB). God's outreach and inbreaking into our lives is unrelenting. As an old Gaelic proverb goes, "There is an ebb to every tide, except the tide of God's grace." Toward us God's grace is ever at high tide. Or to echo the Psalmist, it will always be true that "the earth is full of the steadfast love of the LORD" (33:5).

The questionable side is ours. Can we, will we, see to it that Christian faith endures, that it remains as the great life-flourishing source that it can be for individual persons, for communities, and for the life of the world? St. Paul gave thanks for the "grace of God bestowed on [us] in Christ Jesus," which has "enriched [us] in every way" (1 Cor. 1:4–5, NAB). So, with the help of God's grace, I'm confident that we can see to it that there will be Christian faith on earth, and a flourishing rather than withering one. To imagine a new vision and approach to this good purpose, there is no better place to begin than by reflecting on "to teach as Jesus did" (Chapter 1).

A Few Preliminaries

I use "educator" throughout as a comprehensive term to mean everyone and not only teachers, located everywhere and not only in schools. The Latin *educare* means "to lead out." Thus, anyone who "leads out" others toward faith is a religious educator. In fact, by baptism every Christian bears this responsibility, at the very least by their lived witness to their faith. Therefore, the whole faith community should be an effective religious educator (the theme of Chapter 5). Then, parents and family (including siblings, grandparents, aunts, uncles, cousins, godparents) are the primary educators in faith (Chapter 6). After them, "educator" includes designated religion teachers and catechists, whether professional or volunteer (Chapters 7, 8, and 9). So, although I often explicitly name "parents and teachers"—they are, after all, at the forefront of this good work—I invite every Christian person and community to take seriously their responsibility to be educators in faith. *Will there be faith?* Depends on every Christian!

Readers will note that I often use a plural pronoun to refer to a singular term, as in, "Every *Christian* must take seriously *their* responsibility to educate in faith." This is now deemed permissible by the U.S. National Council of Teachers of English. It is also a return to the practice of Elizabethan English. To quote Shakespeare, "May God send everyone their heart's desire." This old and new pattern helps to honor gender inclusivity in our time, while avoiding the awkward "he/she," "her/his" constructions. Further, when quoting an original text that is not gender sensitive, I take the liberty to adjust toward inclusivity when the latter is clearly intended. I do likewise when an original Bible text is, in fact, inclusive, but the translation fails to reflect this. For example, "God created humankind in God's image" is actually more faithful to the original Hebrew than "God created man in his image" (Gen. 1:27). Although I favor the NRSV Bible translation because it is more gender sensitive, I sometimes use the New American Bible or the Jerusalem Bible when their texts seem more apt to the point I'm making.

When I refer to the formal reality of Christian faith but without using the adjective "Christian," I sometimes alert that I intend it by capitalizing Faith, as in "the Faith." I also capitalize when the intent is a particular faith tradition, as in *life to Faith to life.* Likewise, I capitalize when referring to the normative media of Christian revelation as Scripture and Tradition; however, when referring to "a passage from scripture" I do not capitalize. Similarly, I capitalize "Church" when referring to the universal community of Christian faith or to a particular one, as in "Catholic Church," whereas when used as a generic term, as in "church and society," or as an adjective, as in "church structures," I use lowercase.

Last, note that each chapter reflects a *life to Faith to life* pedagogy for readers. After establishing the generative theme of the chapter, I invite you first to reflect on your own life-based opinions and wisdom before reading my Christian faith–based proposals. Then pause and discern throughout and toward the end of each chapter what wisdom to embrace as your own and how to integrate it into life as your praxis of Christian faith or of religious education. This is signaled by the heading "For Reflection and Conversation." I encourage you to pause and reflect on the questions as posed. Even better, when possible, bring your reflections into conversation with a neighbor.

CHAPTER ONE

To Teach (and Learn) as Jesus Did

Looking to the Master at Work

A t the outset, let me make crystal clear that the defining core, greatest asset, and most enticing feature of Christian faith is Jesus Christ. This may seem obvious, and yet it is worth stating at the outset, because Christians often lose sight of this simple truth: *the heart of Christian faith is Jesus Christ*. It is not the scriptures, or the dogmas and doctrines, or the commandments, or the sacraments, or the Church, or any other one "thing"—important and vital as all these are. Rather, as the *Catechism of the Catholic Church* (*CCC*) so well summarizes: "At the heart . . . we find a Person, the Person of Jesus of Nazareth, the only Son from the Father" (n. 426).

Note well that this statement names the core "Person" as both the *Jesus of history,* the one "of Nazareth," and the *Christ of faith,* "the only Son from the Father." So Christians are called to be disciples to that carpenter from Nazareth who walked the roads of Galilee, who preached the reign of God with its rule of radical love, even of

enemies; who fed the hungry, cured the sick, consoled the sorrow-
ing, and welcomed the marginalized; who claimed to be the kind
of messiah who brings liberty to captives, sight to the blind, good
news to the poor, and freedom to the oppressed (Isa. 61:1; Luke
4:21); who presented himself as "the way, and the truth, and the
life" (John 14:6) and invited all and sundry to "come follow me."
Such is *the way* that the historical Jesus modeled for us.

To follow *the way* of Jesus, however, we need him also to be the
Christ of faith, the Son of God, the Second Person of the Blessed
Trinity, who by his life, death, and resurrection makes it possible
for us to so live. The paschal mystery—Jesus's life, death, and
resurrection—forever mediates to us "God's abundant grace in
Christ Jesus" (1 Tim. 1:14, NAB; see also 2 Cor. 4:15; 9:8; Titus 3:6).
Because of his dying and rising, we *can* live as disciples of Jesus.
Whatever we do by way of educating in Christian faith, then, Jesus
Christ must be its defining center. We must teach disciples to follow
his *way* and then to embrace him as Lord and Savior, and likewise
teach what he taught us of God, of the Holy Spirit, and how to
live as people of God. The defining value of our curriculum is "the
boundless riches of Christ" (Eph. 3:8).

For Christian religious educators, teaching Jesus Christ and
teaching what he taught must be the heart and soul of our educating in faith. At the same time, might it be that we are also *to teach as
Jesus did*?[1] At first blush, this may well sound like a pious platitude
or a naive proposition. After all, we are living in a very different
time and context than Jesus did. Shouting from a hillside to a crowd
below (no microphone) or trudging dusty roads in search of disciples (no Web outreach) is hardly a model for us today. Neither do
we have his miracles at the ready to encourage people to faith. Jesus
was then; we are now.

Admittedly, a time-and-culture chasm exists between us. Nevertheless there is something enduring about human nature, something

true for all time and in every culture, and likewise about Christian faith. Jesus would be the first to encourage us to take full advantage of all the modern means of communication and every instructional technology at our disposal in order to mediate God's word into people's lives. Likewise, Jesus would advise us to craft all communication of his gospel "according to the mode of the receiver," in other words, in ways likely to be effective in our time and place.

This being said, we are ever called "to teach in his name" (Acts 5:28). So our "intended learning outcomes" should surely reflect those of Jesus, and our approach to promoting them should be inspired by his teaching style and be consistent with how he went about it—certainly not inconsistent. For example, our approach should reflect Jesus's welcome for all, his respect for learners, and the way he actively engaged them with the ordinary and everyday themes and symbols of their lives, even while he taught them "as one having authority" (Mark 1:22) and invited them to discipleship (1:17). Conversely, to be inhospitable and excluding, disrespectful of learners, oblivious to their lives, wishy-washy in what we teach, and indifferent about people's responses would be teaching in ways antithetical to Jesus's and the faith he represented.

To detect his style of teaching we have to rely on the hints we find in the Gospels. Jesus never articulated nor do the Gospel writers describe his teaching style per se. On the other hand, the Gospels refer to his public ministry as "teaching" some 150 times. Nicodemus had it right, "We know that you are a *teacher* who has come from God" (John 3:2). So the Gospels contain numerous clues about teaching as Jesus did. Before examining some of those clues, however, pause and take note of how *you* imagine Jesus's teaching style.

For Reflection and Conversation

- From your own encounter with Jesus through the Gospels, what was he hoping to achieve by his teaching? That is, what do you think was the learning outcome he intended in people's lives?

- How would you describe Jesus's pedagogy, his overall approach to teaching? List its most salient features.

- How does Jesus's approach compare with your own?

Educating in Whole Faith for God's Reign

For God's Reign: To appreciate and be inspired by *how* Jesus may have taught, we first need to detect *why* he taught—his purposes in teaching. Surely Jesus crafted his approach to serve his intentions, and every educator in faith should do the same. Otherwise, what we hope to teach may be defeated by how we go about it. In teaching, medium and message are ever intertwined, and this is particularly true of educating in Christian faith.

Scripture scholars now agree that the symbol "reign of God" summarizes how Jesus understood his life's mission and what he intended to catalyze in people's lives by means of his public ministry. Over and over, Jesus's teachings begin with the words "The reign [*or* kingdom] of God is like . . ." Repeatedly he talks about who belongs to God's reign, how to be among them, and so on. As the Synoptic Gospels (Matthew, Mark, and Luke) attest, the reign of God is constantly on Jesus's lips and is clearly the touchstone of his life and teaching.

Though the scholars agree that the reign of God was the focus of Jesus's ministry, they debate what exactly he meant by it. The reign or kingdom of God was a favored symbol in the Jewish faith of the time, yet Jesus gave it his own spin as well. Clearly he intended it to mean the realization of God's intentions—God's will—for all people and all creation. This is the work of God within human history. However, when teaching disciples to pray "Your kingdom come," he taught them to immediately add "Your will be done, on earth as it is in heaven" (Matt. 6:10). In other words, and as reflected throughout the Bible, God takes God's people into covenant partnership, to live as God intends. So we have kingdom hope for what God is bringing about, and kingdom responsibility to do God's will now—*on earth*. Well, then, what is God's will for us?

The response from the whole gamut of biblical revelation is that God intends *the best of everything for everyone, all the time, and the integrity of God's creation*. God's intention is for all people to enjoy and live with faith, hope, and love, with peace and justice, with mercy and compassion, and with holiness and wholeness of life and to fulfill all the authentic desires of the human heart, which are God's desires for us as well. The Hebrew scriptures summarize the realization of God's reign as *shalom* ("peace with justice"). Jesus summarizes it this way in John's Gospel: "I came that [you] may have life, and have it abundantly" (10:10). We can well name God's will as *fullness of life for all*.

The Bible makes clear that what God wills *to* us becomes God's will *for* us—in other words, what God wants us to have is how we should live. God is ever active within human history on behalf of God's reign *and* takes humanity into covenant to so live. Since God wills the integrity of creation, the people of God must be its good stewards (Gen. 2:15); because God wills justice to all, people in covenant with God must do the works of justice and promote it in society (Mic. 6:8); and so on. From the perspective of Christian faith, Jesus is the catalyst of God's reign within human history. The paschal mystery is the powerhouse of grace that works through us to realize God's reign now and to ensure its completion at the end time. Jesus is both "the way, and the truth, and the life" (John 14:6) by which we are to live for God's reign and the Savior who makes it possible for us to do so.

After that, it seems wisest to say that for Jesus, the "reign of God" was a tensive symbol in the sense that it had many meanings, often with "both/and" paradoxes. Thus, Jesus taught God's reign as a symbol of both hope and command, of promise and responsibility, as comforting the disturbed and disturbing the comfortable. He spoke of it as already present in him, but yet to come in its fullness, as a reward in the hereafter and to begin here as well, as something to be realized as both personal holiness and social justice, as a deeply spiritual yet also a social reality, to shape both the prayers and the politics of disciples.

According to Mark, the first Gospel written, this is how Jesus launched his public ministry: "Jesus came to Galilee, proclaiming the good news of God, and saying, 'The time is fulfilled, and the kingdom of God has come near; repent, and believe in the good news'" (1:14–15). At the end of his ministry, the good thief on the cross echoed the central theme of Jesus's life when he requested, "Jesus, remember me when you come into your kingdom" (Luke 23:42). Luke concludes the Acts of the Apostles by saying that Paul spent his time "proclaiming the kingdom of God and teaching about the Lord Jesus Christ" (28:31). Jesus taught God's reign and now we, like Paul and the first Christians, must continue to teach what Jesus taught—the reign of God—and to teach Jesus as our Lord and Savior, God's definitive agent in the ongoing coming of God's reign in human history.

So "to teach as Jesus did" means that the coming of God's reign and God's will being done on earth as in heaven should be our overarching purpose in Christian religious education. God's reign should be the ultimate guideline that helps us decide *what* and *why* and *how* to teach, shaping our whole curriculum in Christian faith. Indeed, God's reign in Jesus of love and compassion, peace and jus-

tice, fullness of life, and the stewardship of creation is to be the overall criterion in how we understand any symbol, text, or tradition of
Christian faith.

A student new to the study of theology came to me greatly per-
plexed by all the apparent contradictions she was finding in her
study of scripture. What was she to make, for example, of Jesus's
two contrasting statements, "I have not come to bring peace, but
the sword" (Matt. 10:34), on the one hand, and on the other, "Peace
I leave with you; my peace I give to you" (John 14:27)? I explained
that we always need what the scholars call "a canon within the
Canon," in other words, an overall "rule" or "measure" (the meaning of Greek *canon*) that guides our interpretation, explanation, and
application of any text of sacred Scripture or teaching of Tradition.
The "reign of God" as God's will and intentions for us can serve as
such a canon. In this light, Jesus's statement favoring peace must be
taken as the overall intent of his gospel. It is important for teachers
and parents, with the guidance of the Church, to have such a ready-
at-hand canon.

Now we need to ask what Christian faith might look like as it
does God's will on earth. This will indicate Jesus's more immediate intentions—within the overarching ambit of God's reign—and
thus guide our own.

In Whole Faith: The Gospels make clear that Jesus's immediate
hopes were that the people he taught would become disciples. His
overarching purpose of bringing about God's reign would be served
as people converted their lives and followed *the way* that he modeled and his dying and rising made possible. Such is the lived faith
to which he invited people. The learning outcome he intended for
disciples was for them to live as people of God after his example.
We can say, then, that his educating intent was precisely that there
would be *faith on earth*—as long as we understand faith as very
holistic.

So often in English, "faith" is reduced to mean "belief," that is, what people claim to accept as true in their heads. Of course, belief is an aspect of Jesus's understanding of faith, but so too is a trusting relationship with God coupled with the morals and values by which disciples are to live. "Faith" for Jesus has a power-packed triple demand—beliefs, relationships, and commitments—all rolled into a single way of life. The Gospels reflect that Jesus educated for a *whole* faith, one that engages people's heads, hearts, and hands— their entire way of being in the world.

There are many particular instances in which Jesus taught what people are to believe, how they are to pray and trust in God, and the ethic by which they should live. Perhaps the best instance of Jesus rolling all three into one for disciples is his preaching of the law of love as the "greatest commandment." First, however, remember that Jesus's preaching of the law of love was set within the greatest good news of his divine revelation, namely, God's unconditional love for all people. Fulfilling the "greatest commandment" must be our re- sponse to the God who has first loved us and will always love us.[2] As we read in 1 John 4:19, "We love because God first loved us."

Responding to God's love, then, is how disciples must live for the reign of God now, the lived faith that Jesus intends us to realize on earth. The three versions of the law of love, Matthew 22:34–40, Mark 12:28–34, and Luke 10:25–38, differ slightly from one an- other, and none quote Deuteronomy 6:5 exactly. The last is the parent text for love of God; Leviticus 19:18 is the parent text for love of neighbor as oneself. Nevertheless, all accounts emphasize that faith lived for God's reign and in response to God's love demands the whole of who we are, all our minds, our affections, and our wills.

In Mark's version (my favorite), a scribe asks Jesus, "Which com- mandment is the greatest of all?" Note that he speaks in the sin- gular and of the great*est*—there can be only one tallest tree in the wood. Jesus responds by first repeating Deuteronomy 6:4: "Hear, O Israel! The Lord our God is Lord alone!" (NAB). This is not in Matthew's or Luke's version; Mark, however, as the earliest Gospel, may be closest to what Jesus actually said. So Jesus was reiterating that the greatest commandment is based on the first of the Ten—to make God the God of our lives, to have no other gods besides God. Therefore, then, to put a God of love at the center of life requires a radical law of love that makes all three mandates—toward God, self, and neighbor—symbiotic with each other.

No Hebrew prophet before him had ever united Deuteronomy 6:5 and Leviticus 19:18, but Jesus does: " 'You shall love the Lord your God with all your heart, and with all your soul, and with all your mind, and with all your strength.' The second is this, 'You shall love your neighbor as yourself.' " At first blush, this looks like two, if not three, commandments—to love God, neighbor, and self. However, just as the scribe asked for the greatest, Jesus ends in the singular, "There is no other commandment greater than these" (Mark 12:31), confirming that the three are as one triangle.

The scribe responds and echoes Jesus with his own gloss of Deuteronomy 6:4: "Well said, *teacher.* You are right in saying, 'He is One and there is no other than he' " (Mark 12:32, NAB). Indeed, God belongs at the center of a life of faith. Then, the same scribe, also departing slightly from the text of Deuteronomy 6:5, summarizes the triple love command as engaging heart, head, and hands: "To love God with all the heart, and with all the understanding, and with all the strength, and to love one's neighbor as oneself" (12:33). No wonder Jesus said to him, "You are not far from the kingdom of God" (12:34).

In Luke's account, the question asked is not about the greatest commandment. Rather, a lawyer asks, "What must I do to inherit eternal life?" In other words, "What life should I live to possess what matters most?" Note well how the lawyer poses the question—

what *to do*? Jesus responds with the greatest commandment and concludes, "Do this, and you will live"; he implies here as well as hereafter. When the lawyer goes on to push Jesus with, "Who is my neighbor?" Jesus tells the parable of the good Samaritan and ends by saying, "Go and do likewise." Note again the *doing;* the faith that Jesus taught must be lived (read Luke 10:25–37).

Matthew's version falls short of Mark's. Matthew rounds out something regarding the law and life of faith, however, with Jesus's account of the last judgment and who will inherit God's "*kingdom* prepared . . . from the foundation of the world" (25:34). This text makes clear that God wants our love for God to be expressed as love of neighbor, a love practiced to bring the best outcome for ourselves as well—to be among the sheep destined for God's eternal reign. God will not say to those to be rewarded, "There was a hungry person one time and you fed him," but rather "*I* was hungry and you gave *me* food," and so on (25:31–46). For Jesus, the faith of discipleship is, indeed, a *whole* way of life. This will be important to remember when we imagine how best to educate for Christian faith. We will return to the theme of faith in Chapter 3 when we subsume these reflections of Chapter 1 to describe the purposes of Christian religious education.

For Reflection and Conversation

- Jesus's teaching had the overarching theme of the reign of God. This is what he hoped to bring about in human history, the ultimate "learning outcome" for which he taught. What do you think? How might this inspire your own sense of grand purpose?

- How might it influence *what* you emphasize and highlight? *How* you teach?

- That people may come to faith was Jesus's more immediate

purpose, to a *whole* faith that shapes their beliefs, relationships, and values toward God's reign. What do you think of such purpose? Anything to adjust in your own sense of "faith"?

• How might this shape *what* you teach? *How* you teach?

Watching the Master at Work

The New Testament word *mathetes* is usually translated "disciple." In the world of the time, however, it also meant an "apprentice." This humbler term reminds us that we are always apprenticed to the "Master." As Jesus himself advised, "Do not be called 'Master'; you have but one master, the Christ" (Matt. 23:10, NAB). So let us take a closer look at Jesus the master teacher at work and imagine ourselves apprenticed to him.

To appreciate Jesus's distinctive pedagogy, I first note four salient features of his whole *way of being with people* as an educator. The particular pedagogy of individual educators is set within and permeated by their *way of being with people*. Even the best teaching methods will be less effective and perhaps defeated if an educator's presence in learners' lives is a negative one, for example, if the educator is authoritarian, elitist, manipulative, mean, or biased. The Incarnation was God's *way of being with us* in Jesus. I detect that Jesus incarnated the divine pedagogy by being:

• Welcoming and inclusive,

• Respectful of learners,

• Compassionate and committed to justice, and

• Encouraging of partnership and servant leaders.

Welcoming and Inclusive: Jesus's style was distinguished by its proactive outreach and radical inclusion. The two go hand in hand. Both would have been distinctive in his time and culture. To begin with, in that culture students would look for a teacher; teachers did not look for students. Jesus, by contrast, reached out into the highways and byways to recruit disciples. Following on, Jesus's outreach was totally inclusive. Rather than focusing only on men or the elite, which would have been typical of teachers in his time, Jesus reached out to men, women, and children and to ordinary people—farmers, shepherds, merchants, homemakers, and fishermen. He reached out especially to the marginalized, to lepers and public sinners, to the physically and psychologically ill, to the poor and hungry, to the suffering and bereaved, to all who were oppressed by the cultural mores of the time.

The *General Directory for Catechesis* (*GDC*), the most authoritative recent document from the Catholic Church on religious education, summarizes this aspect of Jesus the Teacher: "Jesus made himself a catechist of the Kingdom of God for all categories of persons, great and small, rich and poor, healthy and sick, near and far, Jews and pagans, men and women, righteous and sinners, rulers and subjects, individuals and groups" (n. 163).[3] New Testament scholars point to Jesus's table fellowship, his "eating with tax collectors and sinners" (Matt. 9:11), as symbolizing both his outreach and his inclusivity. The etymological roots of Greek *katha holos*—*katholos*—mean "to include all"; Jesus was truly "catholic" in his approach.

It is worth highlighting that Jesus fully included women within his community of disciples. There are many instances of his rejection of the male chauvinism of his time and place. Take, for example, his conversation with the Samaritan woman at the well in John 4. Jesus was not only speaking to a woman in public, but was explaining to her his core message, something teachers of his time would never do. Then he allowed the Samaritan woman to become a witness on behalf of his teaching to her own people, this in a culture where women were not allowed to bear witness. No wonder the disciples came back from the city, where they had gone to buy food (4:8), and "were astonished that he was speaking with a woman" (4:27—the verb there implies conversation). And well they might have been!

The clearest symbol of Jesus's gender inclusivity, however, was that he welcomed women into his core band of disciples. All three Synoptic Gospels attest that the women at the foot of the cross had "followed Jesus from Galilee" (Matt. 27:55). This means that they were with him from the *beginning* of his ministry to its *end* at Calvary. Accepting John's chronology, this would have been a three-year period. The Gospels place Mary Magdalene by name at the foot of the cross and then recognize her as the first witness to Jesus's resurrection: "He appeared first to Mary Magdalene" (Mark 16:9). This made her—as reflected in her early church title the "apostle to the apostles"—the first to announce the resurrection to the rest. Jesus taught as much by such acts of inclusion as by his words of instruction.

Respectful of Learners: Jesus's approach had tremendous respect for the learners. His whole intent was to empower people to become agents of their faith rather than dependents. He was not looking for docile devotees as a cult leader might do. Jesus wanted his disciples to become people fully alive to the glory of God. Matthew makes clear at the end of the Sermon on the Mount that Jesus was teaching "the crowds" (7:28), not just his inner circle of disciples. Imagine the affirmation experienced in the heads and hearts of ordinary peasant people when he taught them, "You are the salt of the earth; . . . you are the light of the world" (5:13–14). Think too of so many of Jesus's miracles of healing; instead of boasting, "I have cured you," Jesus's typical comment was, "*Your* faith has made you well" (Mark 5:34). Note how he affirmed the widow's mite, the prayer of the publican, the innocence of children, and so on. Respect and affirmation for all were hallmarks of his style.

Let religious educators note well the great respect Jesus showed for his learners' discernment and decision-making ability. His call to discipleship was always by invitation and never by dictate. Apparently he always gave people the freedom to decline. For example, when some disciples found his teaching to be too "difficult" and left his community, instead of following after with threats or recriminations, Jesus turned to "the twelve" and asked, "Do you also wish to go away?" Peter's response might imply that they had thought about it; he asks, "Lord, to whom can we go? You have the words of eternal life" (John 6:60, 66–68). The story of the "rich young man" in all three Synoptics (only in Matthew is he described as "young"; see 19:16–26) reflects a similar freedom. When Jesus challenges the man to move beyond obedience to the law and to embrace full discipleship, he declines and departs. Though saddened, Jesus does not threaten or send disciples to bring him back. His approach tells us that educating in faith must respect people's freedom of choice. Anything less is unworthy of Jesus's gospel.

Compassionate and Committed to Justice: New Testament scholars agree that a defining feature of Jesus's public ministry was his compassion for those in need. One of his greatest parables taught that God is like a loving parent whose heart was "filled with compassion" upon seeing the prodigal return (Luke 15:20). We see Jesus's compassion in the way he welcomed anyone who came to him with an open heart; he accepted all regardless of their condition or circumstance. Look at the welcome Jesus afforded Nicodemus, even though he came under cover of darkness (John 3:1–30); to Zacchaeus, though he had imposed heavy taxes upon his own people (Luke 19:1–19); to the bleeding woman, though her touch made him ritually unclean (8:43–48); and to the Roman centurion, though he was a Gentile and military official of the power ruling Jesus's own people (Matt. 8:5–13). The list goes on.

Likewise, the work of justice was at the heart of Jesus's ministry.

His central teaching of God's reign reflects as much. In his Jewish faith, God's kingdom was understood as both a spiritual and a social symbol that calls people to holiness of life, which demands the works of peace and justice (see the Holiness Code of Leviticus 19). It is no surprise, then, that Jesus rejected every form of chauvinism and sexism, of racism and ethnic bias. The story of the Samarian woman hit all those bases. At the opening of his public ministry in Luke's Gospel, Jesus declared that the great promise in Isaiah 61:1 of a Messiah who would be anointed by the Spirit of God to bring about justice was fulfilled in him. Jesus then spent the rest of his public life bringing good news to the poor, liberty to captives, sight to the blind, and freedom to the oppressed (see 4:16–21).

Encouraging of Partnership and Servant Leaders: The previous features imply that Jesus's whole approach was to call people into a community of disciples, a community of partnership with him and with one another. From the beginning of his public ministry, we find Jesus calling disciples not just to follow him, but to become partners in his teaching. To the first two, the fishermen brothers Simon (later Peter) and Andrew, he said "Follow me and I will make you fish for people" (Mark 1:16). In other words, they would be partners in his labors. Midway through his public ministry, Jesus "called the twelve and began to send them out two by two" (i.e., in partnership), giving them the authority to carry on the work he was doing (see 6:7–13). A little later, Jesus called and appointed some seventy more disciples and likewise sent them out "in pairs" (see Luke 10:1–12), that is, in partnership, to teach what he was teaching.

Furthermore, Jesus's community of disciples was to be a collaborative and egalitarian one. Though he designated leaders among them, they were to be servant leaders, serving as he had come to serve. The Gospels recount at least six occasions when Jesus, in one way or another, warned disciples that they were not to "lord it over"

other people. The greatest among them was to be the servant of the
rest (see Mark 10:41–45). Instead of placing themselves in control of
people's lives, he taught his community leaders to practice and encourage others in the egalitarian spirit of "little children" (see Matt.
18:1–5).

Whatever particular teaching methods we may employ, in order
"to teach as Jesus did" we must try to set them within *a way of being
with people* that is marked by being *welcoming and inclusive, respectful of learners, compassionate and committed to justice,* and *encouraging of partnership and servant leaders.* Though always no more than
apprentices, by God's grace and our own conscious efforts, we can at
least aspire to approximate the example of the Master.

Now we're ready to focus more precisely on Jesus's pedagogy—
his teaching style—as evident in explicit teaching/learning events.
Though I'm surely a biased commentator, I propose that Jesus's
overall teaching dynamic was to lead people *from life to Faith to life.*
He did so by:

- Beginning with people's lives,

- Encouraging their own reflections,

- Teaching them his gospel with authority,

- Inviting them to see for themselves, to take his teaching to
  heart, and

- Encouraging their decisions for lived faith as disciples.

Beginning with People's Lives: First, Jesus most often began a
teaching event by inviting people to look at their present lives, their
reality in the world. He turned his listeners to their own experience,
to their feelings, thoughts, and values, to creation around them, to
the beliefs, practices, attitudes, and mores of their religious tradition

and culture, to their work and social arrangements, to their joys and sorrows, fears and hopes, sins and goodness—to life. His favorite teaching method in this regard was his use of parables in Matthew, Mark, and Luke and allegories (e.g., the Good Shepherd) or "signs" (e.g., wedding at Cana) in John. All of these begin with symbols of everyday life through which people could recognize their own lives and situations. In this, his pedagogy was to engage the very souls and thus the active participation of his listeners.

For example, Jesus's parables were engaging stories—as stories always are—through which people could stop and recognize some aspect of their own experience and then see for themselves how to appropriate their teaching into their everyday lives. When he taught the parable of the sower, he most likely was talking to farmers; the parable of the fine pearls was likely told to pearl merchants, the lost coin parable to a group of women, perhaps gathered at the village well, and so on. Jesus engaged people's interests and made them active participants in the teaching/learning dynamic by raising up real-life themes and issues of concern, by turning his listeners on to what was "happening."

Encouraging People's Own Reflections: Second, Jesus invited people to think about their lives in a whole new way. He wanted his listeners to recognize that great things like the reign of God and their own eternal destiny were being negotiated in the ordinary and everyday of their lives. He wanted them to reflect on the falsehood of hypocrisy, the emptiness of ritual detached from doing God's will, the faith contradiction in hating any group or class, the unconditional love of God regardless of one's worthiness or lack thereof.

Again, his commitment to encouraging people's own reflections was epitomized in his use of parables. Indeed, his parables often turned people's perspectives upside down. None of Jesus's first hearers would have expected the Samaritan to be neighbor, or the father to welcome home the prodigal, or the prostitutes and tax collectors to enter the reign of God before the religious leaders. Such "reversals" were Jesus's way of getting people to reflect critically, perhaps to change their minds and hearts, to see their lives and possibilities in a whole new way. We might say today that his teaching style invited people to a *critical* consciousness (in the sense of "discerning"), to reflect upon and question their own reality and to imagine how to live more faithfully as people of God.

Teaching His Gospel with Authority: Third, from the very beginning of Jesus's public ministry, people recognized that he "taught them as one having authority" (Mark 1:22). In the midst of his stories and conversations, Jesus also took strong positions in teaching his gospel. On the one hand, he clearly cherished the Jewish tradition of his people, obeyed its precepts, quoted its scriptures, and said that he had come not to abolish the Law and the Prophets, but "to fulfill" them (Matt. 5:17). On the other hand, Jesus claimed the unique authority to reinterpret the tradition, to point to how people were missing out on the spirit of the law, and to propose a new vision for living as a people of God: "You have heard it said . . . but I say . . ." (5:21–22). Jesus himself did what he recommended by way of drawing old truths and new wisdom from the tradition: "Every scribe who has been instructed in the reign of God is like the head of a household who brings from his storeroom [*or* treasury] both the new and the old" (13:52, NAB).

It is important to note here that Jesus, in fact, had no official authority in his culture. He was neither an appointed rabbi nor a member of the Sanhedrin. So what was the source of his authority? It must have come from the integrity of his life, that is, from his personal conviction matched by lifestyle. Given how radical his teaching was—love of enemies, praying for persecutors (Matt. 5:43–48), loving even as God loves (John 15:9)—it is amazing that no one ever accused Jesus of failing to practice what he preached. Oh, he was accused of eating with sinners, breaking the Sabbath, ignoring dietary laws, and more, but never of hypocrisy. Jesus must have walked the walk as well as talked the talk. That makes for real authority; faith educators take note.

To recap Jesus's pedagogy thus far, he invited people, first, to look at and, second, to reflect upon their lives in the world; third, he taught them "the Faith" with authority, both the old and the new of it. Now, I propose that there were two additional dynamics ever present in his pedagogy, however subtle: he invited people to recognize for themselves what this faith might mean for their lives and then to make decisions for discipleship.

Inviting People to See for Themselves: Fourth, Jesus taught in a way that invited people to recognize for themselves his spiritual wisdom, to take to heart and personally embrace the truth he was teaching. Jesus often blessed those "with the eyes to see and the ears to hear." More than physical seeing and hearing, he wanted people to open themselves up to and make their own what he was teaching. He enabled the Samaritan woman to come to see for herself, and see for herself she did. "Could he possibly be the Messiah?" she wondered (John 4:29, NAB). The same was true for her friends. Although at first the woman was a witness to her village on Jesus's behalf, in time they too came to recognize him for themselves. They said, "It is no longer because of what you said that we believe, for we have heard for ourselves, and we know that this is truly the Savior of the world" (4:42). The greatest example of Jesus's wanting people to "see for themselves" is in the story of the Risen Christ and the two bewildered disciples on the road to Emmaus; we review this in detail below.

Encouraging People's Decisions for Lived Faith as Disciples: Fifth, Jesus's invitation to discipleship—to *lived* faith—was ever on offer. The intended outcome of his whole public ministry was that people might decide to live for the reign of God, following his "way, truth, and life" as disciples. Jesus was adamant that to belong to God's reign people cannot simply confess faith with their lips, saying "Lord, Lord," but must actually "do the will" of his "Father in heaven" (Matt. 7:21). That surely requires decision. After washing his disciples' feet, Jesus told them, "As I have done for you, so you should also do" (John 13:15, NAB), and again, "Love one another as I have loved you" (15:12). Jesus even went so far as to say, "Whoever does the will of God is my brother and sister and mother" (Mark 3:35). From his opening statement inviting people to "repent, and believe in the good news" (1:15) to his farewell discourse ("Abide in my love . . . keep my commandments," John 15:9–10), Jesus invited people to the decision for lived faith.

As seen previously, Jesus had a holistic sense of faith; his was a faith that entailed knowledge, relationship, and commitment. Though it was holistic, however, Jesus didn't necessarily see faith unfolding in that order—from head to heart to hands. Oftentimes he put the doing of faith first, which would then lead to relationship with him, and then on to true knowledge. For example, "If you obey my teachings, you are really my disciples; you will know the truth, and the truth will set you free" (John 8:31–32, Good News Bible). Notice that the living leads to discipleship, which leads to knowledge. In whatever order, discipleship to Jesus calls for decision—cognitive, affective, behavioral—for Christian faith that is realized. As John has Jesus say, "Whoever *lives the truth* comes to the light" (3:21, NAB).

In summary, Jesus engaged people's own lives and encouraged them to reflect on them. He preached with authority the old-and-new faith that was his gospel. He invited would-be disciples to see for themselves how to integrate "life" and "faith" and to make decisions for lived, living, and life-giving faith for themselves, for others, and "for the life of the world" (John 6:51). Jesus's pedagogy was one of bringing *life to Faith to life*—as lived faith.

For Reflection and Conversation

• What is your own response to the above portrayal of how Jesus taught? What would you add to this description? What do you most appreciate about his approach?

• When you compare Jesus's teaching style to yours, what similarities or dissimilarities do you recognize? Are there any decisions you need to make?

On the Road with the Risen Christ

The commitments and dynamics outlined above are evident in Jesus's approach to teaching throughout his public ministry. Nowhere are they as vividly represented, however, as in the story of the Risen Christ and the two disciples on the road to Emmaus (Luke 24:13–35). Read the text for yourself. Imagine being "on the road" with the two disciples and the Stranger they encounter. Experience this teacher at work. Note the rhythm and movements of his pedagogy. It is a classic instance of an educator crafting a teaching/learning event based on *life to Faith to life*.

The story begins on "that same day"—Easter morning. The Risen Christ, appearing only as a fellow traveler, joins two discouraged disciples as they set out on the journey, seven miles or so, from Jerusalem to the village of Emmaus. Clearly these two are in great anguish, traumatized by the fate that has befallen their beloved Jesus. The Gospel reports that they "looked sad" and says that they "*had* hoped"—note the past tense. Perhaps the two were running away from Jerusalem, afraid that as Jesus's disciples they might suffer the same fate. Maybe they were even changing sides? Emmaus was a Roman garrison.

When Jesus encounters them, they are, as we might expect, engaged in a lively conversation about "all the things that had happened." He simply joins their company and walks along *"with* them." What a great description of the primary posture of the religious educator—neither for, nor against, nor behind, nor ahead of, nor under, nor over, but walking along *with* people. Meanwhile, "their eyes were kept from recognizing" their new traveling companion.

We can well ask why they didn't recognize Jesus. Were they blinded by their disappointment and discouragement? Were they simply preoccupied with their own pain and certainly not expecting a Risen Jesus? Note too that Luke's Gospel often portrays faith as seeing for oneself what should be seen; maybe they've simply lost faith? A better pedagogical question, however, is why Jesus didn't introduce himself. An amazing aspect of this Teacher's approach is that he never *tells* these two disciples what to see. Rather, he crafts the teaching/learning dynamics so that eventually they *come to see for themselves.*

Jesus begins the pedagogy by turning the two to life, to look at and reflect upon what is going on for them and within their own souls. He asks, "What are you discussing while you walk along?" They stop, "looking sad," and one of the two, Cleopas by name, essentially responds, "What a silly question." Cleopas infers, reasonably, that Jesus must be a "stranger in Jerusalem" and the only one who doesn't know "the things that have taken place there in these days."

The Stranger simply asks, "What things?" What an amazing question for the Christ to ask. Surely no one knew better than he what had gone on in Jerusalem over the past week. So why ask? Clearly, Jesus wants them to name and reflect upon what is going on in their lives, to tell their own story and vision of it. And that is precisely what they do. They recount their version of how "Jesus of Nazareth, a prophet mighty in deed and word before God and all the people" had been taken and crucified, shattering their hopes that he was "the one who would set Israel free" (JB). They admit their confusion and disbelief at the report from some women disciples who had gone to the tomb before dawn on this third day and had not found his body, but saw a vision of angels "who said that he was alive." They explain that other disciples—they imply men—went to the tomb, found it empty "just as the women had said; but they did not see him."

The disciples' own life situation and its generative theme—sadness and loss of hope—is now out on the table. Only then does the Stranger move the conversation to their shared Faith tradition, prefaced by noting that the two are "slow of heart" to recognize fulfillment of the ancient messianic prophecies. He then reviews with them "the things about himself in all the scriptures" (no wonder it takes all day to walk the seven miles), interpreting his life as the fulfillment of God's promises through the prophets. Further, the Stranger explains that it was "necessary" that the Messiah "should suffer these things and then enter into his glory." Perhaps this is why they still don't recognize him; they were hoping for a great political Messiah who "would set Israel free"—from the Romans—whereas he came as a suffering servant. He has set up a dialectic between their hopes for the messianic promise and how it was actually fulfilled.

At this point, both the story and vision from the disciples' own lives and the Story and Vision of their faith community are in discourse. Even so, the two disciples still do not "see," and the Stranger continues to resist telling them. Reaching Emmaus, he appears ready to travel on. The Stranger intrigues them enough, however, that they press him, "Stay *with* us . . . the day is now nearly over."

The offer of hospitality convinces him to remain; "he went in to stay *with* them."

When the three sit for supper, the Stranger, as a guest, makes the unusual move to act like the host. As a good educator, he is proactive for the desired learning outcome. Luke uses the same four verbs for actions with regard to the bread that appear in all three Gospel accounts of the Last Supper; the Stranger *takes, blesses, breaks,* and *gives* it to them. And with that "their eyes were opened, and they recognized him." The Greek verb translated "recognized" here means that the disciples "knew" Jesus with their whole being, that they were bonded with him.

We can well ask, why now? Was it an echo from the story of the Last Supper that struck the chord? Perhaps. Was it a result of their offering hospitality to a stranger—an important theme in Luke—that is rewarded by the gift of spiritual sight, by which Luke means faith? Maybe. All of us have had experiences of meals that opened our eyes to see something more, that bonded relationships. The Latin *com panis,* literally "with bread," is the root of our word "companion." We've likely experienced the blessings that can come from offering hospitality. Note too that the story reflects the pattern of worship emerging in the first Christian community, with the Liturgy of the Word on the road and the Liturgy of the Eucharist at the table, always a privileged locus for seeing what should be seen. The Risen Christ, however, was already present to these two disciples; they simply needed to recognize him for themselves. Meanwhile, note again the amazing feature that Jesus never tells the two disciples what to see. Rather, he waits and waits for them to come to see for themselves. I've found such patience to be the greatest challenge in my own teaching style.

After they saw him for themselves, the text says, "he vanished from their sight." Again we may ask, why vanish now? Maybe Jesus's work was done? Perhaps teachers can recede when students have come to see for themselves? We can also ask where he went. To another Emmaus road, surely. A student once asked me, "Professor, did this ever happen?" I replied, "Yes, regularly!" The Risen Christ promised to be "with [us] always to the end of time" (Matt. 28:20, JB). We are always on some Emmaus road and the Risen Christ ever walks "with" us—if we would but recognize him. But surely the best response is that the Risen Christ disappeared into them, into us, into the Body of Christ, as Paul imagined the Church (Rom. 12:4–5). With Christ present to us as the "head" (Col. 1:18) and by the power of the Holy Spirit enlivening this Christian body (1 Cor. 12:4–11), we are now his agents in the world, commissioned and empowered to teach both what and how Jesus taught.

So finally the two disciples put it all together. As they think back over the experience, they say, "Were not our hearts burning within us while he was talking to us on the road, while he was opening the scriptures to us?" The Stranger on the road must have had great passion for what he was teaching; that's the only way to make people's hearts—souls—"burn." Now, having come to see for themselves and with faith renewed, they decide to turn around and return to Jerusalem. When people come to know in the depths of their being, they can't just toddle on home as intended. Their very "being" is changed by such "knowing" (more in Chapter 4). These two disciples are compelled to return to Jerusalem, to come back *to life* again with renewed faith. The Gospel says, "That same hour they got up and returned to Jerusalem"; this would have been a hazardous journey, late at night. But when Christians come to know for themselves, as much recognition as cognition, they are called to go share and live the good news.

When the two reach Jerusalem, they find that the little Christian community is gathering together again, beginning to assemble its new faith Story and Vision. They are greeted with, "The Lord has risen indeed, and he has appeared to Simon!" Although the two from the Emmaus road respect this emerging Story of the Christian community, they don't lose their own story either. "Then they told what had happened on the road, and how he had been made known to them in the breaking of the bread." Again, note that the conversation and presentation on the road were important, and yet recognition happened in the "breaking of the bread." It continues to happen today in all the ways that we break bread together, the bread of friendship, the bread of right and loving relationships, and the bread of Eucharist, the ultimate encounter with the Risen Friend—a Stranger no more.

The Emmaus encounter is a paradigm story that can inspire every educator in Christian faith—every teacher and parent—to "teach as Jesus did." The Emmaus road story leaves no doubt that Jesus's approach was to enable learners to bring their lives and their pressing issues to the spiritual wisdom of the Faith tradition, and then to bring that Faith back to new and renewed commitment to lived, living, and life-giving faith. Surely this is the best hope for our own pedagogy as well.

To Learn as Jesus Did?

We know precious little about Jesus's childhood. Except for the "finding in the Temple" incident (Luke 2:41–52, about which more below), the Gospels suggest nothing from shortly after Jesus's birth until he begins his public ministry, usually dated around the age of thirty. In view of the fact that Jesus was raised in the rural village of Nazareth, in the social backwater of Galilee, how do we explain his keen ability—evident throughout his public ministry—to quote and cite the Hebrew scriptures and to debate points of the law? Although Nazareth was an out-of-the-way town, we know that it had a synagogue (see 4:16). Growing up, then, Jesus would have attended synagogue school where the *hazzan,* or reader, was the teacher. Since Joseph was a carpenter—a skilled tradesperson— Jesus's family would have had the resources to pay the *hazzan*'s teaching fee, thus assuring Jesus of a formal religious education.

Beyond Jesus's schooling, he also would have been socialized into the Jewish faith of his culture. He learned from participating with his family and neighbors in Sabbath worship and by keeping the high holy days both within the family and at the synagogue. Add to these the many informal conversations that must have gone on in the home. In those days people had little entertainment other than communal conversation, and favorite topics were faith and politics. Further, there was a strong Jewish tradition of the father instructing the sons. We know from the Gospels that Joseph taught Jesus his carpenter trade: "Is not this the carpenter?" (Mark 6:3). Surely Joseph also taught Jesus about his faith tradition and, with Mary, directly influenced his values and outlook on life.

Contemporary research affirms such extrapolations about the influence of Jesus's family and life context. The social sciences agree that the influence of home and parents is paramount in the formation of children's identity and values. Likewise, numerous doctoral dissertations about teaching style conclude that teachers tend to teach the way that they were taught. Taking both points, we can presume that Mary and Joseph had a very positive influence on Jesus and the kind of person he became. Likewise, they must have modeled a pedagogy that exemplified inclusion, respect, and partnership and must have encouraged their son to bring his life to Faith and his Faith to life.

There is a theological question percolating here. How did Jesus come by his extraordinary values? For example, where did he get his totalizing version of the great law of love? Even love of enemies? Love tolerant enough to turn the other cheek, to go the extra mile? Why did Jesus challenge the racism and sexism of his culture and dare to fully include women in his community of disciples? As already noted, the defining feature of Jesus's public life was his compassion toward any and all in need. Well, where did he get his deep commitment to caring for the poor and hungry? Apart from the resurrection, feeding the hungry is the only miracle reported six times in the Gospels (once in both Luke and John; twice in Matthew and Mark).

Of course, we could respond, "Well, Jesus *was* the Son of God." True indeed. Christians believe that Jesus was God's "one, perfect, and unsurpassable Word" of divine revelation to the world (*CCC*, n. 65). Yet the dogmas of Christian faith insist that the one person Jesus had two natures; he was fully divine and fully human. Likewise they affirm that the humanity of Jesus was assumed, but not absorbed by his divine personhood. In other words, Jesus's divinity did not suspend his humanity. We read in the ancient declaration of the Council of Chalcedon (451 CE): "One and the same Son, our Lord Jesus Christ" was "perfect in divinity and perfect in humanity . . . consubstantial with the Father as to his divinity and consubstantial with us as to his humanity." Echoing Chalcedon, the *Catechism* teaches: "The distinction between the natures was never abolished by their union, but rather the character proper to each of the two natures was preserved as they came together in one person" (n. 468). As a result, Jesus had "to inquire for himself about what one in the human condition can learn only from experience" (n. 472).

Without getting into the timeless debates about how the divinity and humanity of Jesus coexisted in one person, we can surely say that the human and historical figure Jesus *had to be taught* and *needed to learn* throughout his childhood. Clearly, Mary and Joseph were his most significant teachers.

So, now, where did Jesus initially get his extraordinary values and outlook on life? The only answer must be—as for all of us—from his parents. Read the Magnificat (Luke 1:46–55). Recognize the God that Mary believed in, and the source of Jesus's values becomes patent. Mary had a powerful sense of God's presence and rejoiced in God, who intervened in her life as Savior. Mary's was a God whose mercy endures forever, a God who scatters the proud, puts down the mighty from their thrones and raises up the lowly, who fills the hungry with good things and sends the rich away empty-handed, who always keeps promises. In this light, no wonder Jesus came into his home synagogue at Nazareth on a Sabbath day, "as was his custom," looked for what scholars have called the most radical social justice text in all of scripture, Isaiah 61:1–2, and proclaimed that he was its fulfillment (see again Luke 4:16–21).

Christians have long revered Mary, lionizing her great faith, and rightly so. We believe that God chose her from all eternity for an extraordinary role in God's work of salvation, to become mother to the "Son of God" (see Luke 1:26–38). Mary's "let it be with me according to your word" (1:38) was the great human fiat that made possible God's incarnation as one of us in Jesus. Beyond Mary's vital role in parenting Jesus, the Gospels report her presence in Jesus's public ministry. According to John's Gospel, she prompted Jesus's first miracle, or "sign," at the wedding feast of Cana (2:1–12), and John's Gospel places her at the foot of the cross (19:25).

What about Joseph? Consistent with Jewish custom in Galilean villages of the time, Joseph would have had at least as significant a role as Mary in Jesus's education and apprenticeship. In keeping with cultural practice, we can imagine the men who came by Joseph's carpenter shop being engaged in conversations about faith, helping to immerse Jesus in the spiritual wisdom and knowledge of his Jewish tradition.

Matthew's Gospel describes Joseph as "a righteous man," that is, a just person. When he found out that Mary was pregnant "before they lived together," he refused "to expose her to public disgrace" and wanted "to dismiss her quietly" (1:18–19). What extraordinary sensitivity and concern Joseph had for his beloved Mary. He could well have felt personally offended and taken a very different position, even leading to her ruin; presumed adulterers could be stoned to death. Yet, though Joseph was surely bewildered by the turn of events and unable to explain them, he was intent on protecting Mary. We can infer that Joseph helped to nurture Jesus's later respect for women.

Besides being a man of compassion, Joseph must also have been a person of deep faith. He was instructed by an angel in a dream to "take Mary as [his] wife, for the child conceived in her is from the Holy Spirit." It would have been understandable, however, for Joseph to awake, say, "Yeah, right," and dismiss it all as just a dream. Instead, Joseph takes a great leap of faith and does "as the angel of the Lord had commanded him." (Read the whole story in Matthew 1:18–25). Such was the great faith that Joseph modeled to his son Jesus.

After the nativity narratives, the only instance we have in the Gospels of Mary and Joseph in a shared parenting role is the story of the twelve-year-old Jesus being lost for three days before they found him in the Temple (Luke 2:41–52). Setting aside pious sentiment and accepting not only Jesus as fully human but Mary and Joseph as well will help us to appreciate this story all the more.

The Holy Family, along with relatives and friends, had gone up to Jerusalem for the festival of Passover. The text says they did this "every year" (Luke 2:41). Returning home in a community caravan, Joseph and Mary had gone a day's journey before they even realized that Jesus was missing. Each must have presumed that he was coming along with other family or friends. Imagine the absolute panic of Mary and Joseph, maybe even a few tense exchanges: "I thought he was with your people"; "Well, I thought he was with *your* people." As the couple hurried back to Jerusalem, they must have been worried sick about their only son, a young boy, lost in a dangerous city. They searched for another two days without success.

Apparently, the Temple was about the last place they tried, and there he was, "sitting among the teachers, listening to them and asking them questions." (Note that asking good questions, the mark of an open learner, would become a feature of his pedagogy.) According to Luke, Mary, cool as a cucumber, walked up to Jesus and asked calmly, "Son, why have you done this to us? Your father and I have been looking for you with great anxiety" (NAB). But I wager that much more than that happened and got said. Can't you imagine Mary and Joseph rushing into the Temple upon sight of their young son, scooping him up in their arms, smothering him with hugs and kisses, with an avalanche of inquiries about what had happened to him, if he was all right, if he'd had anything to eat, if anyone had hurt him. Then, though the text makes it sound as if Jesus was simply spending a little time in "his Father's house," I imagine his making a typical twelve-year-old's retort: "But you should have known where to look for me." Sound like a preteen? And who knows what Mary and Joseph said next.

According to the Gospel, Mary and Joseph "did not understand," a common plight of parents, especially of twelve-year-olds. Then the Gospel reports that "he went down with them and came to Nazareth, and was obedient to them." In fact, he didn't leave home again until he was thirty years of age. Then, the story ends with the summary report "and Jesus increased in wisdom and in years, and in divine and human favor"—in other words, under Joseph's and Mary's good parenting.

No matter how we interpret this story, it surely assures parents that Mary and Joseph can be their intercessors with Jesus amid the challenges of parenting in any age, including our own. They know about parenting from the inside and also about raising a child in "the Faith."

Beyond this, if we are to enable people to "learn as Jesus learned," then we simply must give priority to parents and the home (our major theme in Chapter 6). Even the Holy Family reminds us that the socialization of the home makes parents the primary educators of their children in faith. I believe Jesus, Mary, and Joseph would assure us of as much.

For Reflection and Conversation

- What are the best insights or wisdom you've recognized for yourself in this chapter about teaching and learning "as Jesus did"?

- How might you take such insights or wisdom to heart and put them to work in your own approach to educating in faith?

CHAPTER TWO

Who Is Involved Here?
Great People, Every One

All Teaching and Learning Together

While writing this chapter, I was party to a three-way fender bender. With no one seriously injured, all three cars emptied, and their occupants formed something of an immediate bond right in the middle of the intersection. Imagine eight people shouting very different but definitive interpretations of what had happened, with the growing backed-up traffic honking to get through. When the police finally arrived, one of them called for order with, "Whoa, now! Just *who* is involved here?" I knew he was asking for the three drivers. Being one of them and wishing I wasn't, I was tempted to divert with, "Well, officer, exactly what do you mean by *who*?" but thought better of it.

The officer's good question, however, helped me to recognize what this second chapter needs to be about, namely, just *who* is involved here in the business of faith education. At the outset, I alert that I intend to debunk the limiting stereotype of "children and teachers" usually located in some kind of "school"—parochial, Sunday, or otherwise. To the contrary, every Christian person and community should be both teacher and learner, involved lifelong in what the *General Directory for Catechesis* calls "permanent catechesis." *Will there be faith?* Depends on every Christian.

Then, beyond addressing the *who* question in the sense of who the participants are, there is a deeper question here. How do we understand *who* people are and their potential for faith? What is our philosophy or, better still, our theology of the person? This may seem too esoteric a question—and I'm glad I didn't put it to the policeman—but our response and our tacit assumptions about people greatly shape how we educate in Christian faith and our hoped-for outcomes.

Do we see people as being capable of participating in teaching/learning events as agents of their own knowledge, as active contributors to the educational process? Do we assume they can personally receive, construct, and reconstruct knowledge as their own? Or do we think that people should be treated as dependent and passive recipients of knowledge from those who already know better (teachers)? Are we more likely to live Christian faith if we come to recognize its spiritual wisdom for ourselves and embrace it with personal conviction? Or should we just accept and submit to it out of unquestioning obedience to its authority (Church, Bible, or whatever). Are people capable, by God's grace, of living the life of Christian faith, or is ours an inherently sinful estate, rendering us incapable of even approximating the ideals of Christian discipleship? Again, are we simply "sinners in the hands of an angry God," as the renowned Calvinist minister Jonathan Edwards (1703–58) preached, or good people in the hands of a loving God? Where we come down on such questions—and even a slight tilt can make a big difference—will shape how we go about religious education.

In fact, there is no more central question for educators in faith than "Just *who* is involved here?"

As we push beyond the stereotype of "children and teachers" for those who actually participate in religious education, this chapter will also challenge some theological stereotypes regarding *who* we are as human beings. Since the Council of Trent (1545–63) and until recently, Catholic catechesis has assumed in large part that people are totally dependent on the Church for salvation (as if there is none outside of it) and aspired to make people into obedient members who submit to its teaching authority. Meanwhile, classic Protestantism emphasized humanity's inherent sinfulness, our justification by faith alone in Jesus Christ, and our incapacity to contribute anything to "the work of our salvation" (Phil. 2:12). Both positions diminish our agency as instruments of God's grace and thus our potential for chosen and lived faith. Drawing on deeper and more life-giving waters of Christian tradition, I will propose an empowering theology of *who* we are as people.

Because communication of the Faith should be crafted "according to the mode of the receiver," that educators take into account *who* is involved is an ancient wisdom of the Church. Parents with more than one child know this principle well. No two kids—even with the same genes—are exactly alike. To communicate effectively, you must honor each one's unique personality. Christian tradition likewise advises that the best way to teach is however people are most likely to learn. This does not mean watering down the gospel to make it more acceptable, as parents don't water down their good discipline. Rather, it requires presenting the Faith in ways that make it more likely that particular people will receive it in its fullness and respond with lived commitment.

As early as the year 200, we find Clement of Alexandria (150–215) advising teachers in his work *The Paedagogos* to craft their pedagogy to first engage and win the souls of their particular participants. A little later, in his classic treatise on teaching, *De Cate-chizandis Rudibus* ("On Catechizing Country Folk"), St. Augustine begins by urging catechists to get to know well the people they are instructing and to pitch their pedagogy accordingly. Thomas Aquinas (1225–74) often repeated that all communication of Christian faith must be "according to the mode of the receiver"; in fact, he coined the phrase.

Aquinas argued that this way of teaching imitates the divine pedagogy. God always communicates with us according to how we, in our particular human condition, are most likely to receive divine revelation. Of course, the epitome of God's communicating with us "according to the mode of the receiver" was in Jesus—God among us as one of ourselves. Even God could not communicate the fullness of divine revelation any more effectively than by coming in person, when "the Word became flesh" (John 1:14). This is why the *General Directory* makes bold to advise that all education in Christian faith is to be modeled on "the efficacious pedagogy of God throughout history" (n. 139).

Before moving on, let me acknowledge that there are some postmodern thinkers who claim that there is nothing consistent or essential about our human condition, that nothing is true of everyone, everywhere, and all the time. In fact, they contend that both who we actually are and our perception of ourselves are but social constructs, shaped by our sociocultural context, by the networks of power and influence that surround us. Before disagreeing, I do recognize that these postmodern authors make a valuable point in highlighting that our social context influences both who we are and who we think we are. For example, the way we finish sentences such as, "I think men are . . ." or "I think women are . . ." is no more than a socially constructed gender stereotype, unless we are referring to biological differences. Likewise many of the "isms" in our societies—sexism, racism, ageism, sectarianism—are social constructs proposing that some people are more human than others. The postmoderns alert us to such false constructs and biases.

Yet I'm still convinced that there are fundamental and consistent features to our human condition. If nothing else, our bodies ensure this. We have a common need for food and elimination, activity and rest, and clothing, shelter, and safety as well as a capacity for emotion, communication, creativity, and relationship with one another and the world around—all these engage our bodies, including our ultimate capacity to love and be loved. Whoever is "in the body" shares some universal characteristics.

It is true, of course, that every person is one of a kind. Note how our law courts accept fingerprints and now DNA as unique to each person. This being said, there yet remain great consistent features that mark our human condition and, I add, universal truths by which we are called to live. Of course, we can always point to exceptions. Just when we think people are basically "good," we hear of a psychopathic ax murderer. Nevertheless, we know that the psychopath is an aberration. And even if we disagree on the basic traits of the human person, the fact remains that every teacher and parent has what we might call a "functioning anthropology," in other words, an understanding of and attitude toward people that is at work in how they parent and educate. Before making some proposals about ourselves, however, I invite you to pause and try to discern what might be your own response to "Just *who* is involved here?"

For Reflection and Conversation

- Who do you think should be involved in religious education?

- How do you rate people's capacity to actively learn, to see for themselves?

- How do you rate people's ability to live the life of Christian disciples?

- How do you tip the scales—are people basically good or sinful? Trustworthy or untrustworthy?

- How do your positions on such questions shape your approach to educating in faith?

Who Are We Before God?

In one way or another, all the social sciences investigate the human condition—who we are—and offer an anthropology. As religious educators, however, our primary concern is a theological anthropology, in other words, how we understand ourselves in light of faith in God, and as Christians, specifically in light of faith in God through Jesus Christ. As the great theologian Karl Rahner (1904–84) proposed, Jesus revealed not only our God to us, but us to us—who we are and can become before God.

When at its best, a Christian anthropology resoundingly affirms who we are as persons and encourages both our personal potential and the kind of community we can become together. These two emphases—personal and communal—are simply two sides of the same coin. As humans we are always "persons-in-community" and "a community-of-persons." I will first lay out a Christian perspective on the person as person and then highlight how our personhood is inherently relational. Significantly, our understanding of both arises from our understanding of God. God as revealed in Jesus Christ is the One who shapes who we are, personally and communally. As our God is One and Good, so is each person—essentially. As our God is Triune Loving Relationship, we are called to live likewise—together as "a people" in right and loving relationships. This anthropology is the bedrock for *what* and *why* and *how* to educate in Christian faith.

It is surely no coincidence that the very opening chapters of the Bible, Genesis 1–3, lay out the beginnings of a faith response to the question, "Who are we?" The biblical authors must have had a sense that everything else begs this question. And so we find in those chapters three great mythical stories describing who we are. They are *mythical* in that they teach abiding truths, even if they are not literal accounts of what happened.

Genesis 1 presents the creation of humankind occurring toward the end of the "sixth day" as the pinnacle of God's work of creating. It sounds as if God is ruminating, even consulting within the Godhead, "Let us make humankind in our image, according to our likeness" (1:26). Clearly in favor, we read, "So God created humankind in . . . the image of God; . . . male and female God created them" (1:27). We have heard this text so often that its amazing truth claim can pass us by. It proposes that we humans reflect the very image and likeness of our divine Creator and that this is equally true of both male and female. In other words, the first creation story asserts that we can expect humankind to reflect the intelligence, relationality, and creativity of God. At the end of each of the previous five days of creation, God looked upon what God had made and "saw that it was good." At the end of the sixth, however, God looked upon the creation of that day "and indeed, it was *very* good," the only time that Genesis 1 uses the superlative.

The second creation myth portrays God as crafting a "person of the earth" (the literal meaning of Adam, not "man," but gender inclusive), a term that reflects our corporality and mortality. God then breathes God's own breath of life into the earth person's nostrils, and it becomes "a living being" (Gen. 2:7). Though perhaps tamed by repetition, here again we have another astounding claim about our condition, namely, that we are alive by the very life breath of God. Our aliveness is from sharing in God's own life. This life that we live and breathe is truly divine—of God.

Genesis 2 then depicts God as differentiating the "earth person" into *ish* and *isha,* the Hebrew for "man" and "woman" in the sense of gender. This is the first time these gender words appear—only after God differentiates Adam. Then, God gives them to each other as *partners,* a term that, scholars now say, is the best translation of the Hebrew *ezer* (2:18). This is often undertranslated as "helpmate" or "helper," as if the woman were only in a helping or secondary role to the man. Instead, each can say of the other, "You are 'bone of my bones and flesh of my flesh'" (2:23). They are equal partners.

In both creation accounts, God gives humankind responsibilities with regard to the rest of creation. In the first account, "God blessed them, and God said to them, 'Be fruitful and multiply, and fill the earth and subdue it; and have dominion'" over all creation (1:28). Clearly, God places humankind in charge, and note again that this commission is addressed to both the male and female, to "them." In partnership, women and men have a profound responsibility from and on behalf of their Creator. "Dominion," however, could be (and has been) overinterpreted to mean that God has given us permission to do whatever we please with creation, as if it were simply a plaything at our disposal. It is precisely this attitude that has brought us to the brink of ecological destruction. So we need the second creation account as well.

In Genesis 2, humankind receives the explicit mandate to be good stewards of God's creation. The key text is 2:15. It says that God gives humankind a twofold mandate, usually translated as "to till it and keep it." The two Hebrew verbs are *shamar,* which means "to sustain with loving care," and *abdad,* which connotes "to cultivate and develop." In other words, God tells us that we are responsible both to maintain and to grow God's creation. In his parable of the talents (Matt. 25:14–30), Jesus reiterates the stewardship commission of Genesis. Good stewards don't simply maintain their gifts; they develop them, and they certainly don't destroy them.

If we could stop there, what a rosy picture we'd have of ourselves. But it would not accurately represent our human condition, marred as it is by the shortcomings of sin, sickness, and death. So Genesis 3 insists that we face the reality of "original sin" and its ramifications as also describing our human condition. It symbolizes so vividly that something is awry and that we need God's saving help in order to live as a people of God.

We often think of original sin as one of disobedience, surely a valid interpretation of this mythic story; the original couple are presented as disobeying God by eating the forbidden fruit. The temptation that attracted Adam and Eve, however, was that they "will be like God, knowing good and evil" (Gen. 3:5–6). In other words, we can also interpret theirs as a positive desire, reflecting their God-given potential to become godlike (remember 1:26–27). Following the lead of St. Augustine, Western Christianity's traditional interpretation has emphasized "the Fall" through disobedience and the passing on of its consequences by procreation to succeeding generations, giving us a proclivity for sin and evil. Eastern Catholicism, however, does not emphasize our sinfulness as much as it does the incompleteness of humankind and our need for God's help in realizing our positive potential. In fact, Orthodox Catholics propose that, made in the divine image, our vocation in life is to grow in divine likeness, in *theosis,* literally, to become ever more Godlike.

Whichever emphasis one accepts, Genesis 3 reflects the reality of our need for God's help, whether to avoid sin, to realize our possibilities, or both. We simply cannot save ourselves by ourselves. Christians have traditionally seen God's condemnation of the snake (the Tempter) and declaration that the woman's offspring would "strike" its head as the promise of a Savior (3:15—often called the "proto-evangelium," the "first good news"). The *Catechism of the Catholic Church* summarizes: "The doctrine of original sin is the 'reverse side' of the Good News that Jesus is the Savior of all people, that all need salvation, and that salvation is offered to all through Christ" (n. 389).

As noted, Western Christianity has tended to highlight human sinfulness and our need for God's grace to offset our sinful condition. Within the Western tradition, then, a great debate broke out at the time of the Protestant Reformation. This is usually dated from Martin Luther's posting of his Ninety-Five Theses of reform in 1517. Thereafter, a focal question became: Just how sinful is our human condition? Or, stated otherwise: Just how much are we in need of God's grace? The great Reformers—Calvin even more so than Luther—placed huge accent on our sinfulness and incapacity for good. They were reacting to what they perceived as Catholicism's overemphasis on doing good works, as if we can save ourselves by our own efforts. For the Reformers, on the other hand, our justification and salvation are entirely by God's grace, *gratia sola,* "by grace alone."

Responding, Catholicism rejected the notion that we are totally corrupt; we are not a *massa peccati* ("mass of sin") as Calvin claimed. The Catholic point was that such a claim would rob us of our responsibility, reducing us to being recipients only rather than participants and covenant partners in "the work of our salvation" (Phil. 2:12). The Catholic preference was to hold on to the conviction that the human condition, though "fallen," remains in the divine image; though capable of evil, we are also capable of doing great good, albeit only with the help of God's grace. This is so because God's life within us is an original blessing that still trumps any original sinfulness. Note that seeing the human condition as essentially good had been the dominant Christian position up to the time of the Reformation, though there were strains in Augustine's writings that were interpreted to highlight human sinfulness.

In fact, we need both emphases—the classic Catholic stress on the essential goodness of our human condition and our responsibility for the choices we make, and yet the Protestant accent on our need for God's grace, without which we cannot even mount our own best efforts. I often think that people in Twelve Step recovery programs most readily recognize the need for this balance. My friend David will often say that he maintains sobriety only by the help of a "Higher Power." Yet he also feels responsible to attend meetings, to receive and give help to other alcoholics in recovery, and, even after twenty-five years of sobriety, to avoid situations of too much temptation (he'd never take a job in a bar). Thomas Aquinas articulated this balance best by saying that God's grace both *enhances* and works *through* human nature (us), yet we remain responsible for our choices and deeds.

Perhaps the social sciences can help to decide this age-old debate between classic Catholicism and Protestantism regarding the essential nature of the human person and whether we are tilted more toward sin or goodness. These sciences generally agree that so much depends on what a family or culture or society projects onto us. Put simply, people who are treated as sinful are more likely to sin; treated as good, they're more likely to act accordingly. This is very important wisdom for parents with younger children to remember and practice. For example, a dad suspects his young son of taking five dollars from his wallet. Now, should he take a Calvinist posture, say, "What a bad boy you are. Already a thief at seven years of age. I hope God will forgive you," and take away the money (he could be wrong; maybe the kid did get it from his aunt)? Or should he be a Thomist and say, "You're such a good boy. I know you'd never steal from my wallet. And if you did, I'm sure you'd put it back," and then hope for the best? Though always a leap of faith, it is better by far to treat people—young or old—as inherently good rather than inevitably sinful.

Although Reformation era polemics exaggerated the differences between Catholics and Protestants, all Christians might accept this argument as settled in favor of our essential goodness, if not by the social sciences, then by our shared faith in Jesus Christ.[1] To begin with, our conviction that God came among us as one of us in Jesus is an unqualified affirmation of the intrinsic goodness of our human condition. How could it be that "the Word became flesh and lived among us" (John 1:14), if our fleshly state is inherently corrupt and sinful? Further, by Jesus's dying and rising, we believe that God's "grace bestowed in abundance" (2 Cor. 4:15) has been poured out all the more upon humankind precisely that we may "have an abundance for every good work" (9:8, NAB). This is why Paul can also write of us as "God's co-workers" (1 Cor. 3:9) and later explain, "God's grace to me has not been ineffective. Indeed, I have toiled harder than all of them; not I, however, but the grace of God that is with me" (15:10, NAB). What a fine summary of God's grace prompting and working through our own best efforts. As the *Catechism* summarizes: "It is in Christ, Redeemer and Savior, that the divine image, disfigured in humankind by the first sin, has been restored to its original beauty and ennobled by the grace of God" (n. 1702).

Christian anthropology, therefore, must affirm and balance— sometimes in tension—at least three anthropological convictions: our innate goodness, our capacity for sin, and the difference effected by Jesus's dying and rising on our behalf. With our collaboration, the last enables our capacity for good to win out, a goodness, I add immediately, that is itself sustained by God's grace. Our freely chosen efforts to do good and avoid evil are required; God's grace never programs our choices. And though God's abundant grace in Jesus is always at high tide toward us, it comes to us as a responsibility or, better, as our "response-ability."

Having reviewed ourselves as individual persons in the light of

Christian faith, let us turn now to the communal nature of our personhood, reflecting the relational nature of our God. Later on, Chapters 5 and 6, on the parish and family, will examine at length the necessary role of community in educating for faith. Here let us anticipate those chapters by reviewing the Christian warrants for understanding ourselves as essentially relational persons.

Our being made in the divine image and likeness takes on new meaning with the revelation through Jesus that our God, though One, is yet a Trinity of distinct and equal divine Persons, traditionally named as Father, Son, and Holy Spirit. Further, not only does Jesus reveal the triune nature of the One True God, but also, as noted above, God's unconditional love for us. As the great scripture scholar Daniel Harrington writes, "Jesus is the revealer and revelation of God's love." Harrington makes the bold claim: "The theme of Jesus as the revelation of God's love for us is, in my opinion, the central and most basic theme of the Christian Bible."[2] This is why toward the end of the New Testament we find the apex of Jesus's revelation summarized in three words, "God is love" (1 John 4:8).

In this light, the symbol of the Trinity means that our God, even within Godself, is a Triune Loving Relationship. St. Augustine's beautiful analogy was that God the Father is the Lover, God the Son is the Beloved, and the Holy Spirit is the Loving between them. And just as God is a Triune Loving Relationship *within* Godself, so is God always in a loving relationship with us. God's three-way love for us as Father, Son, and Holy Spirit is unconditional, the outpouring of the essential nature of God. God would have to stop being God to stop loving any one of us. In other words, because God is love, God cannot not love us.

Therefore, then, created in the divine image, we are made to live like God, that is in right and loving relationship with God, ourselves, others, and all of creation. Because our God is relational, we are made *for* relationship and find our personhood only *in* and *through* relationships. Likewise, as God is in right and loving relationship within Godself and toward us, so we are called to live in right and loving relationship with all. This is our defining human vocation. As I elaborate later, such "right relationship" is the biblical definition of *both* justice and holiness of life.

It is fascinating how the doctrine of the Trinity has returned of late to where it belongs—at the center stage of Christian faith. For too long, we tended to skip over the doctrine of the Trinity as simply a mystery that we cannot explain, which of course it is. Contemporary theological scholarship,[3] however, has helped us to realize that the Trinity is *the* Mystery that explains everything about our God and about who and how we are to live as a people of God. Reflecting the divine image and alive by the divine breath, we too are essentially relational beings who can realize our full potential only in and through community and by trying to live in right and loving relationships all across the board.

The Bible reflects our communal nature throughout, especially in describing how the Israelites were to live as the people of God. Through priests, prophets, and rulers, God called the Israelites into covenant as a people, related with them as a people, and invited them to live as God's own people, through whom all the peoples of the world will find blessing (Gen. 12:3). Every Israelite's keeping of covenant redounds to the whole people, their sins hurt the community, and so their repentance must be communal as well (for the Day of Atonement, see Lev. 16). At the beginning, Cain asks, "Am I my brother's keeper?" (Gen. 4:9). In many ways, the rest of the Bible is a response to Cain's rhetorical question—"You bet you are!" We are all responsible for and to one another—like sisters and brothers.

The New Testament writes large that being Christian is a communal affair. Although we are called to our personal relationship with God in Jesus Christ, the invitation is in and through community, not in isolation from it. Throughout his public ministry, Jesus constantly called people into his community of disciples. As outlined in Chapter 1, his was to be a community of outreach and radical inclusion, of respect and equality, of compassion and justice for all, practicing partnership with servant leaders.

This communal emphasis flows from the Gospels into the other New Testament writings. It is significant that the major images the first Christians had of themselves were communal—people of God, flock of the Shepherd, household of God, temple of the Holy Spirit, and of course Paul's image of the Church as the Body of Christ. Look, for example, at 1 Corinthians 12:12–31 and at how Paul thinks we should function as Christ's Body in the world now. He begins with, "For just as the body is one and has many members, and all the members of the body, though many, are one body, so it is with Christ. For in the one Spirit we were all baptized into one body—Jews or Greeks, slaves or free—and we were all made to drink of one Spirit." Paul goes on to explain that, like a physical body, all the members are vital and have a key contribution to make. "The eye cannot say to the hand 'I have no need of you,' nor again the head to the feet, 'I have no need of you.'" Likewise, "If one member suffers, all suffer together with it; if one member is honored, all rejoice together with it."

Paul is insisting that every person is important and has their own identity, and yet all together make up more than the sum of the parts, namely, a community. His metaphor of the Body of Christ roundly affirms both the person and the community, with the two going hand in hand. In other words, Christian faith reflects human nature—as created by God—in that as communal persons we must be communal Christians as well.

It is worth noting that this Christian sense of a "communal person" is in stark contrast to the hyperemphasis that modernity places on "the self," even lionizing what Charles Taylor calls a "buffered self."[4] Taylor uses this term to mean individuals who claim to be autonomous, standing alone from others and the world, invulnerable within a protective shell, and masters of their own destiny. Taylor and other postmodern authors are recognizing that the buffered self can be a destructive myth. The truth is that we are essentially relational beings. It is not that we are individual persons first, who then may choose relationships when to our advantage; rather, we become persons only in and through relationships.

Parenthetically, this is why I favor the term "person" over "individual." The latter is from the Latin *individuare*, literally "to stand apart," whereas "person" is from the Greek *prosopon*, which means "turned toward another." (The Greek for a person who tries to "stand alone" is *idiotes*. Enough said!) Thus, even the very word "person" bespeaks that we are relational beings, human only through relationship with others.

To summarize, by nature and by faith, we are called to live as communal persons. As members of the human family and as Christians, we are to commit to both the personal and common good of all. Before reviewing some implications for education in faith, pause to note your own reflections thus far.

For Reflection and Conversation

- How does the understanding of the human person as essentially good and communal compare with your own sense of who we are? Do you agree, disagree, or have something to add?

- Recognizing that people are essentially good and graced—empowered by God's effective love—what might be some implications for educating in faith?

- Recognizing that we are communal beings, what are some implications for educating in faith?

Putting Theological Anthropology
to Work in Faith Education

Given the dual Christian emphases on our potential goodness *and* communal personhood, let us tease out some implications for educating in faith. I suggest seven here and others will emerge in later chapters.

1. *Presume that everyone is already spiritual and engage their souls to educate in faith.* Given our creation in the divine image and our aliveness by the very life breath of God, all humans are essentially spiritual beings. Instead of identifying people as human beings with a spiritual aspect, it is better to think of us as spiritual beings with a human aspect. Educators in faith can presume that people have an innate aptitude for God and that the Blessed Trinity is forever relating with us to draw us to Godself. The *Catechism of the Catholic Church* summarizes it well: "The desire for God is written in the human heart, because [the person] is created by God and for God; and God never ceases to draw [us] to [God]self" (n. 27). So parents need not worry about "making" their children spiritual; they are already spiritual beings. Children's spirituality, however, does need nurture and fostering. Likewise, religious educators need not worry about "bringing God" into peoples lives; God is always already "here" with grace—God's love at work—and self-disclosure, revelation. People do need education, however, to recognize, understand, and respond to the divine Presence.

Given the above and quite logically, spiritual beings need a pedagogy that engages and delves into their very souls, into the depths of their human spirit, appealing to them personally and as persons. Indeed, their minds must be well engaged too, but it is in the soul and only through the soul that life-transforming education in faith can take place. We engage and nurture people's souls by turning them to reflect on their own lives and what matters most to them, by inviting them to express their feelings and desires, their hopes and fears. We do so by lending people access to the spiritual wisdom of the Christian faith in ways that are likely to resonate with their own spirits, to strike a chord in their hearts, to give them hope and confidence, to affirm and encourage their potential for goodness. We engage and nurture people's souls by encouraging them to appropriate and see for themselves the wisdom of Christian faith, to make its spirituality their own, to choose to live their lives by its light.

2. *Give people ready access to a rich and persuasive expression of Christian Story and Vision.* God's revelation, which biblically begins with the stories of creation, continues to unfold throughout the Hebrew Bible and reaches its apex in the New Testament. Christians recognize Jesus as the "fullness" of divine revelation. Though we await no new revelation after Jesus, the *meaning* of Scripture continues to unfold throughout human history, particularly as people of faith find themselves with new questions and challenges in different times and places. Christians use the generic term "Tradition" for the faith consensus that the Holy Spirit emerges in the community of faith, the Church, and is well tested by time. Guided by the Holy Spirit, the Church continues to interpret Scripture and Tradition as God's word to our lives in every time and place.

Although Scripture and Tradition are the standard terms for the normative media of divine revelation, for pedagogical reasons I've found it helpful to give people access to them through the symbols of "Story" and "Vision." I use "Story" to symbolize *the whole historical reality and spiritual wisdom of Christian revelation* and "Vision" as *the demands and promises that this faith makes upon the lives of its adherents and communities* (more in Chapter 8).

Religious educators, whether in home, parish, school, or program, are responsible to see to it that people have ready access to the teachings of Christian faith and its rich spiritual wisdom, all as mediated through Scripture and Tradition. People are capable of receiving and are entitled to competent and in-depth knowledge of Christian Story and to know its challenges and consolations, its responsibilities and hopes, its implications and applications—to have a Christian Vision for life. This is their spiritual legacy in faith, which they are entitled to inherit and to flourish within in their time.

Further, without manipulation or indoctrination, educators must re-present Christian Story and Vision in ways that are enticing and attractive to people's lives, that are likely to encourage them in personal conviction of its truths and values. Most older Catholics grew up with an apologetics for faith based on authority and fear. We need, instead, the kind of persuasive presentation of faith that the great Christian apologists offered in the early centuries, one that appeals to people's desires, to their own reason, and to the fruits and witness of lived Christian faith. Chapter 4 will elaborate such a new apologetics.

3. *Invite people to Christian discipleship and present it as a lifestyle that is possible to live.* Christian faith calls people to live as disciples of Jesus Christ. He was truly "the way, and the truth, and the life" (John 14:6) that we are to follow, as persons and as communities. A later chapter will elaborate what discipleship demands. Here, I simply summarize that it requires lives of faith, hope, and love as modeled by Jesus, with the last as "the greatest" of all (1 Cor. 13:13). The love command that Jesus preached requires all of our minds, hearts, and strength—everything we've got—to love God by loving neighbors as ourselves, with neighbor meaning everyone, even enemies. Besides, Christian faith demands living by the Ten Commandments and doing the works of compassion and mercy, of justice and peace in the world. This is certainly not the "therapeutic deism" mentioned in the Introduction, belief in a "nice" God who makes no demands on people's lives. Though following *the way* of Jesus is the greatest mode possible for the living of our lives, it is

also a very challenging one. That is how educators in faith are to re-present it.

Further, although the demands are great and challenging, by God's saving grace in Jesus Christ it is possible for disciples to approximate Christian living. I say "approximate," because we never do it perfectly. Even the greatest saints were keenly aware of their shortcomings and their need for God's mercy. Yet because of Christ's death and resurrection, "grace abounds all the more," and it is God's grace—not sin—that now has "dominion" (Rom. 5:20–21). By God's grace, then, people *can* live and be constantly challenged to grow in holiness as disciples of Jesus.

I make a parenthetical comment here about these first three suggestions for putting a Christian anthropology to work in faith education. The first invites people to turn to and reflect upon their own lives in the world and God's initiatives therein. The second suggests that people have ready access to the spiritual wisdom of Christian Story and Vision. The third calls them to discipleship, in other words, to integrate their own lives and Christian faith into a lived faith. Together, these three amount to the dynamic of *life to Faith to life*. I highlight to make the point that such an approach not only reflects the pedagogy of the Stranger on the Emmaus road, but is entirely fitting to a Christian anthropology, to our nature as human beings.

 4. *Teach people their own dignity, equality, and worth and to respect the same in others.* From the great truths reflected in the creation accounts and reiterated throughout the Bible, Christian faith draws out a deep commitment to the dignity of all people, to their equality and worth, regardless of social condition or cultural context. The truth is that no one is created any more in the divine image than anyone else. All are people of God. To educate in such faith requires teaching this very positive image of the person, so that people embrace it for themselves and promote it for all. However, beyond *what*

we teach as Christian faith, we are to reflect such an anthropology in *how* we teach it.

Such a dignified sense of the person calls for a pedagogy that engages people as agents of their own knowing and becoming in faith. The *General Directory for Catechesis* insists that "In the catechetical process" the one being catechized "must be an active subject, conscious and co-responsible, and not merely a silent and passive recipient" (n. 167). We need to engage all of people's gifts of reason, memory, and imagination, their whole "mind," to pay attention to the data of their lives and to the data of Christian faith, in order to bring them to understanding and then encourage their own good judgments and decisions about how to live as disciples. Anything less than this sort of pedagogy will lack full respect for participants, ignoring their dignity and potential as knowers of truth and doers of good.

5. *Teach people for and through community.* Chapters 5 and 6 will unpack at length this consequence of a Christian anthropology, focusing on the role of parish and family in religious education. Here, however, we can summarize with two key points. First, our educating in Christian faith should nurture in people a sense of themselves as communal beings, encouraging them to be active members in a local parish and likewise good citizens of their neighborhood and larger world. Our challenge is to teach Christian faith in ways that inspire people to be both active members of the Body of Christ and good citizens of society, contributing through each to the personal and common good of all.

Second, the very pedagogy we employ ought to reflect the communal nature of people. So we can encourage conversation and participation according to people's learning styles. We can build up community within teaching/learning events, inviting people to share with neighbors, to work together in partnership, to learn from and with each other. It is significant that much of the current lit-

erature on teaching emphasizes cooperative and collaborative learning, peer teaching, partnerships, and so on. Given our theological
anthropology, education in Christian faith should encourage such
approaches.

6. *Teach to convince people of God's love and mercy.* This may
sound like a pious sentiment and yet, if faith education can help
people to really "know" in their depths—in the very "marrow bone"
of their being—God's unconditional love, what a gift to their lives
this will be. It would surely convince people that life is meaningful
and worthwhile, not because of what we earn or deserve, but as
sheer gift. Our meaning arises out of Ultimate Meaning, from God
who is Love and in love with us. Such conviction would encourage
people in an "attitude of gratitude" toward everything in life and
confidence that "neither death, nor life, neither angels, nor rulers,
nor things present, nor things to come, nor powers, nor height, nor
depth, nor anything else in all creation, will be able to separate us
from the love of God in Christ Jesus our Lord" (Rom. 8:38–39).
What an antidote such conviction could be to the frenetic anxiety
that society creates in people when they have to prove themselves by
achievements, when the truth is that we give glory to God just by
being alive in the divine image and likeness.

As of God's love, we can say likewise of God's mercy. When the
Israelites had already broken their newly minted covenant with
God by worshipping the "golden calf" (still our favorite idol), Moses
went back up the mountain in fear and trepidation, fully expecting
to be blasted by the wrath of God. Instead, Moses encountered, "a
God merciful and gracious, . . . abounding in steadfast love and
faithfulness, keeping steadfast love for the thousandth generation,
forgiving iniquity and transgression and sin, yet by no means clear-
ing the guilty," that is, still holding us responsible (Exod. 34:6–7).
At the beginning of the new covenant in Jesus, we hear Mary echo
these sentiments. She proclaims that "God's mercy is for those who

fear him from generation to generation" and that God remembers "his mercy according to the promise" (Luke 1:50, 54–55). It is true that Jesus heightened the demands of God's reign, radicalizing its law of love, but he also increased the availability and assurance of God's mercy.

These convictions challenge us to bring people to much more than "knowing about" God's love and mercy. We need to help people experience both with deep conviction. This is where parents' love for their children and teachers' for their students will be more convincing than anything we might say. It is our august and daunting privilege to be mediators of God's love and mercy in their lives and to do so perhaps more at the experiential than the cognitive level.

Recently, after a presentation to a gathering of Catholic school educators, a middle-aged man came to me at the lunch break. He took me into a bear hug, while insisting rhetorically, "I'm sure you don't remember me." Out of a thirty-five-year fog, to my amazement and his, I said, "Don, of course I do." With this he came to tears. Don was in the first undergraduate theology course I taught at Boston College, and I still remember many of their names and faces (then), although I have forgotten thousands of others since— it's something like the way we remember our first date.

Don rapidly reviewed the headlines from his life since B.C., all the while interjecting his thanks to me for being so kind when he was in my class. He said that my kindness brought him back to his faith, and he'd clung to it tenaciously ever since—through many challenges. When I asked him what course he'd taken with me, he couldn't remember the title. When I asked what particular act of kindness I'd done for him, he was vague, but mentioned something about my allowing him extra time on a paper when he was sick. But he just remembered that I was very kind to everyone (I was also scared of them—my first year teaching—and figured I could win them over by being kind). But I took his word for it that I had been so and that my kindness was an instrument of God's grace in Don's life. Meanwhile, I knew better than to press him on any theological topic I might have taught; I knew that was long forgotten.

7. *Teach people the vision of becoming fully alive to the glory of God.* The very positive sense I've outlined of people's personal potential for goodness and for right and loving relationship is heavily reflected in the writings of early Christian authors. We already saw Paul's confidence that all the baptized can bond with and have something valuable to contribute to the Body of Christ. Besides, Paul had many other affirming ways of talking about who Christians can become. For example, "If anyone is in Christ, there is a new creation: everything old has passed away; see, everything has become new!" (2 Cor. 5:17). Bonded with Christ and each other by baptism, we become the adopted sons and daughters of God. Now, we too can address God as "Abba"—as Jesus did—because we are "joint heirs with Christ" within God's family (Rom. 8:15–17). Paul also proposed that the damage done to the human condition by Adam's sin has been reversed by God's saving work in the life, death, and resurrection of Jesus: "For as all die in Adam, so all will be made alive in Christ" (1 Cor. 15:20–22).

The author of 1 Peter hails Christians as "a chosen race, a royal priesthood, a holy nation, God's own people . . . called out of darkness into God's marvelous light" (2:9). A century or so later, St. Irenaeus (130–200) declared that "the glory of God is the human person fully alive." In other words, the more we flourish as people, the more God is praised in us. What and how we teach in faith can emphasize the great potential people have for good and for God and help them to flourish as persons in right and loving relationships. Anything that demeans or diminishes people should be entirely foreign to Christian religious education. Instead, we are to enhance and empower people, ever encouraging them to grow into their divine potential.

I'll conclude this section with some advice for educators concerning the fruits of our labors. It helped me when I came to realize—albeit slowly—that the teaching outcome does not depend entirely on me, that I need not accept all responsibility for how my students turn out. *Educators in faith need to strive to do the best they can and then leave the rest to God's grace.* A pious-sounding sentiment, perhaps, but it can help sustain us to "keep on." As Aquinas argued, God's grace builds upon and works through nature, so we are called to be adequate instruments of God's grace. This requires us always to mount our best efforts. This means being well prepared, pedagogically and theologically, and intentional and thoughtful in all that we do. I return often to the importance of "intentionality" to educating in faith. For now, suffice it to say that God's grace typically works through our labors—which themselves are prompted by God's grace—and the better the labors, the more likely is grace to work effectively. This being said, and our best efforts made, let us place the outcome in the hands of God. May we remember that while some plant and others water, it is "only God who gives the growth" (1 Cor. 3:6).

For Reflection and Conversation

- What other implications for faith education might you add from your own anthropology—sense of the person?

- How might these reflections affect your practice of faith education?

- In your opinion now, who are the actors in religious education, the actual participants?

Who Is to Be Educated in Faith?

The title of this chapter responds to the question, "*Who* is involved here?" with, "Great people, every one." Now that we have reviewed the "good people" involved and some implications, I move to the second aspect of *who*—the actual participants. I divide my proposal into two parts, first, who is to be educated in faith and then who is to do it. As hinted, the answer to both questions is *everyone*.

Before we set aside the stereotype of "only children," let us first be sure to say "including children." I stress this because I've come upon religious educators of late who place so much emphasis on the continuing religious education of adults that they can sound as if they are neglecting children's catechesis. Indeed, some evangelical traditions have strongly maintained that children cannot be educated in faith until after they have been personally converted (beginning around the age of twelve). The great Protestant religious educator Horace Bushnell (1802–76) was once tried for heresy and expelled from his evangelical church for claiming that "children should grow up Christian and never know themselves as being otherwise."[5] Effective catechesis of children undoubtedly takes real intentionality and programming on the part of both parish and parents (Chapters 5 and 6). Today, however, all Christian denominations take seriously the responsibility to share their faith with their upcoming generations of children and adolescents. To this I say, amen, and let us redouble our efforts—rather than curtail them—in the catechesis of children (more in Chapters 5, 6, and 7).

We have laid out a very positive sense of the potential goodness of people, enhanced all the more as they embrace and approximate, by God's grace, the life of holiness and wholeness that is discipleship to Jesus. One strong strand within Christian tradition goes as far as proposing *theosis,* that is, becoming ever more like God, as our ultimate potential. For Catholics, and indeed for all Christians, the Second Vatican Council (1962–65) presented an inspiring description of the potential and responsibility of every Christian that come with the turf of baptism. In many ways, the whole agenda of Vatican II can be summarized as a reclaiming (from the early Church) of *a radical theology of baptism.* The council reiterated that baptism, instead of being considered merely a cultural practice or a traditional ritual, should be seen as the root (Latin *radix*) that determines the identity of Christians as disciples of Jesus, that vitalizes their lifelong growth into holiness of life. Let's take a sampling from the council.

The Dogmatic Constitution on the Church, often referred to by its Latin title, *Lumen Gentium,* states that all the baptized are to exercise their rights and fulfill their responsibilities within "the common priesthood of the faithful" and participate with the ordained "in the one priesthood of Christ." This constitution then elaborates: "The baptized, by regeneration and anointing of the Holy Spirit are consecrated into a spiritual house and a holy priesthood" (n. 10). *Lumen Gentium* goes on to boldly state that all the baptized "share a common dignity from their rebirth in Christ, a true equality" (n. 32). In this Body of Christ, no one is any more baptized than anyone else. This egalitarian sentiment is reflected even in the title of the document's fifth chapter, "The Call of the Whole Church to Holiness."[6]

The Constitution also states that "the faithful are by baptism made one body with Christ . . . sharers in the priestly, prophetic, and kingly functions of Christ . . . in the mission of the whole Christian people . . . to the world" (n. 31). Taking seriously our baptismal bond with Christ as "priest, prophet, and ruler," other council documents amplify that baptism calls us to "full, conscious, and active participation" in the Church's worship—to become a priestly people; to side with those "who are poor or in any way afflicted"—to be a prophetic people; and "to express [our] opinion on things which concern the good of the Church"—to be a co-responsible people (Constitution on the Sacred Liturgy, n. 14; Pastoral Constitution on the Church in the Modern World, n. 1; Dogmatic Constitution on the Church, n. 37). In a Church that has been so defined by its hierarchy, these sentiments mark a coming of age for the vocation of all the baptized.

The Council's statements are a clarion call to a new level of co-responsibility for our faith and Church. Rather than being divided into providers and dependents, teachers and taught, baptism unites and calls everyone to lifelong growth into holiness of life after *the way* of Jesus and to active participation with the Christian community—the Church—in carrying on Jesus's mission and ministry to the world. Note, however, that baptism is an act of faith, not of magic. Christians don't grow into such adult and mature faith, into holiness of life and co-responsibility for the Church's mission just by being baptized. As Aquinas would ever advise, "grace works through people"; therefore, such lived and mature faith needs ongoing religious education. Recognizing this truth and subsequent to the Council, Catholic statements on religious education call for lifelong education in faith. Again, let us look at just a sample from the *General Directory for Catechesis*. As noted already, it is the most recent statement (1998) from the Catholic magisterium (the official teaching authority of the Church) on the topic.

On the question of who is to be catechized, the *GDC* leaves no doubt: everyone and throughout life. It repeatedly calls for "permanent catechesis" (n. 51) and echoes this with the phrase "continuous education in the faith" (n. 48.5). It often reiterates that Christian discipleship is "a process of continuing conversion which lasts for the whole of life" (n. 56). For this reason, the *GDC* makes its strongest statement (quoting a previous church document called *Catechesi Tradendae*), that "Catechesis for adults . . . must be considered the chief form of catechesis" (n. 59). I reiterate that this is not to neglect the catechesis of children, adolescents, and young adults, but only to say that all religious education must be aimed at fostering maturity of faith and sustaining the lifelong journey of Christians into holiness of life.

Let me note here that in recent centuries Catholics have focused entirely on the catechizing of children and typically within a schooling model. As a result, this emphasis on adults and promoting maturity in faith, primarily outside of a school model, is a major and challenging paradigm shift. It calls for a whole new consciousness and way to proceed (as I detail in Chapter 5). In fact, mainline Protestant churches have traditionally practiced "permanent catechesis" far better than Catholics. I remember an old Methodist friend in Kansas many years ago who, at eighty-two, prided himself in the fact that he had never missed Sunday school except for ill health. It was as important to him as attending worship.

The pioneering research of James Fowler and colleagues on the developmental stages of faith that people *may* pass through toward maturity lends added warrant for lifelong faith education.[7] From the *intuitive* and *literal* stages of childhood, through the *conventional* and *individuating* stages of youth and young adulthood, to the *paradoxical* and *universal* perspectives of full maturity, the journey of faith may take byways rather than highways or hit roadblocks that bring it to a halt. The research suggests that most people either embrace or reject the mid-level stage of *conventional* faith and travel no farther.

I wager that many people who "lose their faith" do so because the conventional version that they encountered as children fails to meet the complexities and pressures of postmodern life. Often this reflects a failure of their church to provide effective education toward mature faith. If people had ready access to good ongoing religious education, they would be likely to negotiate their way into a more nuanced faith—instead of all-or-nothing choices—and they could embrace the paradoxes that constitute mature faith. For example, when the institutional Church and its leaders scandalize or dreadfully disappoint, a mature faith, while protesting the Church's sinfulness, is likely to focus anew on God, Jesus, and the gospel, rather than being crushed by such human failures. A mature faith is also more capable of embracing a paradox such as great human suffering in the face of claims for a loving and provident God. The truth is that the journey of Christian faith always entails "leaps" along the way, often across chasms of doubt and contradiction, and it has no arrival point until we finally rest in God (St. Augustine). Christian faith ever challenges and beckons us onward toward greater maturity and holiness of life. Good religious education is vital to this ongoing journey.

In the Introduction, I noted that it is imperative to promote interfaith understanding in our time. Without it, the world appears to face escalating violence, counterviolence, and war, much of this religiously legitimated. The challenge is not simply to *learn about* other religions, though this is a start. We need religious education that enables people—according to developmental readiness—to "cross over" into traditions other than their own with openness to *learn from* them for their own faith. This is when and where real understanding emerges, allowing us to move beyond toleration to appreciation of religious traditions that are truly "other" than "ours." For this we need competent programs of adult-centered education that encourage interfaith understanding. The future of our world may well depend on as much.

Who should be educated in faith? To summarize thus far, the answer must be *every Christian*. For a variety of compelling reasons, theological, spiritual, developmental, and even social, every person at every age needs and is entitled to have competent, effective, and lifelong education in faith. Much of the remainder of *Will There Be*

Faith? is about how to provide such education. Here I make a few practical suggestions, an initial response.

How are we to provide competent and effective faith education that is lifelong? Before setting aside the stereotype of "only through schooling," let us first be sure to say, "also through schooling." In Chapters 5 and 7, I will insist that it takes a village with a school (of some kind) to educate well in Christian faith, and I will elaborate on how to conduct good schools (parochial, Sunday, or parish schools of religion) that do effective religious education. Here, however, I imagine briefly how adults can continue their religious education. Surely we must include formal programs of study for adults, whether in colleges, universities, or sponsored by a diocese, deanery, or local parish. Beyond these efforts and thinking "outside the school box," what else can we imagine for lifelong education in faith?

We can, for example, harness the faith-education potential of liturgy and worship (Chapter 5 does this in depth). We may well balk at such a thought, if we understand education as only didactic instruction instead of as learning from and for life. Certainly liturgy should never be used simply to teach; that would be an abuse of liturgy, whose primary purpose always is to worship God. Yet because it is so symbol laden, liturgy is a powerful source of education—or mis-education—in faith. *How* we worship God de facto educates the faith of God's people. It is an ancient wisdom in the Church that our praying shapes our believing—and I add our teaching. Perhaps the most "educational" thing the Church does in the world is the way it assembles and enacts its sacred liturgy.[8] There, through word and sacrament, community and ritual, people can have an in-depth experience in which their lives are brought to God and God's life comes to them, all for the life of the world. Liturgy represents the kind of experiential knowing that most shapes lives, precisely because it engages and appeals to people's souls.

For example, a strategic "curriculum" decision that a faith community makes regularly is what to sing at its worship. That we sing good theology is imperative for education in faith. Likewise, think of the educational potential of scripture readings proclaimed so as to highlight their meaning and encourage good listening, of a well-crafted homily that engages people's lives and mediates the spiritual wisdom of Christian faith that people can take back to daily life, of a Eucharistic Prayer that is prayed reverently and as a "we" *with* the congregation, and so on. Indeed, every aspect of liturgy, even the smallest gesture, has the potential to nurture—or stymie—growth in faith. Nothing is more likely to foster people's faith than participation in good liturgy, and little is more adverse to faith than liturgy done poorly.

Beyond the liturgy, lifelong education can take place through all the ways that people participate actively in the life of their parish or congregation. When carried on within the ambit of faith, even service on the Finance Committee or on the New Church Roof Committee can provide opportunities for growth. Beyond this, it has never been so easy for people to find good books to read, good recordings to listen to, good websites to log on to, good chat rooms to join, good applications to download to a "smart phone." At Boston College we offer a superb array of online courses in adult faith education. Indeed, the resources through the Internet are now endless. Add too that more and more people are seeking out a spiritual mentor and participating in retreats and spiritual renewal programs. The list can go on. And think about it: there is nothing more life-giving than continuing to mature in faith and to grow in holiness and wholeness of life as a disciple of Jesus.

If people are to be disposed to such ongoing education in faith, their openness to it must be built into their early childhood religious education. If we give people the impression as children that "there's only so much to learn" or "they'll soon have all they need, at least by

Confirmation," then we are likely to put an end to their continuing adult education. To teach the Faith "too finally" arrests any faith journey. Years ago, the renowned religious educator Gabriel Moran proposed that adult education ought to begin in kindergarten. I take Moran to mean that the pedagogy we use with people, from the very beginning of their religious education, should be one that gives them the resources, the curiosity, and the disposition to go on growing in faith all their lives.

The pedagogy I describe as "bringing life to Faith and Faith to life" does lend people what Aquinas called a *habitus*—an ability and pattern that enables them to go on thinking about, learning from, and growing in their faith. If habituated into such a process, people are likely to continue reflecting on their lives in light of their Faith and on their Faith in light of their lives. The participative nature of such a pedagogy makes it likely that people so formed will welcome conversation and be open to share their own faith story and hear those of others. All of which are requirements, I believe, for lifelong growth in faith.

Who Is to Educate in Faith?

Who is to educate in faith? Again, the answer must be *every Christian*. Because of our baptism, we can say no less. Nor is this a new idea. Almost eight hundred years ago, Thomas Aquinas argued that in the Church the teachers are to be ever learners and the learners ever teachers. There is, of course, a role for designated teachers. Paulo Freire, one of the three greatest (with John Dewey and Maria Montessori) educators of the twentieth century, argued well that all learners can learn from each other and always have much to teach their teachers. This is surely true in matters of Christian faith. After baptism, no one can say, "This is not my job." It seems all the more true in our time; that there may be *faith on earth* depends on every Christian.

Paul, writing of *all Christians,* says, "We are ambassadors for Christ, since God is making appeal through us" (2 Cor. 5:20). The first letter of Peter says to Christians, "Always be ready to give an explanation to anyone who asks you for a reason for your hope, but do it with gentleness and reverence" (3:15, NAB). Note how Peter advises that we are to share our faith—"with gentleness and reverence"; more on this below. At the end of Mark's Gospel, Jesus tells the disciples, "Go into all the world and proclaim the good news" (16:15). And have you ever tried to keep really "good news" to yourself? If we think it is good, we'll really want to share it!

Perhaps the most inclusive text regarding the responsibility of every Christian to share faith is the account of the first Pentecost. So often religious art misrepresents this founding event of the Church as if it happened only to the apostles. The text of Acts, however, makes clear that present in the upper room were the twelve (by now they had replaced Judas with Matthias) and "certain women, including Mary the mother of Jesus, as well as his brothers." It adds that "together the crowd numbered about one hundred and twenty persons" (1:14–15). Then, at Pentecost, "tongues, as of fire, appeared among them, and a tongue rested on each of them. All of them were filled with the Holy Spirit" (2:3–4). Clearly the whole Christian community there assembled, every member, was now empowered by the Holy Spirit to fulfill the great commission that the Risen Christ gave to his Church, "Go and make disciples of all nations" (Matt. 28:19). Some two thousand years later, the *GDC* echoed this universal mandate: "Catechesis is a responsibility of the entire Christian community . . . [and] the particular responsibility of every member of the community" (n. 220).

Later chapters will dwell at length on how parents and families can share their faith, and likewise people in parishes and programs or schools. Here, I propose that even in the normal discourse and conversations of life, without imposing or proselytizing, all Christians have opportunities regularly to share their faith. This may be as invited or as challenged or as seems opportune.

A favorite time I have found for sharing faith is when traveling on planes, trains, and busses or while waiting for them. There is something about the anonymity of traveling—"ships passing in the night"—that allows complete strangers, in the neighboring seat, to volunteer their life situation or story and the struggles that occupy them. Later chapters will suggest how one might craft a "faith sharing" conversation in such circumstances. For now, the key I've found most effective is a good question. Some examples: "So, what are your best hopes?" "How do you make sense out of it all?" "What brings you joy in your life?" "So what do you most want for your kids?" If the person has already used God language, "So, what do you think is God's desire for you now?" I've found that the conversations that follow such generative questions often provide an opportunity to volunteer how I respond from the perspective of my own faith.

Let me reiterate that we must be careful in doing this. Recall that 1 Peter 3:15 wisely advises Christians to share faith "with gentleness and reverence." I take "gentleness" to mean without imposing, claiming superiority, or being pretentious about one's own faith claims and tradition. I take "reverence" to mean with respect for other persons, openness to share with *and* to learn from them, to hear their faith story that might enrich our own.

"Reverence" may also mean bringing persons back to their own faith, rather than to ours. Some Jewish friends of mine have a young daughter who showed real interest in learning about her Jewish tradition. However, her parents, who were more cultural than religious Jews, were unresponsive. Given the young girl's keen interest, as a friend I encouraged them to enroll her in Sabbath school. They did, and lo and behold, inspired by their daughter, they now celebrate *shabat,* keep the high holy days, and have joined a synagogue. My friends remind me that I was the one who prompted their return to the Jewish faith. I feel privileged to have been an instrument of God's grace in their lives.

Having said that *all* Christians are responsible for sharing their faith as appropriate, we must recognize that every faith community needs its designated religious educators, that is, people prepared and commissioned to see to it that the community intentionally educates and is educated in faith. In the first Christian communities, the *didaskaloi*—"teachers"—had official status alongside other functions of ministry like *episcopoi, presbuteroi,* and *diakonoi,* whom we call "bishops," "priests," and "deacons" today.[9] Every Christian faith community needs such designated ministers as well. The *GDC* states: "While the entire Christian community is responsible for Christian catechesis and all of its members to bear witness to the faith, only some receive the ecclesial mandate to be catechists. Together with the primordial mission which parents have in relation to their children, the Church confers the delicate task of organically transmitting the faith within the community on particular, specifically called members of the people of God" (n. 221). The *GDC* advocates that the community encourage its members who have the needed charism (gift) to consider serving in the "vocation of catechist" (n. 233).

The *General Directory* goes on to declare that nothing is more important to a faith community than the "preparation of suitable catechists" in good pedagogy, in sound scriptural and theological studies, spiritually, and in the relevant social sciences, for example, developmental psychology (n. 216). Catechists' preparation must be followed by ongoing formation and support. The *General Directory* also makes the wise point that catechists themselves should be prepared by the same process/pedagogy that they will use in their own teaching (n. 245). I agree, of course, and—as readers might expect now—will claim that a *life to Faith to life* approach is an excellent way for educating catechists, making it all the more likely that they will employ such an approach to catechesis themselves. All of which calls for competent programs at "catechetical institutes at either the diocesan or inter-diocesan level" (n. 250) and points to the need for "higher institutes for experts in catechesis" (n. 251). Amen!

For Reflection and Conversation

- Do you agree that all Christians need lifelong education in faith? Why or why not?

- In your opinion, is every Christian responsible for sharing their faith? Why or why not?

- What are some implications and decisions for your own faith? For your family? For your parish?

CHAPTER THREE

What Faith and *Why* Educate?

The Nature and Purpose of Educating in Christian Faith

A story is told of some American tourists who were traveling by car through County Kerry, one of the most beautiful parts of Ireland. They got lost along the way and stopped to inquire directions back to Killarney from an old farmer who was jogging along in a donkey cart. He stopped and was only too happy to help. After inquiring about where they were from, whether they knew his cousins "over there," if they were enjoying themselves, and what they thought of the weather, he finally got to directions.

"Well now, go down there a couple of miles to the next crossroads and take a right, and then a left at the next cross, and then go straight a while and then . . . and then . . ." He trailed off with, "No, don't do that. 'Twill take you to Tralee, and sure it's Killarney you want." Then he began again, "Well now, go down there to the next cross and take a left and then go on a while and take a left and a left again and then . . . and then . . ." Again he trailed off with, "No, don't do that. 'Twill take you into Dingle." He paused and said pensively, "You know, I think you can't get to Killarney from here."

It is imperative for educators in faith to choose approaches, directions if you will, that are likely to get us where we want to go—to the learning outcomes that we hope to bring about in people's lives. Conversely, it is imperative to be clear about those hoped-for outcomes, so that we might choose approaches that, with the help of God's grace, are more likely to achieve our intentions. In other words, the purposes of educating in Christian faith and the approaches we employ should harmonize. The purposes should shape the approaches we take, and our approaches should be likely to serve rather than defeat our purposes.

For example, if our intent is that Christian faith be life-giving and emancipatory for persons and societies—if that's our Killarney—we are not likely to achieve our goal using behavioral conditioning or a doctrinaire delivery that tells people what to think and how to think it. We just can't get "there" from such a "here." As another example (elaborated in Chapter 4), the intent to educate for justice requires that we educate justly, in other words, with approaches that within their very dynamic reflect justice toward participants and dispose them to embrace the works of justice in their lives. The method itself should be fitting to the intent of justice; otherwise, we defeat our purpose. The *General Directory* explains wisely that errors and defects in approach "can be avoided only if the nature and end of catechesis as well as the truths and values which must be transmitted are correctly understood from the outset" (n. 9).

What, then, is the "nature and purpose" of educating in Christian faith? This two-pronged foundational question occupies us throughout Chapter 3 and continues into the next. I assure you that these reflections are neither esoteric nor "only theoretical." On the contrary, after some thirty-five years of teaching religious educators at Boston College and hearing reports back from many graduates, I'm more convinced than ever that how we respond to the question of nature and purpose sets the direction for all educating in faith. It is crucial to know our "Killarney" in order to choose the road that takes us there.

To speak of the "nature" and "purpose" of educating in Christian faith is a bit of an artificial distinction. They inevitably overlap and, in practice, function as one. As often in life, stating *what* we are doing already intimates *why* we are doing it. That my spouse and I are trying to raise our little son a Catholic Christian states both *what* we're trying to do as parents and *why* we're trying to do it, our hoped-for outcome. Still, the educator's *intentionality*— our being conscious and very deliberate about *what* and *why* we are doing what we do—is key to effective education in faith. Being clear and intentional about both *what* and *why* can help us do it better—in the home, parish, and program or school. Indeed, we need to expand our imaginations about the nature and purposes of education in faith; some prevalent understandings are very limiting.

One limiting understanding of the nature of religious education is "teaching kids about religion" with the intent that they have religious knowledge of some kind. The previous chapter already broadened our focus beyond children to *all* people. And although there certainly is value in people *knowing about* religion and having knowledge of their faith tradition, such goals are limited in what they effect in people's lives and in the world at large. We can readily do much more, even in nonconfessional contexts.

It may be helpful to distinguish three levels at which we can teach a religion. We can teach so that people learn *about* it, or learn *from* it, or *become* it, that is, they form their identity in a particular tradition.[1] To settle for the first level only (learning *about*), even in nonfaith contexts (like religious education in government schools in England), seems like a lost opportunity. It is better by far to approach all the great religions that have borne the test of time as sources of spiritual wisdom *from which* we can learn for our lives, even if we never embrace a particular one as our identity in faith. The first level also presumes that there is an objective way to study religion, as if it can be taught without perspective—as a view from nowhere. This is a classic Enlightenment myth and a false one, particularly in matters of religion. The pedagogy of *life to Faith to life* can be used in nonconfessional contexts and enable people to learn *from* a religion without feigning objectivity or proselytizing people to embrace a particular religious identity.

Regarding the third level (to *become*), there are, of course, contexts that appropriately intend to form people's identity in a particular faith. This is precisely the purpose of the catechetical program in any parish or congregation. There, teaching for "religious knowledge" is only a beginning, though a necessary one. To settle for it in faith-confessing contexts is to miss out on the need for education that both *informs* and *forms* people in a particular faith identity. Besides, in matters religious at least, we need to broaden what we mean by "knowing" and "knowledge." A negative legacy of the Enlightenment was to so reduce knowledge to a dispassionate rationality that it has no practical influence on the lives of the knowers. Given the general diminishment of knowledge to *knowing about,* I later propose *spiritual wisdom* as the desired cognitive outcome for education in Christian faith (more to come).

I once had a fantasy of being a child again and asking my mother, "Mom, why do I have to study my catechism?" Such was my religion curriculum some fifty years ago in an Irish village. She replied, "Oh, you have to *know your faith*." But I pressed on, "Well, what good will that do?" to which she responded, "It will help to *save your soul*." Still not satisfied, I asked, "And what good would that do?" She replied, "Oh, that's the best reason of all—to *get to heaven*."

Having exhausted my mother's purposes for my religious education, I approached my Dad, who was reading the paper by the fire, and asked his opinion. He responded predictably, "Whatever your mother says." But later, he sought me out and said, "This religion stuff, it's all a bit of a waste of time, unless it puts bread on the table, especially for the poor, or unless it helps to raise up the downtrodden," and then he moved on (he was a politician with strong social justice leanings).

I propose that there was much wisdom in both of my parents' responses. I will try to reclaim and deepen their perceived purposes in these two chapters, convinced that educating in faith still revolves around themes like "heaven," "faith," "knowing," "saving souls," and "justice for all." But first, pause to recognize how you would already respond to such questions yourself.

For Reflection and Conversation

- How do you name the nature of Christian religious education? Stated another way, what are you "doing" in people's lives when you intervene to educate them in Christian faith?

- What do you recognize as your purposes in educating in faith? What do you hope will be the "outcome" for the participants personally?

- The outcome for the faith community? For the society?

What Are We Doing as Christian Religious Educators?

I often use the term "educating in faith," but this is more a statement of our purpose, whereas the better name for *what* we are doing, as favored in the literature of the field, is "Christian religious education." What each word means—"Christian" and "religious" and "education"—deserves some brief description. I will work backward and begin with "education." In large part, my attempt to state the *nature* of Christian religious education is by a "definition of terms."

Education: There is little consensus among scholars about the nature of education, that is, about what educators are doing when they educate. Clearly it has something to do with teaching and learning, but then we could debate those terms at length as well. Instead, let me begin with the ideal of education going all the way back to the ancient Greek philosophers, who saw it as a process of humanization, of *enabling people to learn to live more humanly.* Not all instances equally approximate this ideal, and perhaps need not. For example, humanization would be more the agenda in liberal arts education than in teaching engineering or chemistry. Yet the more people experience this ideal of education, the more likely they are to learn to make and keep life human for themselves and others. Such education, of course, is not limited to schools. As Huckleberry Finn often said, he tried not to let schooling interfere with his education.

Education at its best *informs, forms,* and *transforms* the very "being" of people and does so in ways that are powerfully life-giving for both themselves and their society. Technically, this is to say that education is "ontological," from the Greek *ontos,* meaning "being." I use "being" here as both noun and verb. In other words, good education deliberately attempts to enhance *who* people are and *how* they live by what they learn. As such, education should enable people to realize their potential as human beings and to live moral lives. Good education prepares people not only to "make a living"—the present chronic emphasis—but also to "have a life."

The best of education engages and shapes the whole person,

what I have been calling head, heart, and hands, or the mind, emotions, and will. Good education engages all three capacities of the mind—reason, memory, and imagination—and encourages people to think critically and creatively for themselves and with one another. I use "critically" here not in its colloquial negative sense, but in its original meaning of "discerning" (from the Greek *krinein*, "to discern"). Critical reflection enables people to discern and understand the data from life experience as well as the data they access through traditions of wisdom, science, and the arts. Further, such reflection enables people to remember and discern how their own locus in time and place shapes how they think, feel, and choose. Such personal and life-located reflection engages people's emotions precisely because it brings them to their own story, to their own lives in the world. Life-based reflection, as Aristotle argued, also provides people's wills what they need to know in order to make good choices. Only with their own lives so engaged, and thus their emotions and wills, are people likely to move beyond understanding to considered judgments and wise decisions. It is from such life-located knowledge that wisdom may emerge, practical wisdom that serves fullness of life for all (Aristotle again).

Education should bring people to reflect on the data that arise from their own lives in the world *and* from the various disciplines of humanities, sciences, and the arts. Often overlooked is that John Dewey (1859–1952) championed the latter three as amounting to "the funded capital of civilization"[2] and saw teaching them as imperative for human well-being. Of course, Dewey is most remembered for heralding the conviction that reflection on *experience* is the primary source of learning and the most effective entrée for people into the knowledge and wisdom assembled in the humanities, sciences, and arts. Such experiential knowledge is imperative if people are to *learn from* and not simply *learn about* the latter. Good education will enable people to integrate as personal knowledge these two sources, what they learn from their own experience and what they learn from access to the disciplines of learning—which themselves arose from the experience and experimentation of people before us.

Paulo Freire echoed this sentiment, but went farther than Dewey. First, Freire preferred the term "praxis" over "experience," because the former accents the agency of people. While experience tends to be heard as something we "undergo" or that "comes our way," praxis, as I elaborate in Chapter 8, is primarily what people do and initiate themselves. Continuing on, but echoing Dewey's sentiments, Freire argued that people's critical reflection on their life praxis is key to their forging from their lives and traditions of learning the ultimate intent of education, namely, humanization.[3]

Dewey and Freire both insist, as do all the great philosophers of education, that humanizing education not only informs, forms, and transforms the persons who participate, but the society in which they live as well. Good education is the most likely means of social reform and of liberation from unjust and oppressive structures. In this sense, education is always "political" as well as personal, or political precisely because it is so personal. Education shapes people's very "being" and thus how they participate in society. This is not a new insight. Both Plato and Aristotle always wrote of education as an aspect of politics. The overarching purpose of education in the *Analects* of Confucius is *jen,* a term that seems to be best translated as "humanness." Confucius proposed that the more people are educated to live humanly, the more society will dwell in harmony. He insisted that parents who raise good children are social agents who improve the life of society.[4] Religious educators should also be aware that there is a political nature to what we do; we are influencing how people will live their lives in the world.

I have often heard the sentiment that religious education is more than "just education." True, but let us first make sure that it is at least as much. It seems incongruous to teach a rich and expansive

faith tradition like Christianity with anything less than good education. Let us remember too that, throughout its history, the Church
has been the leading champion and exponent of good education.
In fact, the Christian Church originally sponsored and shaped the
educational system of the Western world. This began with the catechetical schools of the early Church (Alexandria, Antioch, Hippo),
followed by the medieval monastic schools (Benedictine and Celtic)
and cathedral schools, which gave rise to the first great universities, such as Bologna (1088), Paris (1150), Oxford (1167), Cambridge
(1209), and Salamanca (1218). All these universities were founded
by papal charter and staffed by the emerging religious orders, for
example, the Augustinians and Dominicans.

Within these universities, theology emerged as the "queen of
the sciences," deeply committed to *faith seeking understanding*—the
partnership of faith and reason. The First Vatican Council (1869–
70) was summarizing a long tradition when it declared: "Faith and
reason . . . are . . . *mutually advantageous.* . . . Right reason demon-
strates the foundations of faith, and *faith sets reason free* (emphasis
added)."[5] While honoring the role of *reason* and the intent of *understanding* as integral to good education, I will also propose that
religious education in particular needs to bring people beyond the
knowing and understanding of data to making judgments and decisions. This is how what people learn is likely to affect their lives,
perhaps becoming wisdom for life. Meanwhile, the Church's great
scholars (Augustine, Aquinas, and others) have consistently claimed
that good education in Christian faith makes it all the more believable and livable.

In this light, religious education in particular should enable
people to reflect critically on their own lives in the world, lend ready
and well-informed access to the Faith handed down, and encourage
participants to know and understand their faith and then to make
judgments and decisions about its truths and spiritual wisdom for

their lives. We will elaborate on this pedagogy in Chapters 8 and 9. For now, I note that the *General Directory for Catechesis* champions the notion of religious education as good education. It urges a "right understanding of the faith," so that "the truths to be believed are in conformity with the demands of reason." It notes that such critical understanding is needed "to overcome certain forms of fundamentalism as well as subjective and arbitrary interpretations" (n. 175). Note well: the *GDC* is saying that critical thinking is needed to prevent both fundamentalism *and* relativism.

The *GDC* also sees critical reflection on human experience as essential for understanding the faith tradition and for making it meaningful as one's own. Religious education must enable people to reflect on what God reveals through Scripture and Tradition and "in light of the same Revelation . . . to interpret the signs of the times and the present life of [people], since it is in these that the plan of God for the salvation of the world is realized" (n. 39). Many times it reiterates that "experience is a necessary medium for exploring and assimilating the truths which constitute the objective content of Revelation" (n. 152). By encouraging catechesis that includes experiential knowledge the *GDC favors* good education.

Religious: Like "education," when we ask "What is religion?" or "What is the religious?" the great scholars offer a plethora of definitions with little consensus. All we need here is a working description, so that we might know a little more clearly *what* we should be doing as *religious* educators. Of course, this is entirely qualified here by our third term to come, "Christian," and I will anticipate as much.

To begin with, religion has a pervasive meaning of something that relates or mediates between the human and divine. The roots of the word itself are debated. The dominant opinion is that it comes from the Latin *religare,* meaning to "tie fast" or "tie up," as in securing a boat to a dock. Thus, we might imagine religion and the religious as how people try to "anchor well" their lives in a relationship with a Realm or Being beyond themselves. The usual term for this is the "Transcendent," whether this is to be found within (as in Buddhism) or outside, in gods or God. For our reflections here, from the Judeo-Christian tradition, "religion" and the "religious" refer to *a lived response to God's loving outreach into people's lives.*

Note that the initiative is God's, not ours. Both Jewish and Christian faiths are deeply convinced that God intervenes in human history with effective love (grace) and self-disclosure (revelation) to persons and communities in their historical circumstances. Religion, then, is the formal pattern by which people make what is typically a threefold response to God's outreach; they (1) develop a system of beliefs, (2) create rituals for worship, and (3) propose a moral code. Religious education, honoring the spiritual nature of humankind (Chapter 2), enables people to recognize, understand a little, and respond appropriately to God's loving initiative in their lives.

The God or gods that people place at the center of their lives have enormous influence for both good and ill on who those people become and how they live. For example, if God as revealed in the Hebrew scriptures and in Jesus Christ truly becomes our God, this colors in very positive ways our outlook on life, ourselves, and others. Such faith shapes how we make meaning, find purpose, engage in the world, and develop the ethic we live by. In fact, placing the One True God at the center of our lives is our most likely path to flourishing as human beings. The First Commandment calls us to make only God our God, but note its preface: "I am the LORD your God, who brought you out of the land of Egypt, out of the house of slavery; you shall have no other gods before me" (Exod. 20:2–3). It is as if God declares and alerts, "I am your God, who intervenes in human history to set free the oppressed, to enhance people's lives. Now, if you want to remain free and flourish, put Me at the center of your life. Every false god will enslave you again."

Having false "gods" or false images of the One True God can be very destructive for persons and societies. Imagine how a God of anger and punishment breeds fear and trepidation in people's lives. Or imagine the One True God as a narrow sectarian who loves "us" and hates "others," thus legitimating, even encouraging, violence and prejudice. These are false images. And all false gods, whether power or pleasure, fame or fortune, possessions or prestige, eventually lead to destruction or addiction of some kind—lead back to "Egypt" and slavery. A great deal in life depends on who or what our "god" is. Christian religious education should help people to put the One True God at the center of their lives, the God whom Jesus revealed as Love and who is in love with us.

Centering God in one's life is much more than an intellectual choice, even more than an exercise of belief, though it is certainly both of those things. It calls for a "God-consciousness" in every-thing, meaning that we are aware of God as the constant "point of reference," the Presence that colors our whole outlook on our-selves, other people, and life in the world. As such a "God-outlook" emerges, one can come, often explicitly and always implicitly, "to see God in all things" (Ignatius of Loyola, 1491–1556) or, as the poet Patrick Kavanagh (1904–67) put it, to recognize God's presence "in the bits and pieces of every day." I could also name my point here as promoting a "sacramental consciousness." The sacramental prin-ciple, so core to Catholic traditions of Christianity, is the conviction that God constantly reaches out to us, and we respond, first and foremost, through the ordinary and everyday. Religious education, then, is not just to teach people "about God," but to shape in people a God-consciousness about life, a sacramental outlook on everything.

Anyone who does not take religion or the spiritual aspect of people seriously or who minimizes how strategic religious educa-tion is to the well-being of persons and societies is historically naive. I have often been asked, "What is religious education?" I used to give long-winded responses. Now I simply say, "Don't know for sure, but if we have good education and good religion and put the two together, we'll likely have good religious education." It takes both: good religion, which is not inevitable at all, and good education, which requires great intentionality. More to come.

Christian: As I stated boldly in the first paragraph of Chapter 1, Jesus Christ is the heart and soul of Christian faith. This is not to neglect God the Father or the Holy Spirit and all the other Christian dogmas and doctrines, spiritualities and sacraments, virtues and values. Rather, it is to say that everything about Christian faith flows from the Incarnation, the amazing claim we make that God became human in Jesus and that, by his life, death, and resurrection, Jesus was the Christ and Savior of the world. This is why the "definitive aim" of all Christian religious education, according to the *General Directory,* is "to put people in communion and intimacy with Jesus Christ" (n. 80), a theme it reiterates many times. In fact, "Christian faith is, above all, conversion to Jesus Christ, full and sincere adherence to his person and the decision to walk in his footsteps" (n. 53), "the following of his person" (n. 41). In this sense, Christian religious education is "an apprenticeship in the entire Christian life"—apprenticeship to Jesus (n. 30).

It is significant too how the language of discipleship has become so central in official Catholic Church documents. Like the centrality of Jesus to Christian faith, highlighting discipleship may seem obvious. Nevertheless, it needs to be stressed, at least for Catholic Christians. So what does *Christian* religious education "do"? One obvious response is that, by God's grace, it attempts to educate people in Christian discipleship, in apprenticeship to Jesus. That response, in turn, begs the question: What does it mean to be a disciple of Jesus Christ? This is where nature and purpose merge as one. However, I'll focus here on *forming disciples* as *what* Christian religious education should be doing in people's lives. Under "Why," below, I'll

focus on the lived faith that incarnates discipleship and pose this
as the intended learning outcome of Christian religious education.

One can cite hundreds of New Testament texts to portray discipleship to Jesus, and I will do so throughout this book. We can also
get an intuitive sense, however, by looking at the best desires and
highest hopes of the human heart. The dogmas of our faith confess
that Jesus was fully human as well as fully divine. In fact, "Son
of Man" was his favorite title. This is often translated now as the
"Human One," because the Greek word *anthropos* means "human
person," not "man" in the sense of male gender. No wonder, then,
that we find realized in Jesus—the Human One—all the finest virtues and values to which the human heart aspires. He made flesh
our "heart's desires" at their best. So to be a disciple of Jesus means
to live lives that are loving and kind, hopeful and faith-filled, just
and peaceable, merciful and compassionate, inclusive and hospitable, respectful and generous, honest and truthful, faithful and trustworthy, authentic and integral—the list can go on and on.

It is significant too that when people asked Jesus, "What must I
do?" he first cited keeping the commandments. Although the greatest commandment for a disciple is Jesus's law of radical love, it does
not exempt us from the Ten Commandments, but is the spirit with
which we should follow and obey them. Likewise, disciples should
be formed in the attitudes of the Beatitudes: being poor in spirit
and truly humble, hungering for justice, mercy, and peace, living
without guile, and being willing to witness to what is right, even to
the point of persecution. Christian religious education intervenes in
people's lives and aspires to inform, form, and transform them as
faithful disciples of Jesus.

In addition to "Christian religious education," readers will note
that I sometimes use the word "catechesis," a term much favored
in Catholic Church documents (e.g., the *GDC*). "Catechesis," however, is not an exclusively Catholic word. From the Greek *katecheo,*

meaning to teach by "echoing" a tradition, "catechesis" is the ancient Christian term for educating in faith so that it resonates in people's lives. In the literature of the field, some authors distinguish "catechesis" from "religious education"; the former focuses on socialization into Christian identity, and the latter is the academic study of religion. In some cultures and contexts, this distinction may be helpful. For example, in Britain, the Education Act of 1944 requires that religion be taught in government schools, but that it be a strictly "objective" presentation, without influencing the identity of students. Though perhaps helpful in getting that act through Parliament, I see limited value, as indicated earlier, in teaching *about* religion. It is better in all contexts that participants at least learn *from* their religious education for their lives. This can be achieved without forcing or enticing anyone to take on a particular religious identity.

As noted already, there are contexts where it might be more appropriate to encourage learning *from* a religious tradition, and others where the explicit intent is to form people's identity in a particular faith. In the theology curriculum of Catholic universities and perhaps in Catholic high schools, since both now have students from diverse religious backgrounds, the emphasis might be on an academic study, which enables people to learn *from* whatever tradition is being studied. In such cases, the enterprise could be called theology or religious education. On the other hand, in a parish catechetical program the overt intent is to socialize as well as educate participants into Christian identity. So also in efforts to educate their children in faith, parents strive to form them in Catholic Christian identity. Such effort is well named "catechesis."

All this being said, I reiterate that there is not much value in religious or theological education that does not enrich people's identity in faith. People should at least be encouraged to learn *from* such study, finding some spiritual wisdom for their lives. Likewise, I would be worried about catechesis that simply socializes people into Christian identity without offering sound instruction and encouraging people to understand the content of their faith. For these reasons, I use the term *Christian* religious education to reflect the value of both emphases. When the context makes the meaning clear, I sometimes use the terms "catechesis" and "religious education" interchangeably, or "catechetical education" to capture the best of both.

For Reflection and Conversation

• Looking back at your response to the initial questions regarding the nature of Christian religious education, and after mulling over my proposals above, how do you now describe the *nature* of this enterprise? *What* is it?

• How might your renewed understanding of the *nature* of Christian religious education shape your approach to doing it?

The Why of Christian Religious Education

Any one of us can have many reasons to educate for Christian faith, shaped by our own biography, faith journey, and present context. Reasons can range from the noble to the pragmatic, from, "That people may experience and respond to God's unconditional love in their lives" to, "It might help to keep the kids in line." Whether we are parents or teachers or both, our common sense of purpose is likely that we want those we educate religiously to become good people, coupled with the conviction that this way of being human and religious which is called "Christian" can be a powerful resource to that noble end. Christian faith can be a wonderful way to live one's life for self and others, to contribute to the common good of humanity, and to find true happiness here and hereafter. This being said, Christian faith offers its own rationale for why to educate in it and what it should elicit from the lives of those we teach.

Religious Education for the Reign of God

To begin with, our purpose must surely reflect that of Jesus. As reviewed in Chapter 1, Jesus's life purpose was the coming of God's reign. As Luke's Gospel summarizes, "Jesus journeyed from one town and village to another, preaching and proclaiming the good news of the kingdom of God" (8:1, NAB). Two thousand years later, the *General Directory* also summarizes: "Jesus proclaimed the Kingdom of God as the urgent and definitive intervention of God in history, and defined this proclamation as '*the Gospel*,' that is, the Good News. To this Gospel, Jesus devoted his entire earthly life: he made known the joy of belonging to the Kingdom, its demands, its *magna carta* (i.e., the Sermon on the Mount), the mysteries which it embraces, the life of fraternal charity of those who enter it, and its future fulfillment" (n. 34). The ultimate purpose of Christian religious education, then, is to build up this "Kingdom of justice, love and peace" that was "so central to the preaching of Jesus" (n. 102). He is well named, indeed, as "catechist of the Kingdom of God" (n. 163).

Practically, then, the coming of God's reign in Jesus is the overarching guideline that shapes the whole curriculum of Christian religious education, helping us to decide *what, why,* and *how* to teach. Regarding content—*what* to teach—the curriculum should always reflect the whole Story and Vision of Christian faith. As to the *why,* then, we must allow the reign of God to shape how we spin that story and propose its vision. Everything we access from Scripture and Tradition must be slanted toward what promotes the values and realization of God's reign in people's lives. Christians are to be educated both to pray "Your kingdom come" and then to "do God's will on earth as it is done in heaven."

The truth is that God will bring about God's reign in its fullness at the end time. Meanwhile, this great eschatological hope (from Greek *eschaton,* "end time"), should shape our faith, hope, and love now. This ultimate vision is being realized already as we live the values of God's reign here. Our concern is not the *eschaton* in its fullness—this is in God's hands—but for how to live toward such hope along the way. Meanwhile, Jesus made clear that even a small deed done according to God's reign can have huge positive consequences; many of his parables make this point. So the "kingdom of heaven" (Matthew's favored phrase, because, as a good Jew, he was reluctant to use God's name) "is like a mustard seed," which, when sown, "becomes a tree, so that the birds of the air come and make nests in its branches" (Matt. 13:31–32). Or again, it is like the "yeast that a woman took and mixed in with three measures of flower until all of it was leavened" (13:33). Doing whatever we can do as God's will "on earth" always has significant consequences toward God's reign within human history. Then, for us as individual persons, doing God's will in this life is how we will come to do God's will "in heaven," in the eternal presence of God.

God's will, as summarized in Chapter 1, is fullness of life for everyone and the integrity of creation. What God wills for us and by us is that all people experience and live with faith, hope, and love; that they come to holiness and fullness of life; that they live in and promote peace and justice for all; and that they experience and practice mercy and compassion. As discipleship to Jesus reflects the deepest desires of the human heart, so the realization of those values—God's reign—is well described by the poet William Butler Yeats (1865–1939) as "the land of heart's desire." Everything we teach is to advance the ongoing coming of God's reign in Jesus. Stated negatively, if we teach as the content of Christian faith what diminishes some people or retards the realization of the great social values of God's reign on earth, we are in grave error.

The reign of God in Jesus is likewise to shape the *how* of Christian religious education. We need an approach that informs, forms, and transforms people in the *habitus,* in the conviction and constant disposition to do what they discern to be God's will in all circumstances and at every level of existence—personal, interpersonal, and social. Let our approach educate people to look at their lives in the light of Christian faith and to discern how to live in faithfulness to God's reign. Let our approach enable and encourage people to "bring their lives to their Faith and their Faith to their lives," where they strive to realize the values of God's reign in the ordinary and everyday. If people are to absorb this *habitus* into their identity, then such a pedagogy needs to run throughout their religious education.

Educating in the Ways of Christian Faith

The idea of educating for the reign of God can seem a bit nebulous, esoteric, or even dated. At least in this part of the world, we seldom use the language of "reign" or "kingdom." This is why we need more immediate goals and hopes for which to educate religiously. To find them, we recognize again, as in Chapter 1, that Jesus invited disciples to live for God's reign by *a life of faith.* Religious educators, then, must ask what the Christian faith is that we are responsible for teaching. Our concern is not so much to find a precise theological definition of faith, but to understand what constitutes *a life of Christian faith,* that is, what it looks like in peoples' lives. This is the incarnate Faith that should shape our curriculum choices.

A Communal Faith: First, we must echo here our description

of Christian faith in Chapter 2 as radically communal. The early
Christians inherited this emphasis on being "a *people* of God" from
their Jewish roots. Throughout the Hebrew scriptures, the focus is
on Israel as a people in covenant with God and with one another.
God comes to them as a people, and they go to God as a people—*together*. Then, in the fullness of time, Jesus revealed the inner nature
of God as a Triune Divine Community of right and loving relationships. Made in God's image, our human nature is relational. Thus,
for Christian faith to be native rather than foreign to our condition,
it must be communal as well. That is certainly how Jesus presented
it and how the first Christians understood it. Refer again to Paul's
metaphor of the Church as the Body of Christ in the world today.

I highlight here that God's reign is itself a communal or social
metaphor. Jesus launched his public ministry saying, "This is the
time of fulfillment. The kingdom of God is at hand. Repent, and
believe in the gospel" (Mark 1:15, NAB). As he preached on, it became
very clear that to be converted to God's reign in Jesus meant to enter
into right and loving relationships. This is the *metanoia*—the constant and ongoing conversion—required for participation in God's
reign. We cannot be a "kingdom" by ourselves or a "private" Christian. The reign of God and thus its lived faith can only be realized
through right relationships and community.

It is in and through Christian community—the Church—that
we have access to God's word through Scripture, guided by the Holy
Spirit through the shared faith of the community over time, now
mediated as Tradition. It is through the Church that we can receive
the sacraments, which enable us to live as disciples. It is through the
Church that we can find the models and witnesses to Christian faith
and the people to pray with and for us in good times and in bad.
No matter the situation, we do not part ways with this community.
In Catholic tradition, the conviction is that the communal bond of
baptism is never broken, not even by death. So, whether living or

dead, we continue to belong to a great community of saints and sinners, for whom we can pray as needed or ask them to pray for us. The community we forge as Christians must also be an effective one that causes, by God's grace, what it symbolizes. The Church is to be the sacrament of God's reign in the world. Every member of the community has a part to play in its sacramentality, enabling it to be an effective agent of what it teaches and claims to believe.

Chapters 5 and 6 will reflect in depth on the communal context of religious education and on how the faith community and family need both to educate and to be educated. For now, we can say that the purposes of Christian religious education call for curricula that form people in the ways of a faith community, that encourage their active participation in the life and mission of some parish or congregation.

Faith Lived, Living, and Life-giving: Christian faith is inherently communal, but we can still ask: What identifies it as realized in people's lives? Remember, we are an incarnational religion. Just as God's "Word became flesh" in Jesus (John 1:14), so Christian faith must become flesh in individual disciples as well. Looking to the Gospels and how Jesus portrayed discipleship, I propose that Christian faith is to be *lived, living,* and *life-giving* for self, others, and the world.

Clearly the Faith must be *lived.* Many times Jesus repeats, in one way or another, that disciples are "those who hear the word of God and keep it" (Luke 11:28, JB). Or again, those who belong to the reign of God don't simply profess Jesus as Lord with their lips; rather, they "do the will of the Father" (Matt. 7:21). Christian faith is a way of life, following the example of Jesus who was "the way, and the truth, and the life" (John 14:6).

Then, one's Christian faith should also be a *living* faith—vibrant and ever fresh, growing and deepening. Recall Jesus's conversation with the Samaritan woman at the well (John 4); he promised her and Christians ever after that his gospel would always be like "a spring of water gushing up to eternal life" (4:14). Here Jesus was echoing the messianic promise in Isaiah: "With joy you will draw water from the wells of salvation" (12:3). Christian faith should never be presented as stagnant waters; they are deadly. Instead, it should be represented as fresh, living waters that nourish a living faith.

Finally, Christian faith must be *life-giving* for oneself, others, and the world. In John's Gospel, Jesus repeats some ten times that faith in God and in him will bring the reward of eternal life. Note the great summary found in 3:16: "For God so loved the world that he gave his only Son, so that everyone who believes in him may not perish but *may have eternal life*." Clearly, Jesus is referring to everlasting life with God, but even in John's writings this "life" is also for now. In the "bread of life" discourse (6:22–59), Jesus explains that "the bread . . . that comes down from heaven" brings the promise of eternal life for believers, but it also "gives life to the world" (6:33)—now. In fact, Jesus is the "bread of life," given precisely "for the life of the world" (6:51). Later, Jesus says that his function as "the good shepherd" is to ensure that we "may have life, and have it abundantly" (10:10). His gospel should be taught as life-giving for here as well as hereafter.

So, as we teach for Christian faith, we need to structure the whole curriculum so that it educates for faith that is *lived, living,* and *life-giving* for oneself, for others, and for the world.

For Reflection and Conversation

• I've affirmed my mother's "get to heaven" purpose, but broadened it to educating for the reign of God—"on earth as in heaven." How might this enhance your own purpose and practice of Christian religious education?

- What practical differences might it make to our pedagogy if we commit to educate for Christian faith that is lived, living, and life-giving?

Christian Faith as a Way of the Head, Heart, and Hands

Chapter 1 described how faith for Jesus was holistic, a faith that engages people's heads, hearts, and hands. Jesus presented faith as a whole *way of life.* And so discipleship means to follow *the way* of Jesus, what he modeled and made possible. From the very beginning of the Church, Christians were nicknamed "followers of *the Way.*" Recall that Paul sallied forth on the Damascus road looking for "any who belonged to *the Way*" (Acts 9:2)—to destroy them. Then, to his surprise, Paul became a champion of what he came to recognize as the "still more excellent way" (1 Cor. 12:31). We must educate for Christian faith as *a way of the head, a way of the heart,* and *a way of the hands.*

By focusing on each element of this way—head, heart, and hands—we will recognize the sort of comprehensive faith to be embodied in discipleship to Jesus and for which Christian religious educators must aspire to educate. Christian faith as:

- *A Way of the Hands* demands a discipleship of love, justice, peacemaking, simplicity, integrity, healing, and repentance.

- *A Way of the Heart* demands a discipleship of right relationships and right desires, community building, hospitality and inclusion, trust in God's love, and prayer and worship.

- *A Way of the Head* demands a discipleship of faith seeking understanding and belief with personal conviction, sustained by study and investigation, by probing and reflecting, by discerning and deciding, all toward spiritual wisdom for life.

A Way of the Hands: Recall that Jesus often put the *hands* of faith first, something he learned from his Jewish tradition. For example, he explained that it is by *living* according to his teachings that we become socialized into his *community* of disciples, and then come to "*know* the truth that sets us free" (John 8:31–32). Note again that the living leads to the relationship, which leads to the knowing. If he'd been a good Greek philosopher, he would have put the sequence the other way around, from head to heart to hands. So, to emphasize our mandate to do God's will "on earth," we begin here with the hands, in other words, with the lived commitments of Christian faith.

Christian faith is first and foremost a *way of love,* bonding love of God, neighbor, and oneself, with no exceptions. Then, *the way* of Jesus calls us to love and care most of all for people in need. New Testament scholars now agree that the defining character of Jesus's public ministry was compassion for people in need of any kind. Disciples too should be ever ready "to suffer with" (Latin *compassio*) those who suffer and to favor the ones who need the favor most.

Then, true love demands justice—as a minimum. Surely Christians are called to follow Jesus's *way of justice.* Nothing less would be discipleship to the one who defined his life purpose as bringing good news to the poor, liberty to captives, sight to the blind, and freedom to the oppressed and effecting God's year of jubilee (Luke 4:16–21).

Following on, because the fruit of justice is peace (Isa. 32:17), Christian discipleship calls us to a *way of peacemaking and reconciliation.* From when the angels first announced his birth with "peace on earth" (Luke 2:14) to the greeting by the Risen Christ, "Peace be with you" (John 20:19), bringing peace to the world was clearly an intent of Jesus's mission of God's reign. And now, because God reconciled the world to Godself in Jesus, disciples are given the ministry of reconciliation and peacemaking (2 Cor. 5:19).

Because Jesus didn't even have a place to lay his head (Luke 9:58), Christian disciples are surely called to a *way of simplicity*. We must be ever mindful that the "poor in spirit" are blessed and promised the kingdom of heaven (Matt. 5:3), whereas "it is easier for a camel to go through the eye of a needle" than for people attached to riches to enter the reign of God (see 19:24).

The way of Jesus calls us to educate for Christian faith as a *way of integrity*. As I said before, he must have "walked the walk" of what he preached; it is amazing that he was never accused of hypocrisy, given the demanding gospel that he taught. Further, disciples should be honest in their one-on-one dealings, truthful in word and deed, matching their lives with what they claim to believe. We are to make decisions and choose actions that are faithful to the moral principles and values of Jesus.

Then, it is amazing how often throughout the Gospels that Jesus's ministry is one of healing. To do as he did calls disciples to a *way of healing* as well. Though we cannot work his miracles, we must have great empathy and care for every kind of human illness, physical, psychological, and spiritual. In our own time, it has also become abundantly clear that our faith imposes an urgent mandate to be healers of the earth and conservers of its ecological systems.

Last, though our list of faith for *the hands* could go on, Christian disciples are called to a *way of repentance*. Living *the way* of Jesus is a huge challenge, even with the help of God's abundant grace. The most we can do is approximate it and then ask for God's mercy when we fall far short. However, just as Jesus heightened the demands of belonging to God's reign, he also increased the availability of God's mercy. Jesus revealed that there is now no unforgivable sin, as long as we are willing to admit our guilt, say we're sorry, ask forgiveness, and recommit ourselves to live as disciples.

This *way of the hands* calls Christian religious educators to craft curricula that make persuasive presentations of the lifestyle and ethics, values and virtues that constitute Christian faith. What discipleship demands of people's lives—its orthopraxis, or right practice—should be a primary focus and intent of our educating in faith. This would be in contrast to the present nigh exclusive emphasis—at least in Roman Catholic circles—on orthodoxy (right belief). Although our beliefs are integral to our faith (more below), how we *live* our faith is really the nub of Christian discipleship. Therefore, with regard to *how to,* although it is important that our educating bring people to know and understand the data of Christian faith, it is just as important that we invite people to appropriate the practical wisdom of Christian faith into their lives and to make good judgments and decisions in its light.

A Way of the Heart: This category reflects how Christian faith is to permeate people's desires and relationships all across the board, climaxing in our relationship of prayer and worship of God. It should nurture in people *a way of right desires,* disposing them to direct their emotions and affections toward a *way of right relationships.* The latter requires a deep respect for all people and a commitment to their dignity and equality.

Based on what we've already said of its communal and inclusive nature, Christian faith is a *way of hospitality,* of *including all.* Jesus's eating with "tax collectors and sinners" (Mark 2:13) marked his radical inclusivity. Now, hospitality and outreach to all is the responsibility of every member of Christ's Body in the world.

Christian faith calls us to a rock-solid *way of trusting in God's love.* I already cited the claim by the scripture scholar Daniel Harrington that the central theme of Jesus's revelation to the world was the universality of God's unconditional love, a love that prompts us to love God and others as ourselves. May I add that Christians too often forget the "third leg" of the great commandment? The law of God demands that we love not only God and neighbor—not even excepting enemies—but ourselves as well.

To suffuse all other relationships, we are to educate people in a Christian *way of prayer and worship.* Jesus often went aside to pray, and he taught his disciples to pray (e.g., the Our Father). Then he instructed them to take what he had done with the bread and wine at the Last Supper and to do it "in memory" of him (Matt. 26:13). The first disciples heeded Jesus's words. The Acts of the Apostles tells us that, from the beginning, "they devoted themselves to the apostles' teaching and fellowship, to the breaking of bread and the prayers" (2:42). Our worship is the sacramental mode by which we bring our lives to God and encounter God's life to us—through word and sacrament—all "for the life of the world" (John 6:51).

For religious education curricula, this *way of the heart* means that our pedagogy is to nurture people effectively in right and loving relationships with God, self, others, and the world. Educating people's desires and relationships in the ways of Christian faith requires digging deeply into their souls, engaging them with the great generative themes of their lives, with what matters most to them. Our educating in faith should dispose them to belong to a community of faith and, according to ability, to contribute their time, talents, and tithes to its mission and ministries. Our educating should also prepare people to actively participate in the worship life of their faith community and nurture them in a sacramental consciousness by which they might "see God in all things."

A Way of the Head: This *way* refers to the beliefs and convictions of Christian faith. These beliefs and convictions are not just "head knowledge," the kind presumed by our Western Enlightenment heritage. When it comes to biblical faith, knowing and believing engage much more than the mind. In the Hebrew scriptures, for example, the *lev* is the faculty of knowledge and belief. It engages not only intellect, but emotions and will as well. In fact, *lev* is most often translated as "heart." In the New Testament, Paul reflects this tradition when he writes, "One believes with the heart" (Rom. 10:10).

This being said, we still are ever to educate in the rich intellectual aspects to Christian faith. Though it can entail the "foolishness of the cross" (1 Cor. 1:18–31), it is eminently in keeping with *a way of human reason.* As noted already, Vatican I, an ecumenical council of the Church, reiterated a long tradition that "reason and revelation" are partners in the ways of faith. Each needs the other—reason to deepen faith and faith to guide reason. The Church's long tradition of theology as *faith seeking understanding* reflects the conviction that faith's truths are in keeping with human reason and are demonstrable to reasonable people. As I've told generations of students in theology courses at Boston College, if someone is teaching or preaching something that doesn't make sense to you, doubt it immediately.

Christian faith is *a way of believing* with personal and heart-felt conviction the great truth claims of Scripture and Tradition. Christian religious education, then, must ground people well in the Faith's core beliefs. A full list is impossible here, but from Scripture, one thinks immediately of the biblical portrayal of God as One of "loving-kindness" or "steadfast love" (Hebrew *hesed;* Exod. 34:7); how we should live as a people of God, faithful to the covenant between us and keeping its commandments; God's saving work in the life, death, and resurrection of Jesus Christ; and the ongoing salvation of the world through the Holy Spirit. From Tradition, one thinks of the two great creeds, the Apostles' Creed and the Nicene Creed, and the central dogmas of faith, especially those concerning the Blessed Trinity, the divinity and humanity of Jesus, the teaching role of the Church, and the effectiveness of the sacraments to mediate God's grace to our lives.

Vatican II noted and the *Catechism of the Catholic Church* reiterates that there is a "hierarchy of the truths of faith" (e.g., *CCC,* n. 90). Some truth claims are foundational to Christian faith, while others are extrapolations from the foundations. Though we have no agreed-upon listing of either, the consensus of faith that the Holy Spirit formulates through the Church and as taught by its magisterium is our reliable guide for unity in faith. And in all essential matters there should be unity, in nonessentials diversity and debate as called for, and on all issues respect for one another.

Christian faith as believing calls disciples to a *way of studying and investigating,* of being open to learn from and understand more deeply the rich treasury of Scripture and Tradition. It is a *way of probing and reflecting,* ever striving to look at life and its meanings, at the Faith and its meanings, and to integrate the two—life and Faith—into lived, living, and life-giving faith. Vatican II declared that the "split" that Christians manage to maintain "between the faith which many profess and their daily lives deserves to be counted among the more serious errors of our age" (Pastoral Constitution on the Church in the Modern World, n. 43). Christian religious education should facilitate the bridging of this gap, enabling people to bring *life to Faith to life.*

This, in turn, implies that Christian faith is a *way of discerning and deciding,* of attempting to recognize its truths and spiritual wisdom, to personally appropriate its meaning for life, and to make good decisions in keeping with its convictions.

Some of what such *ways of the head* mean for Christian religious education has already been intimated, and there is more to come. In sum, we are to teach the whole rich Story and Vision of Christian faith and enable people to know it well, to take it to heart and life, to come to personal conviction of its truth claims, and to thus be a little more likely to live it. This sets our pedagogical purpose as being much more than "knowledge" of the faith, as we typically understand what it means "to know." As I've reiterated already, our intent is more than that people *know about* the faith; they must at least learn *from* it, so that its truth claims become meaningful in the context of their lives, so that it becomes something that enhances them personally and morally. In matters of Christian faith, we want people to *know* at the very depths of their "being"—as both noun and verb—shaping who they are and how they live. We want them to embrace it in their souls as *a way of spiritual wisdom for life.*

Spiritual Wisdom: The Old Testament portrays education in faith as bringing people to "know God," in Hebrew *daat Elohim.* Note that the verb root of *daat* is *yada,* which the Bible uses for both "knowing" and "lovemaking." Knowing God is deeply relational. As mentioned above, it is centered in the *lev,* which represents the whole person. Thus, to come to "know God" is to fall in love and then to be informed, formed, and transformed by what we love. We find Jesus steeped in this biblical epistemology when he looks up to heaven and says to the Father, "Eternal life is this: to *know* you, the one true God, and Jesus Christ whom you have sent" (John 17:3, JB). Clearly he means a relational knowing, much more than knowing *about.* This is why John can write, "Whoever is without love does not know God, for God is love" (1 John 4:8). On the other hand, "If we love one another, God remains in us" (4:12, NAB).

Given the above, I hesitate to say that the learning outcome of the "head" is simply *knowledge* of the beliefs of faith. If this were true, then all theologians—with their great religious knowledge—would be saints. If we ask the biblical tradition for an educational name for the cognitive outcome that religious educators intend, it would be *spiritual wisdom.* In Chapters 7 and 8 I will elaborate. It is enough for now to say that "spiritual wisdom for life" can guide our pedagogy and enable us to reach beyond knowledge—as the West understands the term—without leaving it behind. And when we push beyond knowledge toward wisdom, our faith becomes a spirituality for life.

In the Bible, the portrayal of *wisdom* evolves from a *craft* (Exod. 31:3–5) to *the* Craftsperson who accompanies God in the work of creation (see Prov. 8:30). Overall, biblical wisdom is *holistic,* engaging the total person—head, heart, and hands. It is *realized,* that is, "done" in a way that goes beyond being known about. It is *located* and *situated* in the social context of life. Finally, it is profoundly *ethical,* for it seeks what is true and does what is good. Spiritual wisdom is always *for fullness of life for all.* In sum, people who are spiritually wise are so because they embody and live their wisdom.

Note too the Bible advises that we must seek wisdom with all our hearts, but that she also comes looking for us—an important conviction for religious educators to keep in mind. In our work, nature and grace are ever intertwined, with our best efforts initiated and met by grace that both sustains our outreach and comes more than halfway to meet us. So, "Wisdom hastens to make herself known in anticipation of human desires," and "she makes her rounds, seeking those worthy of her . . . and graciously meets them with all solicitude" (Wisd. 6:12, 16, NAB). We must seek spiritual wisdom, but it also comes to meet us as grace—free gift. No wonder, then, that Paul can refer to Jesus as the "wisdom of God" (1 Cor. 1:24); Jesus is ever the incarnation of God's wisdom coming to meet us where we are, in the midst of life. Likewise, Paul assures us, "The sacred writings are capable of giving you wisdom for salvation through faith in Christ Jesus" (2 Tim. 3:15, NAB). It is precisely because he is the wisdom of God that Jesus can say of himself, "something greater than Solomon is here" (Luke 11:31) and, "I am the way, and the truth, and the life" (John 14:6).

In this light, I see as eminently appropriate a pedagogy that enables people to bring their lives to their faith and their faith to their lives, as did the Stranger on the road to Emmaus (Luke 24:13–35). This is how *knowing* the faith can educate people to embrace its spiritual wisdom as their own, as their spirituality of life.

For Reflection and Conversation

- How can you educate for Christian faith as a way of the head, heart, and hands?

- Call to mind a person in your life whom you consider to be truly wise. What makes this so? How can you educate people in the spiritual wisdom of Christian faith?

This chapter has focused on the purposes or learning outcomes intended by Christian religious education, highlighting the commitments that such education is to encourage *from* people's lives. I've proposed commitment to God's reign as disciples of Jesus and, more immediately, that people live the holistic faith that Jesus Christ taught, modeled, and made possible. Such purposes, however, are what education in faith is to "draw from" peoples lives—the "outcome" that educators should intend. Now we must also ask: How about what education in Christian faith should "bring to" people's lives and to the world? We might call this the "income." Though *outcome* and *income* are, of course, two sides of the same coin, it is worth dwelling on the latter as well. The fruits that Christian faith is to effect in peoples' lives and world also reflect our purpose—our Killarney—and call for an effective pedagogy toward such consequences within history.

I'll propose that Christian religious education is to bring people a salvation that liberates them and effects justice in our world. This is what lends Christian faith its most persuasive apologetics. So the themes of Chapter 4 are *liberating salvation* and *justice for all,* and then I highlight the contemporary need to weave such purposes into a "new apologetics" on behalf of Christian faith.

CHAPTER FOUR

Liberating Salvation
with Justice for All

Educating in Faith for the Life of the World

Every Christmas I receive at least one card with the beautiful meditation "One Solitary Life"; I love to read it again. Attributed to Rev. James Allen Francis (1864–1928), it was part of a sermon he preached to his congregation at the First Baptist Church of Los Angeles. Although Rev. Francis delivered his sermon in July of 1926, it seems most apt to recall at Christmastime. It begins: "He was born in an obscure village, the son of a peasant woman." After reviewing the notable points of Jesus's humble life, it concludes: "All the armies that ever marched, all the navies that ever sailed, all the parliaments that ever sat, all the kings that ever reigned, put together, have not affected the life of people on this earth as much as that One Solitary Life."

The agenda of this chapter is to ask and propose what the "one solitary life" of Jesus Christ has effected for individual persons, the church, society, and the world. What difference did and does the life, death, and resurrection of Jesus Christ make to our human condition? To the course of human history? What are the fruits of his paschal mystery as it reaches into the very depths of people's being? Into the public realm of the economy, government, and society? Into the natural environment?

We can immediately answer, as does St. Paul, that through Jesus, God's grace is now all the more abundant for us (1 Tim. 1:14; 2 Cor. 4:15; 9:8; Titus 3:6). But what does this really mean? What difference does and should it make for us now? As we have repeated often, though free and unearned, God's grace always comes to us as a responsibility—a response-ability. So this chapter is paired with the previous one on the *why* of Christian religious education. Here, however, our focus is on the effect that the "Jesus event" had on human history and what it empowers Christians to do as agents within this history and as covenant partners in God's grace. Clearly, our responses to these questions must shape our educating in Christian faith. Further, *how* we talk about the fruits of the paschal mystery must be effective and appropriate to the "mode of receivers" in our time and context.

The "mode of *receivers*" is all the more challenging in this age of secularity, which seems to dispose people to be more like "decliners." Even hopeful commentators like the social philosopher Charles Taylor alert that the answer to *Will there be faith on earth?* is not an inevitable yes at all, due to a pervasive secularity that discourages faith. In brief, Taylor makes a convincing argument that an "exclusive" or "self-sufficient" humanism has risen up in the Western world as a real alternative to faith. By this he means a perspective that encourages fullness of life without any reference to God; instead, we presume that we can take care of ourselves. He traces the roots of exclusive humanism to three strands of evolution in human consciousness: people became enlightened about the phenomena of nature (good or bad weather is not from God, but explained by meteorologists); we figured out that the foundation of societies is not the *divine* right of kings, but the consensus of its citizens (i.e., based in "us" rather than God); and that ours is not an enchanted world where we need God "to hold the plentiful forces of darkness at bay."[1] Now ghosts, goblins, and devils are just fun at Halloween.

As a result, "the coming of modern secularity [Taylor means social conditions discouraging of faith] has been coterminous with the rise of a society in which for the first time in history a purely self-sufficient humanism came to be a widely available option"[2]—in other words, a compelling alternative to religious faith. This makes the "new apologetics" I offer on behalf of Christian faith through-out this chapter and summarize at the end all the more urgent. To appeal and win hearts in such an age, people must see Christian faith as clearly promoting rather than retarding what Taylor calls "human flourishing" and as effectively mediating God's abundant grace and revelation to this end. For example, for exclusive human-ism, people no longer have sins but "issues," and the latter can be treated by therapy. Oftentimes, however, the only effective therapy for us is to experience God's mercy and unconditional love. Or again, the warrant for justice toward ourselves (e.g., keeping the Sabbath) or others (e.g., ending oppressions in society) is not just benevolence, a humanist option, but the law of God. The examples go on.

As we embark to find effective language and a persuasive apolo-getics for Christian faith in our time, we must first recognize that the paschal mystery is well named "mystery"—it belongs within the realm of God. It should not surprise that there is no one explanation of its meaning for us and for the world. The first Christians had come to a rock-solid conviction that Jesus's life, death, and resurrec-tion had changed everything about the human condition and even the course of history. The poet William Butler Yeats captured this well when he wrote, "All changed, changed utterly; a terrible beauty is born"—the refrain line from his moving poem "Easter 1916." But what was "changed utterly" by Easter, and how do we talk about it? Our best hope will be to honor what we find throughout Scripture and Tradition and then to weave a compelling response that can engage and educate effectively in our time and place; indeed, this has been the challenge for Christians since the beginning.

Given the mystery, it comes as no surprise that in the four Gospels we already detect slightly varying understandings of *why* Jesus came and *what* he brought about. In Mark's Gospel, Jesus brings the good news of God's reign and is God's definitive agent of its realization. Matthew and Luke echo this sentiment and add their own perspectives. For Matthew, Jesus is the one who fulfills God's promises of *salvation* to the people of Israel. For Luke, Jesus is the great prophet of God who brings light to the Gentiles and extends God's saving work to all humankind. In a shared text in all three Gospels Jesus says of himself that he "came to serve," and then Matthew and Mark add, "and to give his life *a ransom* for many" (Mark 10:45; Matt. 20:28; Luke 22:27). To ransom implies that Jesus rescues or frees us from some bondage for a price—which will be his own life. But perhaps it is John who has the richest Gospel response to this mystery. It is summarized in what may be the most quoted verse of the New Testament: "For God so loved the world that he gave his only Son, so that everyone who believes in him may not perish but may have eternal life" (3:16).

This verse is so familiar that we may miss out on what an amazing statement it makes. Note first that there is no mention of Jesus taking away sins or God demanding redress for human offenses. Instead, the verse declares that God's motive was total love, love enough to send even God's own Son. And the intended outcome or effect? To enable humankind, through faith in Jesus, to come into "eternal life." John repeats "eternal life" many times as the reward for Christian faith well lived.

Belief in an afterlife emerged in the later books of the Hebrew scriptures (e.g., Dan. 12:1–2; 2 Macc. 7). By Jesus's time, it appears that for some Jews (not the Sadducees) "eternal life" had come to symbolize the deepest hopes of the human heart, the ultimate goal of living. Recall how Luke has a lawyer ask Jesus, "What must I do to inherit eternal life?" (10:25); the rich ruler later asks the same question (18:18). John, however, makes "eternal life" the ultimate intent and outcome of God's sending the Son. As noted in Chapter 3, though John's primary reference is everlasting joy in God's presence, this "life" that Jesus effects is also for *now*. It is already present through Jesus: "Anyone who hears my word and believes him who sent me has eternal life, . . . and has passed from death to life" (John 5:24). Likewise, Jesus gives himself as our "bread of life" and "for the life of the world" *now* (6:51). He is the Good Shepherd who came so that we "might have life, and have it abundantly" (10:10). *For fullness of life for all, here and hereafter* will always be a powerful metaphor for talking about the fruits of Jesus's paschal mystery. It certainly remains one of my favorites.

St. Paul uses a plethora of images to capture the meaning of Jesus for us, reminding again that this mystery cannot be exhausted by human language and certainly not by any one metaphor or analogy. Paul first tells the Romans that the gospel of Jesus is "the power of God for *salvation* to everyone who has faith" (1:16). A little later, however, he tells them that they are "*justified* freely by God's grace through the *redemption* in Christ Jesus, whom God set forth as an *expiation,* through faith, by his blood, . . . because of the *forgiveness* of sins" (3:24–25, NAB). In just these two verses, Paul has added to salvation the metaphors of justification, redemption, expiation (sometimes translated "atonement"), and forgiveness of sins.

Then, in his first letter to the Corinthians, Paul opens by saying that "Christ Jesus became for us *wisdom* from God, and *righteousness* [also translated *justice*] and *sanctification* and *redemption*" (1:30)—in a sense, four new metaphors. Paul echoes these a few chapters later, but in a different pattern: "You were *washed,* you were *sanctified,* you were *justified* in the name of the Lord Jesus Christ and in the Spirit of our God" (6:11). When Paul writes to the Corinthians a second time, however, his favored metaphor seems to be *reconciliation*. In great summary verses, Paul begins with, "If anyone is in Christ, there is *a new creation.*" He continues, "All this is from God, who *reconciled us* to himself through Christ, and has given us the ministry of reconciliation" (5:17–18). Note that the reconciliation which God has effected in Jesus now becomes *our* responsibility as well.

Paul repeats these metaphors and adds many more throughout his writings; I highlight two of my favorites from his letter to the Galatians. First, through Jesus, we are now the "*adopted children* of God." What a lovely image! Paul says that Jesus redeemed us "so that we might receive adoption as children." And because we are children, "God has sent the Spirit of his Son into our hearts, crying 'Abba! Father!'" (4:5–6). This amazing passage implies that we have been elevated to a status analogous to that of Jesus, receiving his Spirit and able to address God as he did—as Abba. My other favorite metaphor from Paul's letter to the Galatians is that of freedom: "For freedom, Christ has set us free. Stand firm, therefore, and do not submit again to the yoke of slavery" (5:1). I'll echo this sentiment later in this chapter under "*liberating* salvation."

Throughout the New Testament, there is a tension between the "already" and the "not yet" in the fruits of Jesus's paschal mystery. Chapter 3 noted a similar tension regarding the reign of God; Jesus announces that it "has come near" (Matt. 4:17) and yet urges disciples to pray and work for its coming. Both reflect the same tension between eschatological and historical hope—in other words, between what God will surely bring to completion at the *eschaton* (the end time)—and how this is to sustain our hope and good ef-

forts now, within human history. Our confidence in final fulfillment, both personally and socially, should sustain our hopes and
best efforts along the way, all made possible by God's grace through
Jesus and by the Holy Spirit, ever at work in the world. So Paul
writes about people "obtaining the salvation that is in Christ Jesus"
now *and,* in the same verse, of gaining "eternal glory" later (2 Tim.
2:10). Likewise, 1 Peter 1:5 speaks of "a salvation that is ready to be
revealed in the final time" (NAB). A few verses later the text speaks
of the "indescribable and glorious joy" of people as they already
"attain the goal of faith, the salvation of [their] souls" (1:9). The triumph of the paschal mystery is already assured, yet the Risen Christ
will be "with [us] always," enabling its fruits to blossom "to the end
of time" (Matt. 28:20, JB).

The metaphors from Paul and other New Testament writings all
became foundational to Christian understanding of "God's work
in Jesus." In fact, throughout Christian history we find that varied
metaphors came to the fore in different times and cultural contexts.
About a thousand years after Paul, we hear St. Anselm of Canter-
bury (1033–1109) asking afresh, as if it were a new question for his
time, *cur Deus homo,* literally, "Why did God become a person?"
His response was to focus on redemption and Jesus as Redeemer, the
one who "pays the price" for our sins. We'll see below that Anselm's
choice was particularly effective within the social imagination of his
time and place.

Informed by and honoring the rich tradition of responses that
have preceded, we need to find compelling and relevant responses
to Anselm's question for our time: Why did God become human?
This is needed to offset the negative effects of secularization and the
option of exclusive humanism, so ready at hand. We need a persuasive apologetics on behalf of Christianity to ensure a "yes" to *Will
there be faith on earth?* Before making some proposals, pause and
discern your own responses.

For Reflection and Conversation

- In your opinion, *cur Deus homo?* Why did God become a person in Jesus, and what are the consequences of his life, death, and resurrection—the paschal mystery?

- Do you have a favorite metaphor to express your response? How did you come by it? What do you like best about it? What are its limitations?

- When you imagine educating in Christian faith for such consequences for people and society, what comes to mind? What is to be emphasized? What are the opportunities? The challenges?

Why Did God Become Human?

In the great sweep of Christian tradition, there are three major models or ways of talking about the consequences of Jesus's life, death, and resurrection, all well grounded in Scripture. One classic way is to name *Jesus as Savior* and his work as *salvation.* This highlights that Jesus saved humankind *from* the overwhelming power of sin and evil and *for* life and goodness, conquering all that threatens to destroy us. This is the model favored by the Nicene Creed; we confess: "for us and *for our salvation,* he came down from heaven." Another classic model is to see *Jesus as Redeemer* and his work as our *redemption.* He has ransomed or paid the price (dual meanings of the Latin *redemeo*) for the sins of humankind by making satisfaction to God's justice, thus canceling the punishment due. The third classic model, more favored in Eastern Catholic traditions, understands *Jesus as Divinizer,* who restored the divine image to humanity that was tarnished by original sin. Thus, he renewed people's potential for *theosis,* that is, to become ever more like God. In the pithy summary of St. Athanasius (296–373), "God became human so that humans could become more like God."[3]

All of these models reflect a profound truth that must be carried forward in contemporary understandings of why God became a person in Jesus. As with all human language about divine mysteries, each of these metaphors says something profoundly true. Yet they can never say it all. Further and like all metaphors, if taken too literally, they begin to say what is *not* true at all. For example, pushing the metaphor of Jesus as Redeemer too far (as I've often heard in churches on a Good Friday) can make it sound as if God's scales of justice could be rebalanced only by horrendous suffering on the part of God's own Son. What a terrifying image of God.

Likewise, let us remember that these metaphors have found favor in particular historical circumstances. For example and as noted already, Anselm's answer to his own question was to favor the *redemption* model. Though well grounded in the New Testament, he explained it as analogous to how there is a great imbalance caused to the equilibrium of society when a ruler is offended by a vassal or servant. Such dishonor throws everything out of kilter, and the scales of justice must be rebalanced by some punishment or act of fealty. "Ah," proposed Anselm, "that's what Jesus did for us"—he paid back what was due to God's honor, so dishonored by our sins. Anselm's metaphor spoke powerfully to the people of his medieval society, but perhaps not so well to ours.

Emerging Possibilities: Beginning in the late 1960s, with the emergence of liberation theologies, there was a rich retrieval of *Jesus as Liberator.* As noted earlier, Christians can truly say that "Christ has set us free" (Gal. 5:1). He did so precisely that "we might no longer be enslaved to sin" (Rom. 6:6). Now "freed from sin" by Jesus's paschal mystery, even death has been conquered, "for the wages of sin is death, but the free gift of God is eternal life in Christ Jesus our

Lord" (6:7, 23). From such sentiments—and they run throughout the Pauline writings—it became a standard confession of Christian faith that Jesus has "conquered sin and death" for us, well echoed in both Catholic and Protestant catechisms.

What has deepened of late, however, is the recognition that sin is both personal and social, that besides our personal sins there are many "deadly" things from which people need to be set free (e.g., addictions and social discriminations of all kinds). The social sciences help us to understand that our personal sins give rise to sinful social structures and cultural practices. Personal sins of sexism, racism, or greed coalesce in societies that are sexist, racist, and greedy. Then, vice versa, the sinful structures of society and oppressive mores of culture create conditions that dispose people to personal sins. Since the life, death, and resurrection of Jesus conquered sin and made goodness more possible, this means that he defeated both personal and social sins and freed us personally and socially to live toward the reign of God. In sum, if sin is both personal and social, then the effects of Jesus's life, death, and resurrection must be both personal and social.

It seems totally appropriate, then, to highlight the emancipatory consequences for societies and cultures as well as for individual persons. Jesus's paschal mystery was a catalyst to *free people from* all that diminishes and enslaves, both personal and social, and to *free people for* realizing God's will of holiness and fullness of life for all humankind, for societies, and for the integrity of creation as well. Paul explicitly writes that in Jesus, "creation itself will be set free from bondage to decay and will obtain the freedom of the glory of the children of God" (Rom. 8:21). Recall too how Jesus saw himself as a catalyst of God's reign in human history; its values are the very antithesis of bondage or oppression, personal, social, or cultural. Thus, *liberation* and *Christ as Liberator* are reflected well in Scripture and are particularly apt metaphors to speak of the effects of the paschal mystery in our time.

Another contemporary model gaining traction is of Jesus and his paschal mystery as the catalyst of our *humanization* or, similarly, the one who enables *human flourishing*. This model takes the emphasis off of original sin and places it onto our human potential when enlivened by God's grace. As noted already, human sinfulness was more the emphasis of Western Christianity, whereas Eastern Catholics favored our potential for *theosis,* becoming more Godlike and living "godly" lives. Many contemporary authors, with some feminist theologians leading the way,[4] image Jesus as enabling Christians to live into fullness of life as reflections of God. Again, this is entirely in keeping with Scripture. It echoes well John's Jesus as the catalyst "for eternal life," here and hereafter. It is an inspiring and persuasive apologetics to think of Jesus as enabling people, societies, and cultures to flourish.

A Proposal for Our Time: Liberating Salvation

In 1975, Pope Paul VI promulgated an apostolic exhortation entitled *Evangelii Nuntiandi,* "On Evangelization in the Modern World." It reflected the discussions by a worldwide synod of bishops on the topic. It was, in fact, an excellent statement on religious education that has now reached classic status. Pope Paul VI proposed the metaphor of "liberating salvation" to describe the historical effects of Jesus's paschal mystery. I believe he did so in such a document, because it seems particularly apt for the work of religious educators. To imagine that we are educating in faith toward *liberating salvation* for peoples' lives and for society is surely an inspiring purpose. It can shape our whole curriculum—what, why, and how we teach Christian faith—in very positive and life-giving ways.

I already referred to *salvation* and *Jesus as Savior* as one of three great classic ways of explaining the consequences of Jesus's paschal mystery. I also elaborated a little on the emerging metaphor of *liberation* and *Jesus as Liberator*. The genius of *Evangelii Nuntiandi* is to blend the traditional with what appeals to contemporary consciousness, lending a more holistic sense of the paschal mystery for persons and societies. *Evangelii Nuntiandi* states that "at the kernel and center of his Good News, Christ proclaimed salvation, this great gift of God which is liberation from everything that oppresses people but which is above all liberation from sin" (n. 9). The exhortation goes on to elaborate what the liberating salvation is *for,* not just *from.* It calls for "bringing the Good News into all the strata of humanity, and through its influence transforming humanity from within and making it new" (n. 18). Note the consequence of humanization here as well. Such effects are both personal and social: "Always taking the person as starting point," liberating salvation focuses on "the relationship of people among themselves and with God." At the same time, it pushes out "into all the strata" of societies and cultures, working for "their regeneration by an encounter with the Gospel" (nn. 18, 20).

"Salvation" is still the noun here, so we need to elaborate on it a little. At first, however, we need to consider whether this term will appeal to contemporary consciousness and be heard as relevant to present issues. Will "salvation" communicate the effects of the paschal mystery "according to the mode of the receiver" in a culture of secularity? I believe it can be a compelling metaphor, especially when identified as "liberating," and that it can encourage education in Christian faith that helps to save both souls and societies.

Etymologically, "salvation" and being "saved" have meanings of both *from* and *for.* We are saved *from* danger, threat, oppression, and so forth; but the Latin *salus* also means *for* good health, being safe, and thriving. This dual meaning can ever speak to our human condition, in which there is an enduring sense of threat, what the philosophers call "existential angst." Put more plainly, as human beings in residence, we always have concerns, some of them very deep and threatening. Given our capacities to destroy ourselves and our environment, it would seem that we are more threatened today than at any time in history. Likewise, every person is faced with the ultimate reality of death. As my grandmother would often remind, "None of us will get out of here alive." In Christian faith, however, salvation means precisely that "we *can* all get out of here alive." As Paul insisted, "by victory through our Lord Jesus Christ," death has "lost its sting" (1 Cor. 15:55–57). Meanwhile, we always feel the need to be *saved from* the power of all the sins and evils that beset us, the addictions and violence, the cruelty and exploitation, the injustice and discrimination, and *saved for* living into fullness of life for all. Exclusive humanism addresses the same issues, but has nothing comparable to offer.

The Hebrew scriptures repeat hundreds of times that "Yahweh saves" and that only God saves. The word *yeshuah*—"salvation" (the root of Jesus's name)—has political and spiritual meanings of both being protected from danger *and* made secure in peace and harmony with God and one another. God's greatest saving deed is the Exodus. It is clearly a work of liberating salvation, when God brings people out of slavery into a promised land of freedom. God said to Moses, "I have witnessed the affliction of my people in Egypt and have heard their cry of complaint against their slave drivers, so I know well what they are suffering. Therefore I have come down to rescue them from the hands of the Egyptians and lead them out of that land into a good and spacious land, a land flowing with milk and honey" (Exod. 3:7–8, NAB). Theirs (and ours) is a God who recognizes suffering and intervenes in human history to side with the oppressed and downtrodden in order to liberate them and move them to a place where they can flourish.

The Israelites had firm faith that God did, indeed, free them from slavery in Egypt. In the Exodus, God's act of salvation was liberating, with the two as one. Then, at Sinai, the people recommitted themselves through the Mosaic covenant, promising to live as God's people by keeping the Ten Commandments. So God's liberating salvation in the Exodus was both political and spiritual, communal and yet incumbent upon each member to keep the commandments. In other words, the liberating salvation wrought by God does not give people license to do as they please. Instead, as always with true freedom, God's saving calls to responsibility and points the way with the commandments.

Note well that the Israelites always prefaced the listing of the commandments by remembering that their God was the One "who brought [them] out of the land of Egypt, that place of slavery" (Exod. 20:2, NAB). In other words, they saw these laws as the paths to continue in God's liberating salvation. To put anything other than the one true God at the center of life is likely to enslave—back to Egypt again. In the later books of the Old Testament, this saving work of God merges into the promise of a messianic Savior. This Anointed One (*messiah* in Hebrew, *kristos* in Greek) would save all people, liberating them from every evil, and be a catalyst to realize all the values of God's reign.

Even before Jesus is born, Mary declares in the Magnificat, "My spirit rejoices in God my Savior" (Luke 1:47). Then, from the beginning, the Gospels present her son Jesus as the long promised Savior. Luke has the angels announce to the shepherds, "Today in the city of David, a savior has been born for you who is Messiah and Lord" (2:11, NAB). Likewise, the angel who appears to Joseph says, "You are to name him Jesus, because he will save his people from their sins" (Matt. 1:21). In John, the Samaritans are the first to recognize him as "truly the Savior of the world" (4:42). Throughout his public ministry, Jesus constantly restored people to health—physical, psychological, and spiritual. At the same time, he claimed to have been "anointed by the Spirit" to bring good news to the poor, release to captives, sight to the blind, and freedom to the oppressed (Luke 4:18–21). Jesus's ministry was both personal and social, salvific and liberating.

The remainder of the New Testament represents Jesus as Savior *from* sin and the power of sin and also Savior *for* good health, new life, faith, truth, freedom, and everything needed for human flourishing. Indeed, "the gospel . . . is the power of God for salvation to everyone who has faith" (Rom. 1:16). Salvation is the ultimate triumph over evil, making possible fullness of life for all and for the whole cosmos. "Eye has not seen, and ear has not heard, and it has not entered the human heart" what amounts to the fullness of salvation in Jesus Christ (1 Cor. 2:9, NAB).

Although God assuredly saves in Jesus Christ, this salvation comes as no cheap grace; God's work of salvation engages our responsibility as well. In fact, we are to "work out [our] salvation with fear and trembling; for it is God who is at work in [us], enabling [us] both to will and to work for God's good pleasure" (Phil. 2:13). What a great summary statement of how grace works through nature—us: God is "at work" enabling us to fulfill our side of the covenant. For good measure, James asks the rhetorical question, "Can faith save you?" and responds, "Faith by itself, if it has no works, is dead" (2:14, 17).

Salvation, especially when identified as liberating, can be a compelling metaphor for our time. To craft religious education toward such ends and effects lends it powerful potential to engage, entice, and persuade. I will elaborate specifically in the next section on educating for a faith that does justice, and then as the new apologetics we can mount on behalf of Christian faith in an age of secularity.

Educating for a Faith That Does Justice

It is rather amazing how Christian consciousness has deepened to yield the realization that Faith brings profound social responsibilities and the mandate to work for justice in society. We now realize better than ever, in the often quoted phrase from the International Synod of Bishops of 1971, that: "Action on behalf of justice and participation in the transformation of the world fully appear to us as a constitutive dimension of the preaching of the Gospel, or, in other words, of the Church's mission for the redemption of the human race and its liberation from every oppressive situation."[5] So if what we preach or teach does not require and prompt people to do the works of justice, we are not representing the gospel of Jesus Christ.

The Church has long taught that works of mercy, spiritual and corporal, are integral to Christian faith. From the beginning of the Church, Christians have garnered very positive attention for their practical charity toward the poor and needy. Over the past century, however, there has been a profound deepening of awareness that calls Christians beyond the works of charity, without leaving them behind, to the works of justice as well. It is not enough simply to feed hungry people. Christians must both question and change the structures that cause people to be hungry in the first place as well as empower them to feed themselves.

In mainline Protestant traditions, such figures as Walter Rauschenbusch (1861–1918), proponent of the "social gospel" movement, and Reinhold Niebuhr (1892–1971), who called for "prophetic Christianity," were heralds of the social justice mandate for Christians. The evangelical leader Jim Wallis (1948–), founder of the Sojourners community and magazine in Washington, D.C., is an inspiring voice today in this tradition. And there have always been "radical" Christian denominations like the Quakers, Amish, and Mennonites that have made peacemaking and social responsibilities central to their practice of Christian faith.

In Catholic tradition, the contemporary emphasis on justice is dated from the first great social encyclical of Pope Leo XIII, *Rerum Novarum* ("Of New Things"), issued in 1891. Since then, popes have followed with many social encyclicals and myriad justice teachings, beginning with concern for the rights of workers, moving on later to the responsibilities of wealthy nations toward developing ones, to halting nuclear proliferation, and most recently to emphasizing care for the environment. It is significant that this huge corpus of teachings is now referred to as the social *doctrine* of the Church. In Catholic parlance, this places the Church's teaching for justice and peacemaking in the top echelon of its "hierarchy of truths."

We might well ask why the works of justice and peace have come now to center stage for Christians. There are a number of reasons. To begin with, the developments in biblical studies have been very significant. Good Bible scholarship has made us realize that biblical justice does not simply mean the punishment of sinners, as had been the dominant portrayal, but rather fulfilling the social responsibilities of the covenant, with emphasis on caring for those most in need: widows, orphans, and strangers in the land.

Literally hundreds of biblical texts, especially from the prophets, clearly mandate works of justice. As an example, I take a favorite, Micah 6:8. Bible scholars point to this one verse as summarizing the core preaching of the prophets. To appreciate it fully, however, we might begin by looking at Micah 6:1–7. It portrays a dramatic courtroom scene in which Yahweh puts Israel on trial and acts as both plaintiff and prosecutor. The charges are that Israel has forgotten its liberation by God from slavery in Egypt (6:4) and what such emancipation requires of God's people. God calls the mountains and foundations of the earth as witnesses. Israel doesn't deny the charges, but tries to "buy off" the prosecutor, perhaps to settle out of court. Maybe God can be appeased by more generous sacrificial offerings, for example, better-quality calves or upping the number of rams or the volume of oil. Israel even offers God the unspeakable, the sacrifice of its own "firstborn" children.

In the face of this pathetic bribery, Yahweh looks out over the head of Israel and addresses all humankind as well: "This, O humankind, is what Yahweh asks of you, only this: that you *act justly, love tenderly,* and *walk humbly* with your God" (6:8, popular translation). These are not three separate mandates, but a whole. *Justice, love,* and *faith* are integral to the covenant of "right relationship" that God expects to have with and among God's own people.

Parenthetically, note that the biblical sense of justice and holiness are two sides of the same coin. Both call people to right and loving relationship with God, self, others, and creation. For example, the great Holiness Code of Leviticus 19 begins with, "Be holy, for I the LORD your God am holy" (19:2). Reading on, however, we find that the holiness demanded is doing the works of justice—at every level—with a special favor "for the poor and the alien" (19:10) and to "love your neighbor as yourself" (19:18). Biblically, to be holy means to keep the covenant, but only by the works of justice can people keep covenant with this kind of God.

Note too that biblical "rightness" is modeled on God's relationship with us. There is a largesse and munificence in God's relationships, and God's people should have the same in theirs. Biblical justice, then, is not the "blind Lady Justice" balancing the scales, as represented by many a statue outside our courthouses. Such justice gives "everyone their due" and no more (Aristotle's proposal). Biblical justice, however, is that of a "compassionate mother." The Hebrew word *rachum* can be translated as "compassionate," a frequent designation for God. Note well, however, that the similar word *racham* means a mother's womb. Our God is "womblike" toward all God's people. Like every good mother, God shows special favor to those children who need the favor most, "the poor" of whatever kind. God's people should be and do likewise.

Regarding the New Testament, scripture scholars agree that Jesus's preaching of God's reign was a clarion call to works of peace and justice, to the *shalom* that God intends for all humankind and creation. This was how people understood the symbol of God's reign in Jesus's time. Beyond this, we've already referred to Jesus's feeding the hungry (the only miracle, besides the resurrection, reported six times across all four Gospels), his outreach to the marginalized, his inclusivity at table, his having women disciples, his commitment to peacemaking, and so on. Likewise, I've many times referred to the two classic texts that reflect Jesus's social commitments, Luke 4:16–21 and Matthew 25:31–46.

In Luke, Jesus begins his public ministry by going to his home synagogue at Nazareth on a Sabbath day, is asked to read, and searches for the text of Isaiah 61:1–2 (and mixes in Isa. 58:6). Jesus then proclaims that he is God's promised and Anointed One, bringing good news to the poor, liberty to captives, sight to the blind, and freedom to the oppressed and proclaiming God's jubilee year (Luke 4:18–19). The jubilee occurred every fiftieth year; the land was left to lie fallow, debts were forgiven, and all slaves were set free. Then, toward the end of his ministry in Matthew, Jesus reviews how we will be judged. In sum, God will judge between "the sheep and the goats" by whether or not we've fed the hungry, sheltered the homeless, cared for the imprisoned, and generally helped those most in need (25:31–46).

It is likely that Jesus himself understood his paschal mystery as effecting a liberating salvation with justice for all. For example, Luke's version of the Transfiguration depicts Jesus conversing with Moses and Elijah about "his exodus that he was going to accomplish in Jerusalem" (9:31, NAB). In John's Gospel, when Jesus first appears in public, John the Baptist hails him with, "Here is the Lamb of

God who takes away the sin of the world!" (1:29), an echo surely of
the paschal lamb, whose blood saved the people of Israel during the
first Exodus. Jesus's last supper was also a Passover meal. There he
associated his own body and blood through bread and wine with
the death he was about to undergo the next day, forging a new covenant. Later, Paul teaches that "our paschal lamb, Christ, has been
sacrificed" (1 Cor. 5:7). We can say, then, that Jesus's paschal mystery echoes well the first Exodus; both are God's great acts of liberating salvation for justice and fullness of life for all.

Beyond biblical studies, the centrality of justice to Christian
faith also received initial impetus from eighteenth- and nineteenth-
century political movements coupled with the insights of the emerging social sciences. Both sent the Church back to reread its own
scriptures and traditions and to rediscover what had been largely a
recessive gene for justice and peace. For example, the French Revolution, with its emphasis on human rights, dignity, and equality,
though at first roundly resisted, helped the Church to rediscover
social values like the *imago Dei* tenet (all in the "image of God")
so central to early Christian theology and ethics. Likewise, the
threat of Communism and its growing success with the workers in
Europe, many of them Catholic, was a catalyst for Pope Leo XIII
to write *Rerum Novarum* (1891). He could readily build upon principles of justice evident in the Bible and developed in the tradition
by great theologians like Augustine and Aquinas.

From the social sciences, the Church learned about the systemic
nature of our public realm, the way systems work (or don't work),
and the fact that the personal and social are so intertwined. Much
of what we accept as "the way things are" is in fact due to social
constructs that can be changed. Though systems are powerfully re-
sistant, we can be agents and re-creators within our sociocultural
context, not just passive creatures who accept things as they are as if
they should be so. This brings a new perspective to Matthew 25:31–

46 and our interpretation of the criteria by which we will be judged. In the example I gave already, it will not be enough simply to feed the hungry and shelter the homeless, though such charity is always a mandate. We'll also need to try to change the social conditions that cause people to be hungry and homeless.

Note too that the works of justice and peace are deeply inter-twined; justice promotes peace, while injustice brings on violence and war. We can say, then, that justice and peace are symbiotic. The prophet Isaiah said as much: "Justice will bring about peace" (32:17, NAB). Pope Paul VI in his Peace Day address of January 1, 1972, paraphrased Isaiah in the now famous phrase, "If you want peace, work for justice."

For Reflection and Conversation

- Reflect again on your own understanding of "why God became human" in Jesus. In light of my proposals, is there anything to shift or state differently?

- Liberating salvation! How might this shape what you teach as Christian faith and how you teach it?

- Faith that does justice! How might this shape what and how you teach?

What Justice and How to Teach It?

What Justice: We've fallen into the pattern of using *"social* justice" as a blanket term. Indeed, all justice does have a social dimension. However, we must be committed to justice at every level, personal, interpersonal, and social, making commitment to justice what the late Joseph Cardinal Bernardin (1928–96) of Chicago called "a seamless garment."[6] Thus, the following distinctions from Christian ethics may help.

Commutative justice demands honesty and fairness in all exchanges between persons or private groups. *Distributive* justice requires society to ensure that its social goods—culture, economic wealth, and political power—are fairly distributed, so that all people have enough to meet their basic human needs and to live with dignity. *Social* justice, strictly speaking, then, is the responsibility of society to create structures that protect the dignity of all people and allow each member to participate in and contribute to public life. In practice, social and distributive justice get lumped together as two sides of the same coin, ensuring that people have what they need and can contribute what they have to the common good. Commutative justice may now be the one that we underrate in Christian religious education. In our concern for the structural and public realm, we must continue to teach the demands of Christian faith for honesty, fairness, and truth telling, the one-on-one justice of everyday life.

More recently, a movement has emerged to promote *restorative* justice, especially regarding crime and punishment. The standard justice of our legal systems is *punitive;* it tries people for alleged crime and, if they are found guilty, punishes them. By contrast, *restorative* justice intends to rehabilitate offenders and to give some sense of recompense to the those hurt by the offense. Restorative justice requires that all parties to a particular conflict or crime come together to resolve collectively how to deal with the aftermath. Offenders have the opportunity to admit their guilt, to ask forgiveness, and to make reparation. Likewise, victims have their harm or loss recognized and amends made—if possible. The offended may then choose to forgive the offender(s).

The Peace and Reconciliation Commission of South Africa,

led by Archbishop Desmond Tutu, was a fine example of an attempt to practice *restorative* justice. As parents, we try to practice it with discipline issues; most parents do this by instinct. Instead of simply punishing children for wrongs done, they give them positive things to do that can make up for their offenses. A favorite "consequence" that my spouse and I give our son, Teddy, for misbehaving or disobeying is loss of television time. However, by doing some extra chore or act of kindness, he can win back his TV allowance. Such restorative justice surely has a place in the discipline policy of a church-sponsored school or parish program. It is entirely in keeping with a Christian sense of justice, which at its best is always tempered by mercy and the possibility of redemption for all.[7]

How to Educate for Justice: As I keep promising, I will address the *how to* question in depth in Chapters 8 and 9. Yet there is something particular about educating for justice, so I offer some preliminary suggestions here, having here proposed this as a purpose of education in Christian faith. Note too that educating for justice is within the ambit of educating for liberating salvation. The following suggestions pertain to both.

First, we should realize that educators in Christian communities are crucial to whether members commit to a faith that does justice. Put in the negative, if people come through a curriculum of Christian religious education and remain sexist, racist, classist, ageist, homophobic, negligent in their responsibilities to the poor and marginalized, for the abused and oppressed, for the environment and ecology, then their program or school has not educated them in Christian faith. On the other hand, the content, process, and purpose of how we do Christian religious education should enable all to grow in social consciousness and commitment to the works of justice and peace.

Second, educating for justice demands that we educate justly. This self-evident principle may surprise, but it is worth stating. Unfortunately, we can go about education in ways that are inherently unjust. For example, we can "lord it over" people—even on behalf of justice—act self-righteously, forgetting the democracy of sin, or create unhealthy guilt. Likewise, our pedagogy can rob people of their own word, tell them what to think and how to think it, and discourage their discernment and decision making. All of this would be unjust. A faith that does justice demands a pedagogy that is itself a work of justice and is likely to promote it in people's lives.

Third, as a result, our pedagogy needs to engage people's "souls," reaching into the depths of their being, raising up what really matters, what Freire calls the "generative themes" of their lives. Likewise, it should encourage people's active participation in the teaching/learning event, according to their learning style, placing them in conversation and encouraging community among them. Then, having so engaged participants with social themes that matter, the pedagogy should turn people to "look at" and reflect critically upon their lives and sociocultural reality in connection with the generative theme of the occasion. Here social analysis is needed, in other words, looking at the structures of society to see what is just or sinful and to discern why we see things as we do. Such critical reflection can enable people to "see" what should be seen and to imagine what should be imagined. Remember how the goats at the final judgment will claim, "We never saw . . ." the poor, the homeless. It will not be a sufficient defense (Matt. 25:31–46). Educating for a faith that does justice should help people "to see."

Fourth, we must enable people to reflect on social realities in light of the spiritual wisdom of Christian faith, especially its social doctrine. We must highlight the aspects of Christian Story and Vision that promote the works of justice and peace. Indeed, within all the great symbols of Christian faith, we can find an aspect that encourages justice and a liberating salvation. So, rather than being one topic among many, commitment to justice and peace ought to permeate the whole curriculum. For example, when teaching the Trinity, raise up that the "right and loving relationship" within the Godhead calls us to live the same way, which is the biblical notion of justice. Highlight that the presence of the Risen Christ in the Eucharist makes us responsible to care for those who have no "bread"—of whatever kind.

Fifth, our pedagogy should intentionally invite people to integrate their reflection on social themes with the spiritual wisdom of Christian faith and to make choices that advance justice and liberating salvation. As we encourage people to bring their lives to their Faith, we must also prompt them to bring their Faith back to their lives in ways that fulfill their social responsibilities. This requires people to personally appropriate the social commitments and convictions of Christian faith in their context and to decide for the praxis of a faith that does justice.

A New Apologetics for Christian Faith

My religion curriculum in high school had a whole course on *apologetics*. This had nothing to do with "apologizing." On the contrary, posing as a reasoned exercise, it was an ideological exposition proving that Catholicism is the one true faith and that all others fall very far short. This approach was a faint shadow of the apologetics practiced by the great Christian apologists of the early Church. I propose that we have an urgent need in this age of secularity and perhaps a new opportunity to return to the original apologetics. This would seem all the more possible as we foreground education for *liberating salvation* and a *faith that does justice*. What could be more persuasive in any age?

Both the Greek and Latin roots of *apologetics* have the dual meanings "to defend" *and* "to persuade." Christian faith always needs to do both—to defend against attack and to persuade of its truth. "Always be ready to give an explanation to anyone who asks you for a reason for your hope, but do it with gentleness and reverence" (1 Pet. 3:15, NAB). And Paul assures that "All scripture is inspired by God and is useful for teaching, for refutation, for correction, and for training in righteousness [*or* justice]" (2 Tim. 3:16, NAB). However, the apologetics that people of my vintage remember (and which ultraconservative blogs and websites still advocate) defended the Faith by force of naked authority requiring submission and persuaded more by fear of punishment than critical reason or appeal to human desires. The argument ran: God revealed the one true faith through Jesus Christ; Jesus entrusted this faith to the Catholic Church; everyone must accept it from this Church without question; and refusing to do so is to run the risk of eternal damnation.

For example, the *Roman Catechism,* which popularized the teachings of the Council of Trent (1545–63), offered such a coercive apologetics: "Faith is that by which we yield our unhesitating assent to whatever the authority of our Holy Mother the Church teaches us to have been revealed by God; for the faithful cannot doubt those things of which God, who is truth itself, is the author." It also warned: "This heavenly knowledge of faith should be free from an inquisitive curiosity." In fact, "Faith must exclude not only all doubt, but all desire for demonstration."[8] This is why many Catholics presumed that they could not question their Faith. They were simply to submit to it with passive acceptance. Augustine, Aquinas, and others would view such discouraging of "faith seeking understanding" as very un-Catholic.

Note that such apologetics demanded "unhesitating assent" to the Church's stated beliefs as if all were equally constitutive of Christian faith. There was no sense, as in the current *Catechism of the Catholic Church,* of a "hierarchy of truths." Thus limbo and Easter were presented as equally important, and obtaining indulgences was made to seem as central as the Real Presence of the Risen Christ in the Eucharist.

Even if such an apologetics—more by legislation and coercion than persuasion and conviction—was effective at one time, it is certainly no longer so. Besides being ineffective, such authoritarianism becomes repulsive to the exclusive humanist mentality and its attendant secularity, which Charles Taylor describes as now prevalent in Western society. So, rather than persuading, a coercive apologetics actually gives Christianity a bad name and makes the virulent attacks of the "new atheists" seem all the more credible. Authoritarianism is also antithetical to the beauty, truth, and freedom of Christian faith (refer to Chapter 1 on Jesus's call to discipleship as a free choice). Instead, we need a *new apologetics* that appeals to people's deepest desires and human longings, that persuades by rational coherence, that prompts them to see for themselves that Christian faith is a most life-giving and nourishing way to live— personally and "for the life of the world" (John 6:51). We need a persuasive representation of Christian faith to entice people's freely chosen commitment in this postmodern age.

As is true so often throughout church history, the "new" apologetics actually would be the truly "old" one renewed. Note first that the New Testament writings are all, in their own way, apologetical documents, intent on persuading and bringing people to embrace Christian faith with personal conviction. Perhaps the opening verses of Luke's Gospel can represent the apologetic agenda of all the New Testament writers. Luke begins by saying that he intends to "set down an orderly account of the events that have been fulfilled among us"; in other words, Jesus was the fulfillment of Old Testament prophecies—a persuasive argument to much of Luke's audience. Then, Luke will recount what has been "handed on . . . by those who from the beginning were eyewitnesses and servants of the word"; he is assuring that his sources are reliable—another persuasive argument. Then, Luke claims that it is only "after investigating everything carefully from the very first"—in other words, checking the evidence—that he can now write "an orderly account." So this account will make good sense, will have order and logic to it. Luke's overall purpose is that his friend Theophilus and Christians ever after "may *know the truth* concerning the things about which [they] *have been instructed*" (1:1–4). Clearly, Theophilus has already been well instructed; Luke's Gospel will offer further persuasion to assure his friend's personal conviction (one translation has "may realize with certainty").

The first great apologists of the early Church followed in the same spirit as Luke and the other New Testament writers. They defended Christian faith by coherent argument and appeal to human desire, and they were fully intent on persuading people of its great moral and spiritual assets. For example, St. Irenaeus presented Christian faith as the path "to become fully alive to the glory of God." What an enticement!

Avery Cardinal Dulles (1918–2008) describes St. Justin Martyr (100–165) as "the most important second-century apologist."[9] Justin devoted himself to demonstrating how Christian faith is both reasonable and responsible, intent on attracting the well educated and on winning civil toleration from the Empire. A little later, Clement of Alexandria crafted his apologetics to make people enthusiastic for living as disciples of Jesus. To this end he presented Christ as God's incarnate Wisdom to the world and as teaching people the wisest and most fulfilling way to live. In other words, the early apologists' rhetoric of defense and persuasion was not by authoritarianism or threat, but by the reasonableness of Christian faith and by appeal to people's fondest hopes, using emotive and enticing language. Imagine the excitement of neophyte Christians, most of them poor peasants, as Cyril of Jerusalem (d. 386) welcomed them "to the brighter and more fragrant meadows of this second Eden," for "in the laver of regeneration, the Lord God has wiped away all tears from every face. No more shall you mourn . . . but you shall ever keep high festival, clad in Jesus Christ as in a garment of salvation."[10]

Rhetoric and the New Apologetics: Many of the apologists of the early Church were well trained in rhetoric, the classical art of persuasive speech. We need to relearn this art for out time. To this end, it is helpful to recall Aristotle's categories of the three main forms of rhetoric: *pathos, logos,* and *ethos. Pathos* is an appeal to people's emotions and especially to their deepest desire for happiness. *Logos* uses the rhetoric of logic and reasoned argument; persuasion is by demonstrating the rational coherence of a particular truth claim. *Ethos,* then, is persuasion based on the credibility of the speaker or by the good fruits in the lives of people and communities who live the truth proposed.

With regard to *pathos,* religious educators can surely re-present Christian Story and Vision to appeal to peoples' desires and concerns. We can teach boldly that *the way* modeled by Jesus is the best way to live one's life; that there is no better "way, truth, and life" to emulate. Imagine what a rich life I would live if I would faithfully follow Jesus. I would be the most loving, the most hopeful, the most faith-filled person imaginable. How just, peaceful, and reconciling I would be; how hospitable, compassionate, and empathetic; how inclusive, sensitive, and caring; how integral and trustworthy; how full of courage, prudence, fortitude, and temperance. The list would include all the highest values and virtues to which the human heart can aspire. And imagine the true *happiness* such a life would bring. Indeed, the Beatitudes can be presented as "*Happy* are the poor in spirit . . ." (Matt. 5:3). The Greek word there is *makarios,* which means "happy" as well as "blessed."

Certainly we must never represent Christian faith as a "therapeutic deism," as if God is there simply to make us feel good, with no demands on our lives. On the contrary, to follow *the way* of Jesus is a most challenging life, loving one's enemies, doing good to those who hate us, going the extra mile (see Matt. 5:38–48). As Paul and Barnabas alerted the new Christians in Antioch, "It is necessary for us to undergo many hardships to enter the kingdom of God" (Acts 14:22, NAB). With a vision of working for justice and peace and living into a liberating salvation, this is no Pollyannaish religion. And yet being a disciple of Jesus, in the midst of a community of disciples that functions as a sacrament of God's reign in the world, is indeed a fantastic way to live. What a life! The best possible! We can confidently re-present it as such.

With regard to *logos,* we can persuasively represent Christian faith as making eminent good sense, as ringing true to people's experience and offering a coherent worldview. Its truth claims are never true simply "because the Church says so." They are always true for a better reason, which is why the Church says so. Christian faith can stand up under the most rigorous analysis, challenge, and questioning. Why? Because it can ring true to people's heads and hearts. Indeed, its greatest theologians, such as Augustine and Aquinas, Rahner and Lonergan, were all convinced that the questioning and probing of Christian faith are likely to deepen it. The quest to understand the Faith can bring us ever closer to God, not as the Mystery that we cannot explain, but the Mystery that explains everything and *is in love with us.*

Even Christian faith's paradoxical aspects—like loving your enemies—which can seem like nonsense when compared to the ways of the world, upon deeper reflection can demonstrate their truth and wisdom. How else will Belfast, Baghdad, or Benares come to peace unless enemies learn to live together with respect and acceptance? Christian faith always entails what Paul calls the "foolishness of the cross" (1 Cor. 1:18–31), yet it also poses persuasive and wise responses to the great questions of life: Who are we? What's life all about? What time do we have? Who is our neighbor? In fact, there is no philosophy, no faith, and no combination thereof that makes more sense than does Christian faith. And more than making sense, it offers a spiritual wisdom that works *for fullness of life for all.*

The *ethos* of Christian faith, then, is the credibility lent by disciples who live it. Here, let us first recognize that we find it most believable as we live it ourselves. Trying to live it a little can persuade us to live it all the more. This should not surprise. In fact, Jesus advised people to live as disciples in order to know the truth that sets them free (John 8:31–32). Everyone is inspired by the good example of other Christians and by those who practice what they preach and teach. Recall here that one of the first comments made about Jesus's public ministry was that "he taught as one having authority" (Mark 1:22). But Jesus had no authority of office. His authority must have come from the credibility of his own life.

Most of us will readily recognize that our own faith has been nurtured by the living witness of good people we've known who were inspired by Christian faith. In addition to famous examples like Francis of Assisi, Dorothy Day, Mother Teresa, Jean Vanier, and Oscar Romero, we likely have had family members and friends who lived it well and with joy. Seeing it so lived, we wanted to be like them and to embrace the Faith that made them the good and wise people they were. *Lived Christian faith* will always be the most effective form of evangelization. It is "by their fruits" (Matt. 7:16) that Christians give the most persuasive witness. Not that any of us live it perfectly; let there be no perfectionism here. Our constant good efforts, by God's grace, to live as disciples of Jesus are all that's needed.

Implications of a New Apologetics for Educating in Faith: How are religious educators to embrace and practice such a *new apologetics*? Here again I make a few summary suggestions. They echo what

I've already said about educating for liberating salvation and a faith that does justice, and there is more to come in Chapters 8 and 9.

First, we must engage people's desires, appealing to their best interests, to the depths of their being—their souls—and to what they long for in life. Of course, the most effective way to do this is to craft our pedagogy in response to the real issues of people's everyday lives, that is, in ways that help people to recognize and name their own needs and questions, fears and hopes. In a word, our pedagogy must be "meaningful" to its participants.

Second, we must encourage people to reflect on themselves and their lives in the world, to reason, remember, and imagine, to probe, question, and analyze what is going on regarding the things that matter most to them.

Third, we must share with them the dogmas and doctrines, sacraments and spirituality, morals and values of Christian faith in ways that are both appealing and rationally persuasive, in ways that entice and make sense—again, to be meaningful to their lives. Without manipulation or indoctrination, we must present this Christian life as the best way to live. We must show people that to live its responsibilities and truths is the surest path to fullness of life and real freedom. We can lend such persuasive access to Scripture and Tradition by correlating them with people's desires and good sense, accompanied with our own witness. Educators in faith need to both "talk the talk" and "walk the walk."

Fourth, and perhaps most imperative to the *new apologetics,* we must educate so that people can appropriate and make their own the truth and beauty of Christian faith, so that they come to personally embrace the spiritual wisdom it offers for their lives. Much like the two disciples with that Stranger on the road to Emmaus, even though their "hearts were burning" as he catechized them, they had to "come to see for themselves" before they could turn back toward Jerusalem and a renewed life in faith.

Fifth, just as the Emmaus disciples reembraced their faith, so our catechetical education must invite people to choose, by their own convictions, to integrate life and Christian faith into lived faith. Our *new apologetics* will be effective only as religious education brings people, by God's grace, to decisions to believe, pray, and live as Christians in their daily lives, to live into a liberating salvation and a faith that does justice for peace. As they do so, the effectiveness of Christian faith and the false promises of exclusive humanism will become all the more evident.

For Reflection and Conversation

- What might you add to the description of justice that I've proposed?

- What apologetics have helped to convince you of Christian faith?

- How might you make a more persuasive apologetics for Christian faith in your own work as a religious educator?

So far, *Will There be Faith?* has laid out some key foundations. We have recentered the ideal to teach as Jesus did (Chapter 1) and offered some clarity about who is involved (Chapter 2), for what ends to educate (Chapter 3), and what consequences to promote for persons and communities (Chapter 4). We are now ready to begin reflecting on the *how* of Christian religious education—the make-or-break question. How should we to go about it so that there will be *faith on earth*? The next chapter begins a response by locating catechetical education within its communal and cultural context. I highlight the role of community in Chapter 5, and then the role of family or household in Chapter 6; both are crucial to ensuring that there will be faith on earth.

CHAPTER FIVE

Faith on Earth Requires a Village

Intentional Christian Nurture in a Secular Age

Many times I've asked gatherings of educators, "What kind of a community or family does it take to raise a Polish person?" Those who aren't offended by my so obvious question call out, "A Polish one." Then I ask about forming a Hispanic person, an Irish person, a Korean person, and a few more. By now few are responding, because the questions seem beneath their intelligence. Then I ask the zinger, "So what kind of a community or family does it take to raise a Christian person?" Again, the answer is patently obvious, yet people recognize the deep insight implied. For there to be *faith on earth,* we need good programs of formal religious education. Much more strategic, however, is the role of community and family. It takes a family in a village to raise a Christian, albeit a village with a "school" of some kind. We need both intentional socialization and good religious education if Jesus is to find faith on earth when he returns in glory.

The fact is that *where* we've been and where we are now located (our sociocultural context or "life-world") greatly influence our identity as human beings. *Identity* can be described as a person's consistent *self-image, outlook* on life, and *values* across time. The social sciences, sociology, anthropology, and psychology all agree that our identity is formed and maintained, in large part, by our family and community, by our "village." Personally, I don't think we're determined by our context, though some social scientists might say so. We always retain some level of freedom and can make personal choices that shape who we become. Yet it would be naive to underrate the influence of family and friends, culture and society on our identity. The primary socialization of the family is the most formative; its influence remains paramount throughout life. Then, the secondary socialization of subsequent communities and cultures also has great influence on our identity.

Social scientists explain the formative power of the sociocultural context as a threefold dynamic. First, as human beings we inevitably *exteriorize* ourselves; we put ourselves "out there." By nature, we reach out to enter into relationships and common life with other people. Second, by doing so we *realize* or construct a life-world with other people that takes on a "reality" of its own. We can never simply wish our life-world away and start over from scratch. In fact, even minor changes come slowly. Every sociocultural world has structures of self-maintenance and ideologies of legitimation, convincing members that the way things are is the way they should be. This life-world that we create together, however, does not remain "outside" of us. The third dynamic is that we *internalize* our sociocultural context; we embrace its reflection of ourselves, its thought patterns and attitudes, its rules and values as our own. This is how we're socialized or enculturated into our particular identity. And we tend to become agents of social maintenance, committed to our life-world precisely because it holds our identity.

Of course, all of this must be nuanced, for it never quite works as the social scientists describe. Likewise, from the perspective of Christian faith, we must allow that, if need be, God's grace can work both through and against our sociocultural influences. On the one hand, we've all known contexts that were eminently Christian and yet did not prove effective in socializing some members in Christian identity. On the other hand, we're familiar with situations in which the sociocultural conditions discouraged faith, but people of deep faith emerged anyway. There is always a mystery to faith that cannot be accounted for from the human side. Yet the conclusion from my silly questions remains compelling: given a holistic understanding of Christian faith, we are most likely to raise Christian people within Christian community (this chapter) and within a Christian family or household (Chapter 6). In addition, both parish and family need a parish program or school of some kind that formally educates people in faith. The more truly Christian our parish, family, and educational communities are, the more likely that they will be effective instruments of God's grace in forming the Christian identity of members.

The *General Directory for Catechesis* says that formation in Christian faith requires an "apprenticeship" in Christian living; this is why the *GDC* situates catechesis first and foremost within community: "Catechesis is a responsibility of the entire Christian community" and "of every member of the community" (n. 220). Given the communal nature of Christian faith, education therein must be communal: "The Christian community is the origin, locus and goal of catechesis" (n. 254). By "community" the *GDC* means "the family, parish, Catholic schools, Christian associations and movements, basic ecclesial communities" (n. 253), in other words, wherever Christians gather.

For Reflection and Conversation

- Pause for a moment and recognize some of the communities of faith that have nurtured your own Christian identity. What are they? How did they do it?

- Look at your present faith community. How well does it educate in faith?

- How might it enhance its effectiveness as a Christian religious educator?

Challenges to Christian Socialization in a Secular Age

When considering education in Christian faith, we need to be realistic about the times and contexts in which we live. Too often I've heard easy comments about how poorly the Church is doing in its religious education, without any advert to the complexity and challenge for faith in our time and place. The implication seems to be that once the Church did it very well, whereas the current crop of religious educators is failing. But these are very different times. Again, the analysis of Charles Taylor is illuminating here. Only a few hundred years ago, our sociocultural context was what Taylor calls "an enchanted world," where faith and the spiritual suffused daily life, making it nigh impossible *not* to believe. Today, the social commentators agree that ours is a secular age, at least in Western societies, where the social conditions actively discourage religious faith.

The whole process of *secularization* is much debated among social commentators. What does it mean? Is it inevitable? Are there exceptions? Will it be lasting? Many cite America as an exception to the secularization that has happened in Europe, with varied explanations as to why. The debates notwithstanding, it is clear that a very significant shift has emerged throughout the Western world in religion and faith, and "secularization" sounds like a good description. Of course, much depends on what we mean by the term. Taylor makes some distinctions that I find helpful.

He distinguishes three meanings. Secularization can mean: (1) that religious practice has fallen off; (2) that the secular and religious powers have been separated in society; or (3) that the current sociocultural conditions discourage religious faith.[1] There are ample statistics to verify the first meaning, for it seems that religious practice, usually gauged by attendance at Sabbath worship, has fallen off significantly. The second meaning—separation of secular and religious powers—is surely a positive aspect of secularization. The remaining examples of theocracy (e.g., Iran) readily convince us that both "religion" and "state" fare better when structurally separated. The third meaning, however—that the conditions of contemporary society discourage religious belief—Taylor sees as more ominous to our concern here, *Will there be faith on earth?* Rather than socializing people into religious identity as of old, the sociocultural conditions are now likely to do the opposite. Taylor summarizes: "It is obvious that a decline in belief and practice has occurred, and beyond this, that the unchallengeable status that belief enjoyed in earlier centuries has been lost."[2] The prevailing "exclusive humanism" that I noted in Chapter 4 makes faith all the more challenging in our time.

Then, with regard to my call for community, Taylor sees an uphill battle as well, and for many reasons; two I'll mention. First, as I touched on earlier, the contemporary person has become a "buffered" or "bounded" self. He explains, "For the modern buffered self . . . my ultimate purposes are those which arise within me, the crucial meanings of things are those defined in my responses to them."³ Such a "bounded" self becomes the center of its own universe and is certainly not an avid candidate for community. In fact, such a self is distinctly antisocial. Following on, in more recent times "expressive individualism" has become a dominant social trend. In this attitude, "people are encouraged to find their own way, discover their own fulfillment, do their own thing." Rather than being the preserve of elites, expressive individualism, posed attractively as the quest for "personal authenticity," is now "a mass phenomenon."⁴ Again, such individualism discourages community.

Another way of talking about our time is as "postmodern." This is not as much in vogue as it was ten years ago, yet we can readily see that there have been extraordinary shifts within our era. One can pile up the examples: the typewriter was modern, and the word processor is postmodern; the steam engine was modern, and the *Challenger* spacecraft is postmodern; the mail system was modern, and e-mail is postmodern. I heard a story of grandparents taking care of their two grandchildren for the weekend. The grandmother is reading aloud. "Grandpa, it says here in the newspaper that the post office won't be delivering letters on a Saturday anymore." One of the grandchildren looks up and asks, "Grandma, what's a letter?" The other adds, "Yeah, Grandma, and what's a newspaper?" Now that's postmodernity for you.

It is not easy to describe postmodernity, much less its effects on our consciousness and identity. We are like fish in its water. Two of its agreed-upon features, however, make education for Christian faith all the more challenging. The first is that postmodern people resist "metanarratives," in other words, systems of thought and belief that presume to explain everything to everyone all the time. Christian faith presents itself as such a metanarrative. Can it also allow for diversity of perspectives, even welcome them? If not, postmoderns seem less likely to embrace it. A second feature of the postmodern mentality is to consider all universals—truths, values, principles—as purely the product of their context; we can "deconstruct" or "reconstruct" them as needed. Such radical "relativism" (i.e., all ideas are *related* to their context) poses steep opposition to the universal truth claims of Christian faith. What to do?

As I suggested in Chapter 4, rather than simply lamenting the sociocultural state of affairs, we must regroup as religious educators to discern and devise ways that can be effective "according to the mode of the receiver." Justin Martyr claimed that every cultural context has "seeds of the gospel," in other words, native aspects that can be assets in nurturing Christian faith. So the challenge now is to oppose the "weeds" of exclusive humanism and postmodernity and to take advantage of the "seeds." I believe there are some.

For example, humanism's quest for fullness of life makes an ideal entry point for Christian faith. Such fullness, however, cannot be achieved by "buffering" one's personhood and becoming a self-sufficient automaton, but only by joining in community and with the help of a "Higher Power" or, as we would say, God. The full potential of our personhood can be realized only by living in response to God, who first loves us unconditionally and calls us to love our neighbor as ourselves. For this, we always need help—"saving" if you will.

Commentators maintain that postmodernity has far greater openness to spirituality than modernity had. Why, Wall Street has declared spirituality to now be a "growth industry." Likewise, postmodernity is said to encourage greater respect for "the other," hospitality toward people who are different from "us." Christians should surely embrace this, given our greatest commandment and the fact that there are no limits to who qualifies as the neighbor to be loved. Then, postmodern authors, in contrast to modern ones, champion a holistic way of knowing, involving feelings and experience rather than reason alone and abstract thinking. The list of contemporary "seeds of the word" could go on. Jean-Marie Cardinal Lustiger

(1926–2007), the late great archbishop of Paris, insisted that this is an opportune time for authentic Christianity, for a personally chosen, mature, and lived faith. I agree! That we may sometimes need both to be countercultural *and* to stretch our own faith horizons can make it all the more committed and "interesting."

In light of such prevailing conditions, my proposal is that the Christian socialization that was once acquired in the village simply by osmosis must now be intentionally organized and planned. The parish is still crucial to this effort, as are the family/household and school/program, as we will review in the following two chapters. This is not to say that parishes can be the "lifestyle enclaves"—we used to say "ghettos"—of fifty years ago. Yet with intentionality and imagination I believe we can enhance the potential of our local faith communities to socialize people into Christian identity. Then, if such socialized faith is to weather the storm of leaving the village and surviving in a secular world—beyond childhood—socialization alone will not be enough. We also need formal programs of religious education that are substantive, reflective, and comprehensive, lending people ready access to the whole Story and Vision of Christian faith with pedagogy that engages their souls and makes its truths and spiritual wisdom relevant and meaningful to their lives. I begin to outline this proposal within the paradigm of *total community catechesis*.

A Total Community Affair

There is a growing movement in Christian religious education to shift beyond a schooling paradigm ("beyond" still means to "include") toward a broader, community-based approach. It has a number of names, but the one I favor is *total community catechesis*. Over twenty years ago, in my first published essay recommending this communal paradigm,[5] I used "total" for a number of reasons. First, it echoes the total nature of Christian faith: to engage head, heart, and hands; to become lived, living, and life-giving; to require that people be informed, formed, and transformed in Christian identity. Second, "total" signals that the Church's mission to educate in faith should engage all Christians in teaching and learning together. Third, it suggests that parishes harness every aspect of their shared life and ministries to maximize their educational potential. Instead of limiting catechesis to one ministry among many, all have the potential and can be crafted to educate in faith. Whatever we call it, we need a 360-degree, total approach.

I understand total community catechesis as *an intentional coalition of parish, family, and program/school that engages every member and all aspects of each community, by and for people of all ages, teaching and learning together for Christian faith toward God's reign in the world.* Within this paradigm shift beyond school to community, there are many subshifts: beyond children to all people; beyond didaction to conversation; beyond religious knowledge to spiritual wisdom; beyond teachers and taught to communities of teachers/learners who share faith together.

The key requirement for total community catechesis is that every designated ecclesial minister and then every Christian develop a "faith-education consciousness." This means being alert to maximize and take full advantage of the faith-education potential of every aspect of shared life and parish ministry. As I proposed in Chapter 2, ordinary Christians have constant opportunities to witness to their faith and, as appropriate, to explicitly share it. Then, parents and guardians, grandparents, aunts and uncles, godparents and mentors (coaches, scout leaders, etc.) have unique opportunities to share and educate in faith.

Total community catechesis is the primary responsibility, however, of the designated ministers of a faith community. Beginning with the pastor, all parish staff members must see their particular and combined ministries as participating in total community catechesis. All ministers must be alert to maximize the faith-education opportunities of their ministry. I give many practical suggestions in what follows. Total community catechesis also requires that every parish have its own designated catechetical leader who has the theological, pedagogical, and spiritual formation for this specific ministry. This "director" (by whatever title) needs to recruit a cadre of volunteer religious educators and see to it that they are well trained and then sustained for their ministry. By getting everyone involved, total community catechesis requires all the more competent leadership. Although this is challenging, we should be inspired by the conviction of the early Christians that every faith community has the gifts it needs to carry on the full ministries of the Church. Total community catechesis is possible in every parish and congregation.

Implementing Total Community Catechesis: All Hands on Deck

To say that we must be "intentional" in organizing the faith formation potential of a Christian community requires us to be alert for how every ministry and activity, committee and program, gathering and event can be structured to educate in faith. All aspects of a Christian community's shared life can be made to nurture, sustain, and grow people in Christian identity, even the fun events and ones that don't seem to have any faith dimension at all (e.g., the Leaking Roof Committee). There is absolutely nothing "secular" about the life of a parish—even if it dwells in a secular age and context. Its whole shared life can be approached "in faith" and thus can nurture the faith of its people. Now, it is fair to ask: How does a parish mount and maintain such intentionality to educate in faith?

It is a big shift from a "schooling model" of religious education to a "community of faith" approach. My experience is that parishes grow into it the more they try it. Total community catechesis gradually becomes a community *habitus*. Meanwhile, an approach I've found helpful to intentionally harness the faith-education potential of a parish is to review all of its ministries, imagine how each can educate in faith, and then take advantage of every opportunity. This begs the question: What are the core ministries of a parish?

Within the Church's overarching purpose of being a sacrament of God's reign in Jesus Christ, one can draw out of Christian tradition a sixfold schema of its essential ministries. In other words, we can name at least six core functions that the Church should always be doing in the world. From the first Christian communities, all six can be named by an ancient Greek term. I'll use the Greek terms here, but for easy remembering also some English ones, all of which, with a bit of a squeeze, I've made to begin with *W*.

Welcome: Koinonia, with a Greek root meaning "to share in common," is usually translated "communion." This names the task of the Church to be a real spiritual community within itself, an assembly of Christian disciples bonded in faith, hope, and love, one that includes all disciples in full membership, without exception. I designate it as a ministry of *welcome*.

Witness: Marturia literally means "bearing witness." To fulfill this ministry, the parish must practice what it preaches, must bear witness to what it professes by how it lives. By extension, every Christian disciple must bear such witness, if necessary, even unto death. The Church and every member are always called to this ministry of *witness*.

Worship: The etymology of *leitourgia,* the root of "liturgy," means "public work of the people." Fittingly, it came to designate the task of a local church to assemble in public and worship God together. This is forever the Church's ministry of *worship.*

Well-being: Diakonia means "service." In the early Christian communities, it referred to the ministry of care for human needs, physical and spiritual, personal and social, with special service to the poor. In our time, this broadens beyond compassion to include the works of justice. It could be called the ministry of *welfare,* or, if preferred, *well-being.*

The Word/Preaching: Kerygma means "proclamation" and came to designate both the act and the content of the Church's preaching. The Church always has the ministry to preach God's word of revelation that comes through the Old and New Testaments and, guided by the Holy Spirit, continues to be mediated through Christian Tradition. Here, I call it the Church's ministry of *the Word/preaching.*

The Word/Teaching: Didache literally means "teaching" and is likewise a ministry of "the word." In the early Church, *didache* named the more educational aspect of its mission. Beyond initial evangelization, it was the work of informing, forming, and transforming disciples in Christian identity. I designate it as *the Word/teaching.*

Let us now imagine how to maximize the faith-education potential of each of these designated ministries of the Church in the world. Of course, the categories overlap; it is difficult to talk about the communion of parish life apart from the liturgy, or the quality of liturgy apart from preaching. And yet to unpack them separately can help us to be intentional about crafting the whole mosaic of parish life to educate in Christian faith.

Koinonia: The Parish as a Community of Welcome

First, let's be clear that the parish is called to be a real "communion" of faith, hope, and love. The more a parish is such a community, the more likely that it will educate in faith effectively. I have already highlighted how Jesus called disciples into a community of outreach and inclusion, of respect and empowerment, of compassion and commitment to justice, of partnership with servant leaders (Chapter 1). Further, it is very clear that Christian faith is inherently communal (Chapter 3). So that an essential ministry of the Church, local and universal, is to build up community comes as no surprise, nor does it need further warrant here.

I note only that a central achievement of Vatican II was to retrieve Paul's original understanding of the Church as an egalitarian community: "For in the one Spirit we were all baptized into one body—Jews or Greeks, slaves or free—and we were all made to drink of the one Spirit" (1 Cor. 12:13). Beyond the warrant of baptism, more recently scholars of ecclesiology have highlighted that the Church shares in and is a sacrament of the inner life of God to the world. Therefore, by nature and purpose, the Church is a "communion," since our God is a Triune Divine Community of right and loving relationship.[6]

Vatican II's communion ecclesiology is epitomized in its Dogmatic Constitution on the Church, or *Lumen Gentium*. The word "dogmatic" in the title signals the authority with which the Council, in union with the pope, promulgated the Constitution. In the hierarchy of truths of faith, there is nothing higher than a dogmatic

statement. *Lumen Gentium* declares that the Church must be understood first and foremost as a community. It is the whole Church
together with all of its members enjoying a profound equality that
expresses and mediates God's grace. All members are responsible
for the mission and ministries of this faith community.

The drama that surrounded the writing of and debate on *Lumen
Gentium* reflects the profound shift that it represents in recent
Catholic ecclesiology. Before the Council, various theological commissions prepared draft documents. When the first draft of *Lumen
Gentium* was brought to the council floor on December 1, 1962 (the
earliest document to be discussed), it was roundly criticized for its
unduly hierarchical understanding of the Church, for emphasizing
the authority and juridical power of its leaders. Indeed, its opening
theme was "the hierarchy"; "the laity" was only mentioned later,
more as an afterthought. The draft was sent back to committee,
whereupon Pope John XXIII stepped in and appointed a new one.

The fourth and final draft was very different from the first.
Chapter 1 reflects on "The Mystery of the Church" and its essentially spiritual nature. It says that "the Church is a kind of sacrament
of intimate union with God and of the unity of all humankind"
(n. 1). Then Chapter 2 presents the Church first and foremost as
"The People of God" (the chapter title). We read that "God has
gathered together as one all those who in faith look upon Jesus as
the author of salvation and the source of unity and peace, and has
established them as the Church, that for each and all she may be
the visible sacrament of this saving unity" (n. 9). In other words, the
Christian people *are* the Church; it is defined first by its members.
Only then does the Constitution address "The Hierarchical Structure of the Church" (Chapter 3). This "community" ecclesiology
went on to permeate all of the Council's other documents.

I nickname the *koinonia* ministry of the Church as *welcome* because its hospitality is a make-or-break issue for being an authen-

tic community. Remember, the roots of *koinonia* mean "to share in common," but how can this be so unless all are welcome and included as equal members? Every disciple of Jesus should be welcome at the table, have a voice and be heard, be invited to participate actively in the Church's life and mission, not just as a recipient, but as an agent of their faith. Our best model here is Jesus and the inclusive community he forged, epitomized, and symbolized in his table fellowship. There all were welcomed and cherished, with special outreach to sinners and the marginalized.

Of course, the Church cannot compromise the truths and values of Scripture and Tradition just to attract people. There will always be a tension, however, between those ideals and their practical application in the concrete circumstances and stages of people's lives. Who among us can claim to live the "full gospel" already—turning the other cheek, going the extra mile, loving enemies? Who is entitled to tell anyone else that they are not welcome here? As Jesus once said to the self-righteous, "Let anyone among you who is without sin be the first to throw a stone at her" (John 8:7). May we agree that it is far better to bring people along with the Christian community than to drive them away?

With this community understanding of the parish before us and the demand that it be one of true welcome and inclusion, I offer five suggestions to heighten the faith-education effect of the Church's communality.

Strategy 1: Get people involved in the life and ministries of the parish. Going to Sunday Mass has not been Teddy's favorite family outing. I know, he's early in his rebellion. However, at the family Mass on a recent Sunday morning (in our home-away-from-home parish), they were looking for kids to help with the collection. Teddy jumped at the opportunity, and he loves the job. I wouldn't say that he's an enthusiast about Mass now, but this bit of participation has vastly improved his attitude toward going. Besides participation in the liturgy, every parish should have dozens of ways to get people actively involved, ways by which they can serve the whole community. Our home parish has over a hundred different ways that people can volunteer their time, talent, and tithes, from serving on the Parish Council to a prayer network among its housebound.

I once asked an old friend if being a Eucharistic Minister had deepened her own faith, and she waxed eloquent about how it had done so. I've heard lectors say that the time they spend preparing to read the scriptures at liturgy has helped them to encounter God's word to their lives at a deeper level. I've often asked parish religion teachers if their efforts to teach the Faith have deepened their own. Again, it's another silly question, because the answer is self-evident—of course it has. The list can go on. Getting people, including children and youth, actively involved in serving their faith community will nurture their own faith as well.

Strategy 2: Imagine old and new ways to bond people into community. Here we can list old favorites like parish suppers and picnics, seasonal celebrations, graduations and anniversaries, coffee after worship, and then the activities of the various societies and organizations within a parish. All help to build bonds, to lend a sense of belonging and inclusion. Beyond these familiar ways, we need to imagine new strategies for building community. For example, the *Generations of Faith* program (more below) recommends that the whole parish be given a "question of the week" for faith reflection and sharing. The question is suggested by the scripture readings from the Sunday lectionary and is meant to encourage people's appropriation of "the word" to their lives throughout the week. We also need to develop and take advantage of the potential of the Web (Twitter, Facebook, blogs, and chat rooms) to build up faith communities; they may be "virtual," but they can be effective nonetheless.

Strategy 3: Network people according to special interests. A key to the success of megachurches is that they sponsor umpteen smaller communities within their large one consisting of thousands of members. This is where people can be on a first-name basis, speak and be heard, be prayed with and prayed for as needed, celebrate their joys, and feel supported through the vicissitudes of life. The groups may be of grandparents, new empty-nesters, young marrieds with kids or without kids, parents of teenagers, youths interested in Christian rock, young adults in the workplace, people struggling with addiction, and so on. Another example of such bonding is the *comunidades de base* ("base communities") movement throughout Latin America. These are small groups—often ten or twelve families in a neighborhood—who meet regularly (e.g., one evening a week) for faith sharing around life and the scriptures, prayer, ritual, mutual support, and sharing in food and drink. Such interest groups and base communities are possible in every parish.

Strategy 4: Implement the Church's own canon laws regarding representative councils. The new Code of Canon Law (1983), prompted by the communion ecclesiology of Vatican II, calls for establishing an elected Parish Council and a Finance Council in every Catholic community (can. 536–37). Likewise, the Code calls for synods and councils at the diocesan level that represent both laity and clergy (can. 461, 511–14). Although "on the books" since 1983, the vast majority of Catholic parishes have yet to establish such councils. Further, although Canon 536.2 states that the Parish Council is *tantum consultivo*—"consultative only"—surely it should have a real voice in the life of the parish and not be simply a token body. It would be against Christian charity to pretend to consult people, but to consistently ignore their advice. It should be the very rare occasion that a pastor would do so. All such representative councils educate in faith, for they give people a sense of both ownership and responsibility for the Church.

Strategy 5: Reach out to the alienated and invite them "home." Pope John Paul II often said that his "new" evangelization must include outreach to those who have become estranged from the Church. He encouraged programs to invite and welcome them to return to their faith home. Parishes and dioceses have sponsored some very successful "come home" and "re-membering" programs. Even a cursory check of the Internet will yield suggestions for how to organize such an outreach.

I'm convinced, however, that for a successful "return" program, a parish must be ready to truly welcome people home. There's no point in saying, "You're welcome home as long as . . ." and then lay down, either explicitly or implicitly, a list of conditions, the very things that may have driven people away. Here the story of the Prodigal Son—or the Forgiving Father—should be our model. Note that the Prodigal was coming home with an apology ready, willing to be treated as a hired servant. The old parent, however, was on the lookout for the son, hoping he might return. Upon seeing the Prodigal, he was "filled with compassion; he ran and put his arms around him and kissed him" (Luke 15:20; read the whole story in 15:11–32). Note well, however, that the father offers the hearty welcome *before* the son makes his apology. What a risk for the father. What if the young man is coming home to ask for more money? Taking the risk of unconditional welcome is the ideal for every Christian community. Such true *koinonia* will teach far louder than words.

Marturia: The Parish as a Community of Witness

The rationale for the Church being a *koinonia,* community of *welcome,* calls it to be a *marturia,* community of *witness,* as well. Yet this aspect of its ministry in the world is worth highlighting, precisely because it is truly about educating in faith. As St. Francis of Assisi

(1181/82–1226) put it, we are to teach the gospel all the time, only sometimes using words.

Vatican II states: "Christ, rising from the dead, sent His life-giving Spirit upon His disciples and through this Spirit has established His Body, the Church, as the universal sacrament of salvation" (Dogmatic Constitution on the Church, n. 48). First, note that it is the *whole* Church that is to function as a universal sacrament of salvation. Then, remember the traditional understanding of a sacrament. Echoing Thomas Aquinas, it should be an *effective symbol of what it symbolizes*. In other words, every parish must look at its common life and ask if it is bearing credible witness to what it preaches, teaches, and claims to believe. The parish must constantly ask, "Does the life of this parish and everything about us bear credible witness to *the way* of Jesus Christ?" This question must be put to its worship, shared prayer, and care of souls, to its community ethos, modes of participation, and communal structures, to its human services, outreach, and social values, to its preaching, catechesis, and faith-sharing programs. To the extent that a parish can answer yes, it witnesses to and thus educates effectively in Christian faith.

To be a sacrament, an effective symbol of what we claim to believe is to realize that appearances do matter. In other words, the witness of a parish must be patently consistent with the faith it professes. It must be *seen* to be a just and compassionate community within its own structures and in service to the world (more under *diakonia*), to be welcoming and inclusive, to be transparent and equitable, to be clearly a community of faith, hope, and love. Instead of hiding its light "under a bushel basket," the parish must put it on a lamp stand as a light to the world (Matt. 5:15–16). This does not mean "showing off" to impress the neighbors, but rather bearing authentic witness to Christian faith for its own sake.

I'm in mind of a group of Catholic educators I met in Pakistan.

In one particular school, they told me that in almost two hundred years they had never had a convert to Christianity. Yet they were totally convinced that they were "evangelizing the culture" (in the sense of improving it from within) and bearing witness to Christian faith through the good education they provide. This is how local Muslims perceive them as well. That is real witness.

The "new evangelization," a rich legacy of Pope John Paul II, can be portrayed as a shift in emphasis. The *old* evangelization was more about "bringing in" converts to Christianity. This mission *ad gentes,* that is, to those who have never heard the good news of Jesus Christ, will always be a responsibility of the Church. The *new* evangelization, however, is not so much about "bringing in" people as it is about "bringing out" Christians into the world to live their faith with joy and credibility as its faithful witnesses. Ironically, this may also be the most effective way to "bring in" people as well as to keep our own faith vital and life-giving. Effective witnessing surely wins the gospel promise of a hundredfold return. A witnessing Christian community receives the return of being an effective educator in faith. I'll now suggest some specific strategies, noting that many under *koinonia* also echo here.

Strategy 1: About every aspect of parish life, ask, "What does this say to people?" and then, "Does it witness to Christian faith?" Social scientists advise that a community forms identity primarily through its symbols. Truly, then, its symbols are a community's most effective form of "education," of shaping the self-understanding, outlook on life, and value system of its members. Sociologist Clifford Geertz adds that a community's religious symbols are the most formative of all.[7] But just about every aspect of the life of a parish can take on the power of a religious symbol. All of parish life is loaded with religious meaning, because it appears to be done in the name of heaven—God.

The work of *marturia,* then, requires a parish to ask of everything, "What does this say to people?" and then "Does it witness of Christian faith?" Both questions are important. We need the first not because we want to please or displease, but simply to be conscious of how and what parish life is communicating. We need the second to make sure it is Christian. Indeed, the latter may cause a parish to communicate things or values that don't please everyone, for example, when it takes a prophetic stance on some consistent ethic of life issue. But being aware of how it gives witness and trying to ensure that it reflects the gospel of Jesus Christ are permanent responsibilities of every Christian community. Such consciousness can greatly heighten the community's effect as educator in faith.

Strategy 2: Remind parishioners to be intentional about witnessing to their faith. This requires both raising consciousness and lending confidence, making people aware that they have opportunities in daily life—at home, at school or work, during recreation, in the neighborhood—to share their faith and then lending them the confidence that they have a rich Faith worth sharing. In Chapter 2 we reviewed the sensitivity and respect that this requires. As 1 Peter advises, we must share faith "with gentleness and reverence" (3:15). This is the antithesis of an aggressive, imposing, or proselytizing approach. My colleague Jane Regan says that proselytizing is telling other people what *they* should believe, whereas evangelizing is letting people know, as appropriate, what *we* believe.

Many people's daily lives are in need of a word of faith to give them meaning and purpose or a word of hope to lift them up in tough times, and all of us are in constant need of love. Christians should be ready to share as much and to receive the same in return. As the wind "blows where it chooses," so does God's Spirit (John 3:8). We must be open and respectful of what the Spirit may "do" in people's lives. For example, instead of bringing them to Christian faith, our witnessing may well send people from other traditions back to their own. Praise be God!

Strategy 3: Establish a catechumenal program. Catholic Christianity has drawn no more effective strategy for renewal from Vatican II than the restoration of the ancient catechumenate, better know as the Rite of Christian Initiation of Adults (RCIA). This is an intentional process of socialization and education into Christian faith. Every parish needs to have its RCIA program for people from other traditions or no tradition who are interested in Christian initiation. True to the two-way dynamic of all evangelizing (sharing faith renews it), a good RCIA program is a powerful source of faith education for the parish itself in at least three ways.

First, getting the parish involved in the formation of new members renews the faith of the parish itself. At the "scrutinies," for example, when the parish community at liturgy asks the catechumens if they are living lives of prayer and good works, of justice and peacemaking, everyone present must surely ask themselves the same questions. Second, the RCIA is a great vehicle for getting parishioners actively involved in sharing their faith. Candidates need sponsors to accompany them. The program itself needs all kinds of instructors, facilitators, ritual coordinators, and so on. The more, the merrier, for their own education in faith. Third, the faith life of a parish is renewed by the advent of *neophytes.* These fresh new Christians who come into the Church with enthusiasm can invigorate the tired faith of old-timers. Every community might say to its neophytes, "Please don't come and settle in and embrace the status quo. Instead, bring your enthusiasm and expectations to us, confront and question us as needed, challenge our attitudes that take faith for granted." When neophytes do so, great education in faith takes place.[8]

Strategy 4: Use contemporary media to witness to faith. Our age is distinguished by a communications explosion. Church documents urge Christians to use the modern and postmodern media. The *General Directory for Catechesis* says: "The Church would feel guilty before God if it did not avail itself of those powerful instruments" of modern communication "in order to address the multitudes" (n. 160). A parish can be imaginative about how to use the Internet to educate in faith, how blogs and chat rooms can be means of community building, how the Sunday homily and reflections on the scripture readings can be made available to housebound or busy people—giving a bit of mileage beyond weekly worship. It is indeed possible, now, to "address the multitudes."

Strategy 5: Tell the stories of martyrs, old and new. As the English equivalent suggests, *marturia* brings to mind the fact that countless numbers of people have died and continue to die because of their commitment to Christian faith. An often repeated adage from the early Church, coined by Tertullian (160–225), says, "The blood of martyrs is the seed of Christians." People became disciples when they saw the commitment of those who went to their death rather than deny their Christian faith. In the West, we tend to think of martyrdom as something of long ago. In fact, however, it is very much present today. And the martyrs are not only Christians. Many people from other traditions are killed because of their faith commitments.

As in the early Church, the stories of martyrs, ancient and modern, can stir hearts to faith and faithfulness today. Who would not be inspired by the stories of Oscar Romero, Maximilian Kolbe, and Edith Stein, of Dietrich Bonhoeffer, Simone Weil, and Steven Biko, of Sr. Dorothy Stang and Jean Donovan, of the University of Central America martyrs in El Salvador. The list is long. Such martyrs can inspire the *marturia/witness* of people today, not necessarily to die for Christian faith, but to live for it daily. The martyrs can continue to educate in faith.

For Reflection and Conversation

- Looking at your own parish or base faith community, how might it improve its ministry of *koinonia*—of being a truly Christian community of faith, hope, and love, with *welcome* and inclusion for all?

- How well does your community do in bearing public *witness* to its faith? How might it improve upon this ministry?

- Think of another strategy for your parish to harness its community life to educate in faith.

Leitourgia: The Parish as a Community of Worship

A defining ministry of the Church, and thus of every parish, is to worship God together. This is ever "the work of the people." Although liturgy includes communal prayer such as the divine office and the celebration of all seven sacraments, my focus here is the Sunday celebration of the Liturgy of Word and Eucharist—the Mass.

From the very beginning, the first disciples gathered to hear "the apostles' teaching" and for "the breaking of the bread," the latter being a code term in Luke for the Eucharist (Acts 2:42). Vatican II summarized a two-thousand-year-old tradition since then when it said, in the Constitution on the Sacred Liturgy, that, though "the sacred liturgy does not exhaust the entire activity of the Church," nevertheless, it is "the summit toward which the activity of the Church is directed; the fountain from which its power flows" (nn. 9, 10). That is an amazing statement—the Mass is the summit and source of the life of the Church and parish!

Of the liturgy, the Council declared, "No other action of the Church can match its claim to efficacy, nor equal the degree of it" (n. 7). Here I add that no other action of the Church can match its power to educate in faith. I hasten to say, however, that the liturgy should *never* be "used" in a didactic way, that is, simply to teach. To do so would be an abuse of liturgy. Its primary purpose is always to worship God. As the Council recognized, however, liturgy teaches inevitably. "Although the sacred liturgy is above all things the worship of the divine Majesty, it likewise contains abundant instruction for the faithful" (n. 33) and educates precisely because it is so symbol laden. Remember Geertz's claim that the religious symbols of a community are the most effective? Well, Geertz went on to say that the symbols of worship are the most formative of all.[9] In this light, nothing that a parish does is more "educational" than its liturgy.

While liturgy can powerfully inform, form, and transform people's faith, it can also misinform, malform, and domesticate it. So much depends on the quality of the liturgy. It is an act of faith not of magic, so the symbols must be effective for people to express *true* worship of God and in the *spirit* that empowers them to live lives of faith. Here, I echo and return to another aspect of that amazing conversation between Jesus and the Samaritan woman at the well. He tells her, "The hour is coming, and is now here, when true worshipers will worship the Father in spirit and truth" (John 4:23). This statement begs the question: What would make for liturgy marked by *spirit* and *truth*?

A now classic quote from Vatican II suggests a response. It poses worship "in spirit and truth" as actively engaging its participants and mediating their encounter as a priestly people with God. I quote in full: "Mother Church earnestly desires that all the faithful be led to that full, conscious, and active participation in liturgical celebrations which is demanded by the very nature of the liturgy. Such participation by the Christian people as a 'chosen race, a royal priesthood, a holy nation, a purchased people' is their right and duty by reason of their baptism" (Constitution on the Sacred Liturgy, n. 14).

"Full, conscious, and active participation" surely requires participants to pray, sing, listen, respond, move their bodies, and so on in the enactment of liturgy. Such participation will be a source of education in faith—by how they worship God. Beyond such obvious participation, the liturgy is to engage people at a more existential level. Liturgy should gather up and re-present people's lives to God, enable them to experience God's life being mediated to them through word and sacrament, and send people forth renewed in their own faith and empowered to serve "for the life of the world" (John 6:51). Those words are Jesus's stated reason in John for why he gave his "body and blood" in the first place.

My guiding principle, then, for what makes for liturgy "in spirit and truth" is that it must *bring people's lives to God and God's life to them for the life of the world.* (As readers will recognize, this is a liturgical version of *life to Faith to life.*) The more the liturgy mediates what the collect prayers of the Sacramentary frequently refer to as "a wonderful exchange of gifts"—between God and ourselves—the more effectively it educates in faith.[10]

As I see it, this "wonderful exchange" between God and ourselves happens at least twice at Mass, first in the Liturgy of Word and then in the Liturgy of Eucharist. With the opening call to worship, repentance, and praise (if there is a Gloria), people bring their lives to God, sins and all. In the readings from scripture and it is hoped in the homily, they receive God's life to them. Then, with the Creed and Prayers of the Faithful, they recommit themselves to a lived faith. As an old adage runs, we must be willing to work for what we pray for. Then, in the Liturgy of Eucharist, the Offertory brings peoples lives to God, represented by their gifts—bread, wine, and stewardship. With the Eucharistic Prayer, followed by Holy Communion, God's life comes to them as the body and blood of Christ. Then, they are "sent forth"—*missa*—back to life again to "love and serve" in faith.

In this light, let us imagine some strategies for parish liturgy in *spirit* and *truth,* thus heightening its potential to educate in faith.

Strategy 1: Assemble as a worshipping community that brings its whole life to God. The opening rituals and symbols of liturgy should make people feel welcome and included in a bonded community to worship God together. The symbols should reflect clearly that this is the work of the people, albeit presided over by a priest for holy order. The opening rite should mediate that "all are welcome" and "you are the Church." Further, the call to worship, to repentance, to prayer, and to praise should help this people recognize that they are bringing their lives to God, warts and all.

Strategy 2: Have the assembly sing well throughout and with good theology. St. Augustine was wise when he said that "to sing is to pray twice." Singing heightens participation, and good music can turn the soul toward the Transcendent. A choir or song leader may lead, but the guiding principle of the liturgy's music must be to encourage the active participation and sung prayer of the congregation.

Then, we must also harness the formative power of hymnody. One of the most important curriculum decisions a parish makes regularly is what to sing at Sunday Mass. I have a Baptist friend who often gets mad at her church (who doesn't?) and says she'd love to leave, but that she'd have to forget all the songs. The point is that what we sing, and especially what we sing in church as sacred song, goes to our hearts with powerful effect. It is imperative, then, that we sing "good theology." I was at a liturgy recently in which all the songs were in praise and thanksgiving to God, imperative sentiments, indeed, to express in worship. We sang nothing, however, to remind us how we are to respond to God's love and blessings. All the hymns reflected what the great Lutheran theologian Dietrich Bonhoeffer (1906–45) called "cheap grace"—placing all responsibility on God and none on us. This does not make for liturgy "in spirit and truth."

Strategy 3: Proclaim the scriptures in ways that enable people to encounter and appropriate God's Word into their lives. (I take up the homily under preaching below.) Now almost fifty years since Vatican II, Catholics are still learning how to proclaim the Word for hearing, so that people are disposed to listen and take it to heart. Before the readings, there needs to be some ritual or comment that invites people to "pay attention," to open themselves to the texts and to the possibility that they might well mediate a "word of God" into their lives. Then, there's a way to set the readings out in front of people so that they really hear and engage them, catch their meaning, and take them to heart. To proclaim the scriptures well requires preparation, taking the time to become thoroughly familiar with the words, the flow and punctuation in order to read them without stumbling or garbling. The reader needs to have figured out what the text might say to these listeners and thus what to emphasize in tone in order to bring out the meaning of the text. Blessed John Cardinal Newman (1801–90) said that he took up to an hour each week preparing to proclaim the Sunday gospel. Too many lectors and presiders still read as if they were seeing the text for the first time.

Strategy 4: Re-present people's lives to God in the Offertory, pray the Eucharistic Prayer as a "we," receive Holy Communion with reverence, and send the community forth to become what they've received—the Body of Christ in the world. In my humble opinion, the Catholic liturgical renewal made a slight mistake when it renamed the Offertory "Preparation of the Altar and the Gifts." From the Latin, meaning "to carry into presence," the word "offertory" lent a better sense that people were "bringing [their] gift to the altar" (Matt. 5:23, NAB). The bread and wine represent ourselves, and the monetary offering our stewardship. As fitting, we can carry forward other symbols to represent the lives of this congregation.

The Eucharistic Prayer should be prayed with solemnity and as *from the people*, not just from the priest. As has been so from the beginning, the Eucharistic Prayers of the Church are set in the first-person plural: "We offer," "We ask," "We remember." The priest is to pray as if from the heart of the community. The reception of Holy Communion should always be done with reverence, reflecting the Catholic conviction that the appearances of bread and wine remain, but their substances are now the body and blood of Christ. One cannot think of a sacred moment that deserves more reverence. Finally, the community needs to be sent forth (*missa*) with a clear sense of commission that they are to be what they have received, Christ's effective presence in the world (St. Augustine).

Strategy 5: Let all the prayers, like the songs, reflect good theology. There is an ancient conviction in the Church of *lex orandi, lex credendi,* that what we pray is really the measure of what we believe— and teach. How and what we pray for certainly reflects our faith and thus is vital to religious education. The Church's official Sacramentary provides the collects for the Opening Prayer, Prayer over the Gifts, and Prayer After Communion for any given day or feast. There is some latitude, however, in the Prayers of General Intercession. The *General Instruction of the Roman Missal* directs that the sequence of intentions should be for the needs of (1) the Church, (2) the world, (3) the needy, and then (4) the local community. Too often this sequence is not honored. Oftentimes, these prayers seem to begin and end with the purely personal, for example, "for my aunt who is sick."

It is even more troublesome and mis-educating when the Prayers of the Faithful reflect poor theology. For example, "For the hungry of the world, let us pray to the Lord" hopes for the "cheap grace" I referred to above. This is telling God to take care of what we should be caring for ourselves, with God's help. Better by far to pray, "Loving God, give us the grace we need to care for the hungry in our world, in our community, in our midst." In other words, we ask for the grace we need to be agents of our faith, grace working through nature, not replacing our responsibilities. As Paul explains, God's grace abounds precisely that we might "have an abundance for every good work" (2 Cor. 9:8, NAB). Isn't it amazing that something as innocent looking as a bidding prayer must be scrutinized for what it teaches.

Diakonia: The Parish as a Community of Well-being

We've well established throughout that the Church must carry on the ministries of justice and peacemaking, compassion and reconciliation. Here the rationale can be brief.

There was a designated ministry of deacons in the first Christian communities. The one extended New Testament reflection on the diaconate makes clear that women were included (see 1 Tim. 3:8–13). From the beginning, the defining ministry of deacons was to be of service to human needs; the word *diakonia* has this etymological meaning. The scriptural text accepted as describing the specific function of deacons, Acts 6:1–7, declares that they were appointed to distribute food to those in need. Thus service (*diakonia*), not liturgy (*leitourgia*), should be the primary focus of the diaconate today. For a long time the diaconate was simply a stepping-stone toward priesthood. Recently, however, the Catholic Church has revived the permanent diaconate and opened it to married men. There are now some fifteen thousand permanent deacons working in the U.S. Church.

Beyond the diaconate as a designated ministry, however, from the first Christian communities to the present day, Christians have recognized that their faith demands the works of compassion and mercy. More recently we think likewise about working for justice and peace. The Church, and thus the local parish, must care for human well-being, physical and spiritual, personal and social.

The awareness I wish to raise here is that a parish's works of welfare or well-being are key to its educating in faith. Its religious education program can teach people about commitment to justice and compassion, but if the surrounding Christian community doesn't practice and give opportunities to practice likewise, then they are less likely to embrace such commitment and integrate it into their identity. To be educated for Christian service, people need to see it lived and must be given the opportunity to do it themselves. I suggest some strategies.

Strategy 1: Appoint some group (a committee or the Parish Council) to monitor the parish's internal life for consistency with Catholic social doctrine. The key here is to have a group that keeps the parish's "feet to the fire" of its own justice commitments. It must constantly raise and monitor the answers to questions like these: How does our parish collect, count, and hold its money? Do our investments reflect the values of social justice? What are our budget priorities and do they reflect commitment to justice and compassion? Do we treat the people we employ justly and provide decent working conditions? Are our communal meals tasteful and enjoyable, but without waste and extravagance? As a parish, do we recycle and strive to be energy efficient? Do all manner of people feel welcome and included among us, respected and equal? As a parish, do we strive to be free of all traces of sexism, racism, homophobia, ageism, militarism, of all forms of discrimination? Do we have structures of mediation to handle community disputes? Does every parishioner have opportunity to speak their piece and vote their preference, at least through their representatives on elected councils and committees? As a parish, do we try to avoid gender-favoring language? Do we offer communal celebrations of the sacrament of Reconciliation?[11] And the justice questions go on and on. Every parish should designate some group to "keep it on its toes" with regard to its social justice responsibilities.

Strategy 2: Establish some designated group to lead the parish's works of mercy and justice. The committee for strategies 1 and 2 may be the same, especially in smaller parishes. However, there are two foci to attend to, one directed inward, the other outward. Every parish ought to provide its members with varied and user-friendly opportunities for works of compassion and justice. These can include old reliables like sponsoring clothing drives and food pantries; helping to staff a homeless shelter or meal program; outreach to shut-ins; help with health care to those who need it (the "parish nurse" movement is growing); care and sanctuary for victims of domestic abuse; counseling services to the bereaved and troubled; volunteering at a local prison; working with troubled teenagers; garbage cleanups; and the list goes on. Immediate service to people in need, if not done as a token or presumed to satisfy all responsibilities, can help to maintain social consciousness.

Beyond such works of mercy, a parish needs to get involved in the structural (systemic) struggles for justice for people and the environment. It will be more effective for a parish to take on one or two causes, rather than trying to engage all possible social issues; this would be overwhelming. According to context, the issues chosen should be likely to engage the interest and commitment of *this* community. If located in a social context that still needs to struggle against persistent racism, a parish may choose to take this on as its focused commitment. Or a parish with a large immigrant population may focus on immigration reform or promoting debt forgiveness and economic justice in a country of origin. I know of a parish that chose to involve itself deeply in environmental issues, triggered by an industry nearby that was polluting the local waters.

Strategy 3: Sponsor educational programs that focus explicitly on justice and peace. Under *the Word/teaching* below, I propose that educating for justice and peace is to suffuse the curriculum of all parish programs. This being said, every parish needs educational programs that focus specifically on the works of justice and peace. Thus, the people in charge of youth ministry should see to it that the curriculum regularly has something explicit on social justice as well as a project that engages the youth in works of compassion. The parish adult education program can frequently offer something on a social justice topic, and so on.

Strategy 4: Encourage justice- and peace-focused organizations and invite all organized groups in the parish to embrace such commitment. There are long-standing and revered Catholic organizations that commit themselves to the works of compassion, justice, and peace. A Catholic Worker community within a parish or area is a great blessing and catalyst in this regard. The same is true of a parish or deanery that has a St. Vincent de Paul Society or a Pax Christi group. Parishioners who want to "do more" might consider joining or associating with such groups. Their communal support and spiritual charisms will sustain and deepen commitment.

In addition, the parish can encourage all of its clubs, organizations, and societies to take on the works of mercy to those in need. In my home parish, the Knights of Columbus do a lot of such good works (clothing drives, toys for children at Christmas, Thanksgiving baskets), as do the men's and women's clubs. Every parish group can encourage their members to be involved in some works of mercy.

Strategy 5: Consider twinning with a parish in a different economic and social context. A growing practice is the twinning of two parishes, preferably from different socioeconomic or cultural contexts, with each other. Each can enrich the other in all kinds of ways. The benefit of such partnership is not only from the wealthy to the poor parish, but vice versa as well. Poor parishes, either at home or abroad, have much to offer to wealthy ones. Done well, such twinning is always an "exchange of gifts."

No parish can do everything that could be done by way of compassion and justice, and there are many other strategies beyond mine here. We do such works because Christian faith mandates them and because they need to be done. And I add a third reason. The more diaconal ministry that a parish does, the more effective it will be in educating for compassion, justice, and peace—all mandates of Christian faith.

Kerygma: The Parish as a Community of the Word/Preaching

Catholicism has long claimed that God's revealing Word comes through Scripture *and* Tradition. Its emphasis on both was heightened by arguing against the Reformers' cry of *sola scriptura,* "Scripture alone." Vatican II's Dogmatic Constitution on Divine Revelation, also known by its Latin title, *Dei Verbum,* summarized a defining aspect of Catholic faith: "Sacred tradition and sacred Scripture form one sacred deposit of the word of God which is committed to the Church" (n. 10). But let's be honest. In the Reformation-era polemics, the more Protestants emphasized the Bible, the more Catholics emphasized Tradition, and the more Catholics emphasized Tradition, the more Protestants emphasized the Bible. As a result, prior to Vatican II, Catholics ended up with mostly Tradition and Protestants with mostly Bible.

One of the legacies of Vatican II is its efforts to return the Bible to center stage in Catholic faith. In *Dei Verbum* the Council declared that "easy access to sacred Scripture should be provided for all the Christian faithful" (n. 22). It urged the whole Church to "move ahead daily toward a deeper understanding of the sacred scriptures," constantly providing "the nourishment of the scriptures for the People of God" (n. 23). We have made much progress since then, but Catholics have miles to travel before we know Scripture as well as our Protestant brothers and sisters do and become competent to read, study, and pray it for ourselves.

I gave some presentations in Northern Ireland recently, and a participant commented that she was amazed at how often I quoted or cited Scripture. She was very pleased, but also alerted me that I sounded "very Protestant." The false notion that the Bible is a Protestant book would not be unique to Northern Ireland in Catholic consciousness. We are still in the process of embracing the Bible as central to our faith. Here, under *the Word/preaching* I'll focus on sacred Scripture; in the next section, under *the Word/teaching,* I'll focus more on Tradition. This is only for convenience. In practice, of course, preaching should reflect good theology as well as biblical scholarship, and catechesis should be deeply biblical as well as reflect the teachings of the Church.

Catholics have been largely free of biblical fundamentalism. We are often doctrinal fundamentalists, but not biblical ones. We agree that many parts of the Bible are not to be taken as literally true. Although the Bible always conveys great truths of faith, it does not intend to teach scientific knowledge, for example, in the stories of creation. So it comes as no surprise to Catholic consciousness when Vatican II states, in the Dogmatic Constitution on Divine Revelation, that the Bible is "the words of God . . . expressed in human language" and "made like human discourse" (n. 13). In other words, the Bible's revelation is mediated by human media, and these reflect their sociocultural context. As such, Scripture always needs interpretation. It is not direct communiqués—e-mails from God—but divine truths mediated by human language. This being said, the

Council can still summarize that "the sacred Scriptures contain the word of God and, since they are inspired, really are the word of God" (n. 24).

For so long, Catholics stereotyped Protestants as "reading the Bible for themselves," as if presuming to make up their own individual minds about what to believe. Of course, this is not true of authentic Protestant faith, but it was enough to put Catholics off of personally reading the Bible, fearful that its complexities and potential for varied interpretations could lead them astray in their faith. As Shakespeare has Antonio say in *The Merchant of Venice,* "The devil can cite the Scripture for his purpose." Every Christian, however, can and should read the Bible for themselves, but, the Catholic perspective adds, not by themselves. In other words, read it personally, but within the faith community and with the guidance of the Church. As Vatican II teaches: "Sacred tradition, sacred Scripture, and the teaching authority of the Church are so linked and joined together than one cannot stand without the others" (n. 10).

All this being said, huge work remains for Catholics to embrace God's Word through sacred Scripture. We've made progress since Vatican II, but still have a long way to go. Here are some strategies to consider and, I'm sure, you will think of others yourself. The point I highlight again is that for a parish to recenter the Bible at the core of its Catholic faith is a mighty effective mode of religious education.

Strategy 1: Make the Sunday homily a priority in the life of a parish. Let's face it, the quality of the Sunday homily depends on preacher and preparation. Yet there *are* ways that congregations can encourage the preachers to prepare well. Positive comments after a good homily or demurring after a poor one can be effective. Catholics are not good at giving their priests honest feedback on their preaching. I also know of parishes where the priest meets with a sermon idea group (of whatever name) on a Monday or Tuesday evening

to begin to imagine the homily for the following Sunday. People reflecting on the lectionary texts together with an eye toward the needs of their own parish can be a rich homiletic resource.

My simple formula for a good homily is one that first raises up a "generative theme" from the readings, something likely to be of real interest in the lives of the people who will hear it. It begins by getting the congregation engaged with the theme and offers reflections on it. Then it turns to the spiritual wisdom of the scriptures of the day apropos the theme. It ends by inviting people to take this wisdom to heart and into daily life. There are other ways to craft a homily "in spirit and truth," but this sequence is most effective. Again, it reflects a *life to Faith to life* dynamic.

Strategy 2: Let the Bible permeate all of parish life and the lives of its families. I have a pastor friend who launched a campaign to recenter the Bible at the heart of parish and family life. First, he purchased some five hundred Bibles and gave one to every family or household. He then offered a series of one-shot sessions on a user-friendly approach to sharing faith through the use of Scripture. He spread Bibles throughout every room in the rectory and parish plant; even the bathroom stalls had one. He insisted that every meeting—Parish Council, Picnic Committee, or whatever—begin with a ten-minute "Bible study." This study involved a simple process of reading a text—usually from last Sunday's or next Sunday's lectionary—and inviting people to share what they heard as a word of God for their lives. Soon it was known far and wide as "the Bible parish."

Strategy 3: Provide parish-wide opportunities for Bible study and faith sharing around Scripture. Every parish or combination of local parishes needs to have formal programs of Bible study that enable people to appropriate its wisdom into their lives. With many fine published programs readily available, Bible study that reflects good scholarship is within the reach of every Christian community.[12]

I know of a parish that has a consistent Bible group that meets every Wednesday evening throughout the school year, beginning with Mass at five thirty, followed by a soup supper, and then faith sharing centered on a scripture reading. When the study is to begin, the anchor person (who varies from week to week) calls the group to order and says something to encourage careful listening, such as, "Let us open our hearts to hear how this text might be a word of God to our lives at this time." Then a reader proclaims the text. The reader has usually become effective at reading to be heard, so that the text might touch people's lives. The first cycle of conversation follows, usually centered on two questions, both of which can be asked in myriad ways: "What did you hear for your life and why?" and "Where does this text invite you?" The first round of conversation is usually filled with stories, hopes, and concerns from people's lives.

The group then reads the text again, and following that, the anchor person, who has spent prior time with the text and read a scripture commentary on it, offers some insight from scholarship. This also includes what the Church has heard over time and now hears from this text. The focus here, however, is the spiritual wisdom for life that might be in this text for these participants, what it offers and invites at this time. After these reflections from the resources of Bible scholarship, Church teaching, and present possibilities, the dynamic returns to all participants again and invites them to appropriate and make decisions in response to the spiritual wisdom they discern. Here the questions are: "What are you coming to see for yourself now?" and "How will you/we live the spiritual wisdom of this text going forward?" Again, notice the *life to Faith to life* dynamic, inviting people to bring their lives to the scriptures and the scriptures to their lives. When used in scripture study, *life to Faith to life* is very similar to the dynamics of *lectio divina*.[13]

Strategy 4: Give children and youth "easy access" to sacred Scripture. I love Vatican II's phrase that every Christian should have "easy access" to God's Word. This must surely include a parish's children and youth. There are many ways to do so. My home parish has had success with a "children's liturgy of the word" at the nine o'clock Sunday Mass. The children exit after the Call to Worship and return just before the Offertory. Likewise, our parish youth ministry program has regular moments of faith sharing based on Bible readings. All youth ministry gatherings, even social events, could easily begin with such an opportunity.

Strategy 5: Consider a back-of-church bulletin board of seasonal biblical or liturgical themes. I've seen this done most effectively in my home parish in Ireland. For full disclosure, the anchor person is my wonderful sister-in-law, Doreen. Every liturgical season (Advent, Christmas, Lent) or parish milestone (First Communion, Confirmation), she takes a relevant Gospel quote, creates a large mural on an extended roll of newsprint, and installs it along the back or side wall of the parish church. It is amazing how many people take note, talk about it, and anticipate each seasonal or event mural. The murals help to rivet some primary biblical or liturgical theme into their consciousness. Besides having a good biblical background and a rich spirituality, Doreen is also a gifted artist. To repeat, however, every community has the gifts it needs to carry out its mission. So every parish has artists who could create such murals.

Didache: The Parish as a Community of the Word/Teaching

The claims and proposals already made in this chapter are well summarized by the African proverb, "It takes a village." This is eminently true of educating in faith, which is rarely achieved apart from a Christian community and family or household. I use "rarely" instead of "never," because God's grace can also work miracles in unfortunate circumstances. Our side of the covenant, however, requires that we be fitting instruments of God's grace by providing "a village"—parish—that is likely to socialize people effectively in Christian faith and identity.

Now I add, "It takes a village *with a school.*" Well, not literally a school, though some parishes and areas have church-sponsored schools (our focus in Chapter 7). By "school" here I mean an intentional program of religious education with well-crafted teaching/ learning curricula. Such programs need to be anchored by trained catechetical leaders. Even if or especially if they are volunteers, all catechists need basic training. Likewise, the parish should provide them with age-appropriate textbooks that reflect both good theology and effective pedagogy. In a Catholic parish, the published curricula used must have been reviewed and deemed "to be in conformity with the *Catechism of the Catholic Church*" by the U.S. Bishops' committee for such review. We are blessed to have many fine basal religion series available that are so approved and are catechetically effective. Meanwhile, my point here is that every Christian community must have well-planned programs that educate in faith. Although the parish educates by its shared faith, it also needs to be formally educated itself; although it evangelizes, it needs ongoing evangelization.

The social sciences alert us that socialization alone, though essential to formation, is hard pressed to sustain identity in faith "beyond the village." Because the influences and diversity of postmodernity are so pervasive—through communication, transportation, relocation, and more—there are few "villages" left. In this day and age, not many people live out their lives in their original "lifestyle enclave." Even if they do, to mature in faith requires more than accepting the faith of one's socializing community and family.

In addition to basic socialization, people need a critically reflective pedagogy that promotes religious literacy and understanding of Christian faith, a pedagogy that enables people to become personally convinced of its truth claims and values, to appropriate its spiritual wisdom as their own, and to be both formed and informed to integrate it into daily life.

Developmental psychologists advise that socialization alone will not sponsor people beyond a conventional faith, stage three in James Fowler's sixfold schema of faith development.[14] To mature beyond the conventional requires effective religious education throughout the life cycle, from kindergarten onward. In sum, it takes both socialization and education to bring people, by God's grace, to a maturity in faith that can not only survive, but thrive outside "the village."

In its formal catechetical curricula, a parish program must commit to teach what I call "the whole Story and Vision" of Christian faith. This includes all the constitutive truths, sacraments, and morals of the Faith and what they mean for people's lives. Further, religion curricula should reflect a scope and sequence that is age appropriate—whether participants are in preschool or their golden years. This is best achieved by what the great educational psychologist Jerome Bruner called a spiral curriculum. This is one that constantly teaches the core themes of Christian faith in language understandable to each age level, and yet continues to deepen and expand as the years go by.

Beyond the essentials of Christian faith, adults need opportunity to delve ever deeper into the depths of Scripture and Tradition, accessing their rich legacy of spiritual wisdom for life. There is always a "surplus" in Christian faith. Like God's love, the Faith's founding story, the "breadth and length and height and depth," can never be fully plumbed (Eph. 3:18). There will always be more to learn.

Parishes can provide people the opportunity, as they desire or need, to go on studying their faith lifelong. It is hard to imagine a more important pastoral task for a parish.

There have been attempts to produce comprehensive basal curricula (grades K to 8) that are guided by the readings from the common Sunday lectionary. My concern here is that the lectionary was not designed to be a systematic presentation of the whole Story and Vision of Christian faith and in age-appropriate ways. Yet the catechetical curriculum of a parish does well to correlate with the Sunday liturgy and to echo the various liturgical seasons. Indeed, formal catechesis must be in partnership with all the parish ministries as outlined above, not just with the liturgy. The formal catechetical programs should provide opportunities for people to contribute to building up Christian community, to practice their faith through works of justice and compassion, and to take part in shared prayer and worship. We now turn to some strategies for a parish to be an effective *community of the Word/teaching*.

Strategy 1: Provide comprehensive religious education, making lifelong learning in faith available to all parishioners. This sounds like a tall order, especially for small parishes. Yet we're in a better position to achieve it now than ever before in the history of the Church. There are vast resources readily available through print materials, online continuing education, good-quality video and audio programs, not to mention highly developed basal curricula.

There is great promise too in total community catechesis programs that are intergenerational, such as *Generations of Faith*.[15] This approach is tied closely to the liturgical season and Sunday lectionary. People meet in extended gatherings once a month, usually on a Sunday afternoon. They have shared food, prayer, and ritual, followed by age-specific curricula based on a common theme, then intergenerational faith sharing, and a closing ritual. It has resources for family follow-up, a "question of the week" suggested by the

Sunday Gospel reading, and many other engaging features. Though demanding to organize, *Generations of Faith* offers comprehensive and intergenerational religious education in one fell swoop. Then, within commitment to comprehensive religious education, there should be basal programs that fulfill the needs of different generations. Some suggestions follow.

Strategy 2: Offer a good preschool and grade-school basal program of catechetical education. Although the Church insists that "Catechesis for adults . . . must be considered the chief form of catechesis" (*GDC,* n. 59), it would be foolhardy to neglect the formal catechetical education of children. Of course, parents and guardians have primary catechetical responsibility, as Chapter 6 will review. However, parishes must partner with parents to see to it that their grade-school children receive a thorough education with a basal curriculum that gives them ready access at age-appropriate levels to the foundations of Christian faith. As I've stated before, such programs need teachers— even if volunteers—who are well prepared, supported, and resourced by a trained and designated parish leader. Further, they should use curricula that reflect good theology and effective pedagogy.

Strategy 3: Provide a teen ministry program with strong adolescent catechesis. Nothing is more important to the life of a parish than the ministry it offers to its youth. We've made great strides in developing approaches that actively engage young people in the life and mission of the parish. Certainly they are interested in social justice activities that are fun, and a parish program can provide as much. It is clear, however, that they are deeply engaged and inspired by the social justice teachings of the Church and that they have a "fire in the belly" for Jesus. This points to the fact that youth ministry programs need to have a strong component of adolescent catechesis, enabling youth to both learn and practice their faith.

Strategy 4: Offer programs of education in faith across the life cycle. This requires no further elaboration beyond what I've said already. I'd simply highlight two points. First, there is great benefit for people of like interests and challenges to get together and share their faith, for example, young adults. Second, we need to be more imaginative about how to use the modern communications media to provide such programs and curricula across the life cycle.

Strategy 5: Sponsor attractive programs for senior members that both nurture and draw upon their faith to benefit the whole community. As life expectancy rises, many parishes have large numbers of parishioners in their golden years. This age has great opportunity for spiritual development. As people look back over their lives and look ahead into eternity, they need spiritual accompaniment from one another and from the broader Christian community.

It is also true that people who have "borne the heat of the day" in living their faith have great spiritual wisdom to share with the community. Every parish can tap the rich resources of their senior members. It just takes a little imagination and organization. Many years ago, I was in charge of a parish program preparing children for First Holy Communion. I encouraged all the children to have at least one parent sponsor who would accompany them throughout the preparation. One little friend could not manage to convince her parents to get involved. However, I knew her grandmother in a local retirement home, and she happily signed up as the child's sponsor. It was a great experience for both grandmother and granddaughter and a bonding in faith between them.

For Reflection and Conversation

- What are your own reflections on the power of liturgy to educate in faith?

- Think of a specific strategy—either listed above or one of your own—to enhance the worship life of your faith community.

- How do you evaluate the preaching in your parish? Even if it's good, what might you suggest to improve it?

- List all the efforts at formal catechesis in your parish or base community. How comprehensive and effective are they? What strategies might you suggest to improve them?

Our next chapter turns specifically to the role of family and home in faith education. While Jesus is the heart of *what* and *how* we teach as educators in Christian faith, the family or household is the heart of *where* we teach it.

CHAPTER SIX

It's (Almost) All in the Family—with Help

Faith Formation in Households of Faith

Some years ago, a young Jewish student working on a Ph.D. in education at another university asked to join my doctoral seminar in Theology and Education at Boston College. I'm so glad I welcomed her. Among other gifts, she brought us her Jewish emphasis on the family in faith formation.

I vividly remember one early seminar conversation that was becoming a dire lament about the sad state of families. Students cited the high divorce rate, mixed-faith marriages, parents who don't practice their faith, the fact that everyone's too busy, religious ignorance among young parents, lack of supervision of media in the home—the dismal listing went on and on. The consensus solution seemed to be that the Church should somehow step in and save the day by providing more and better religious education.

Sounding frustrated with the tone of the conversation, our

Jewish colleague eventually crashed in with something like: "I'm so amazed at how you Christians mistrust your families. You assume that *they* can't do faith formation and that you have to do it for them. In my tradition, whether families are observant or not, keep kosher or not, are orthodox, conservative, or reformed, we tell them that *they* have first responsibility for the Jewish identity of their children, and then we give them the help they need to fulfill their role as parents. Sure, our Sabbath school is important, but it is a far second to our families." She refocused our conversation toward how to put families back at center stage in the faith education of their children. Instead of doing it *for* them, we began to imagine how to do it *with* them and to empower them to do it themselves.

Among other things, her point was that it doesn't take a *perfect* family to raise and sustain people in faith. As far as faith is concerned, there is probably no such entity. Many times I've said to large groupings of people, "Hands up, anyone who comes from a perfect family." No hand is ever raised. "And yet," I continue, "you are all here because you are people of faith. That imperfect family of yours must have functioned as an instrument of God's grace. Of course, God's grace rarely has perfect instruments and maybe doesn't need them." This being said, the local parish or congregation can be a fruitful resource to its parents. I proposed in the previous chapter that we need to heighten the capacity of the parish to educate in faith. Now I insist that we must do likewise with the capacity of its families, with the parish or larger community giving them the help they need. The parish can lend its families the resources, training, suggestions, networking, support, and active involvement to help them fulfill their function as the primary religious educators.

By "family" I mean *all sustaining networks of domestic life*. Since there are many one- and two-parent families, blended and extended families, traditional and postmodern families, this definition seems broad enough to include them all. Also, because there are family-like domestic communities that may not be headed by a legal parent, besides "family" I will sometimes use St. Paul's lovely phrase "household of faith" (Gal. 6:10, JB). Whatever the structure or leadership of the household, the key is that it be one of faith.

For most of its history and for the vast majority of its members, the Church entrusted the faith formation of children to the home and village. Apprenticeship and family tutoring was the primary paradigm of education for all but the elite. With the advent of universal education, a profound shift occurred in Western consciousness that embraced schooling and schools as the primary mode and locus of education. Religious education and the Church followed suit. Soon the assumption was that education in faith belonged in a school of some kind and that it replaced more than supported the work of parents and home.

The emergence of denominational schools, Sunday schools,[1] and the Confraternity of Christian Doctrine (CCD)[2] all greatly enhanced the effectiveness of religious education. The disadvantage, however, was that they removed the family from its central position as educator in faith and gave the impression that the school—of whatever kind—could educate better than and instead of parents. Even the Church helped to convince parents of this schooling paradigm. As a result, most parents still assume that if they simply take their children to a parish program, say one hour a week for about thirty weeks a year, it will make them Christians. Although I've already argued for a strong parish catechetical program (Chapter 5) and will review the value of denominational schools (Chapter 7), neither can ever replace the role of a household of faith.

There have been prophetic voices that have championed the centrality of the family to education in faith. I think immediately of Horace Bushnell and his classic work of 1860, *Christian Nurture.* Bushnell took seriously the New Testament admonition to parents that they "bring up their children in the nurture and admonition of the Lord" (Eph. 6:4, KJV). Bushnell insisted that "the *atmosphere* of the home" is the key to Christian nurture. I agree and return to his insight below. Confident that "religion never thoroughly penetrates life until it becomes domestic," Bushnell opposed the evangelical emphasis of his time on adult conversion. Instead, he argued, "The true idea of Christian education" is "that children grow up as Christian and never know themselves as being otherwise."[3]

More recently, the Church has put in place strong rhetoric about the primacy of the family. Though our practice still lags, the rhetoric can help keep our feet to the fire. I'll take some examples from Catholic documents. The family's primacy begins at baptism, when the celebrant addresses the parents as "the first teachers of their children in the ways of faith" (Rite of Baptism). Vatican II declared: "Parents must be acknowledged as the first and foremost educators of their children" and especially in faith (Declaration on Christian Education, n. 3). Even the Code of Canon Law legislates: "Parents above all others are obliged to form their children in the faith and practice of the Christian life by word and example" (can. 774.2). The *General Directory for Catechesis* states boldly that "nothing replaces family catechesis" (n. 178), and the *Catechism of the Catholic Church* advises: "The home is the first school of Christian life" (n. 1657).

Pause for a moment to reflect on these statements, and the wisdom you might glean from your own experience of the family as educator in faith.

For Reflection and Conversation

- Thinking back to your family of origin, how do you rate its success in nurturing your identity in faith?

- What were some of its most effective ways of doing so?

- What wisdom can you learn for educating in faith through your present family context?

The Incarnate Transmission of Faith

I've repeated many times throughout this work that Christian faith is a "total" affair. It demands our heads, hearts, and hands. It pertains to our whole identity and way of "being" as both noun and verb, to who we are and how we live. A standard summary states that Christianity is an *incarnate* religion—a faith that reflects the centrality of God's incarnation in Jesus Christ and calls disciples to "make flesh" the faith they profess. Looking at faith this way heightens all the more the catechetical role of family. The social sciences testify that no influence is more formative of people's identity than their primary socialization. The *GDC* is absolutely correct, then, that "the family . . . is the primary agent of an *incarnate* transmission of faith" (n. 207).

Given our current mind-set, which equates education with schooling, we could mis-hear what it means to say that the family is the primary religious *educator.* From habit, we could hear "educator" and think "school"—as if parents were to set up a school corner at home with desks, textbooks, and chalkboard (or smart board). I've actually had parents hear the proposal this way and rightly resist. Instead, and broadening education far beyond schooling, I follow Bushnell's lead and point to the *atmosphere* of the home. Atmosphere entails the family's shared lifestyle and the values and ethic that suffuse it, the self-understanding it nurtures, the outlook on life it encourages, and the patterns of relationships and language that shape its shared life. The whole atmosphere of the home is what matters most, because family nurture comes much more by osmosis than direct instruction. Family catechesis is "more witnessed to than taught, more occasional than systematic, more on-going than structured into periods" (*GDC,* n. 255). Although some direct instruction might be appropriate at times, the family's primary role is to provide a "positive and receptive environment" and the "explicit experience and practice of the faith" (n. 178).

Vatican II revived the ancient image of the family as functioning like "a domestic church" (Dogmatic Constitution on the Church, n. 11). The *GDC* picked up on this image and proposed that the family catechizes by reflecting within its shared life "the different aspects and functions of the life of the entire Church" (n. 225). In other words, we can strategize about the family as catechist precisely through the functions of ministry that I outlined in the previous chapter regarding the parish. Of course, the family is not to replicate a parish. So parents are not to preach the word of God as if from a pulpit, but they can "break open the word" in many ways as a family, even in everyday conversations and storytelling. They are not to feign a celebration of Eucharist, but their mealtimes, especially on celebratory occasions, can inculcate many of the values of Eucharist. When a family eats together, much more than food passes among its members. They can experience a sense of presence to and for each other, of a love that bonds. This anticipates the Real Presence they encounter in the Eucharist and how it bonds the community as the Body of Christ in the world. A simple "grace" before and/or after meals can help to echo the correlation between "Eucharist" in the home and Eucharist at church.

In summary, then, the family can and should educate in faith by being a community of *koinonia,* welcome, and of *marturia,* witness, by its *leitourgia* of shared worship, by its common *diakonia* toward well-being, and as a community that shares the *kerygma* and *didache* of God's Word. Let us imagine some strategies under each of these functions of family ministry. Remember, our aim is to heighten the intentionality of the family to educate in faith through its communal life.

Koinonia: The Family as a Community of Welcome

Every family needs to be a truly human community. In addition, a Christian family should strive to be a community of Christian faith. The ideal is that the *communio,* "communality," of the Church and, indeed, the very inner life of God as Triune *communio,* be reflected in the family.

It would seem that the sine qua non for a family being a community is its hospitality and welcome for all. Even for healthy human development, the family needs to make every member feel fully included, respected, welcome, and at home. This seems all the more imperative if family members are to embrace the deep truths of Christian faith about their own dignity and worth, to understand their rights and responsibilities, and to respect themselves and others. No family is perfect, yet every household of faith must strive to be one where all members are equally loved and cherished, protected and safe, challenged and enabled to flourish.

There is a spate of postmodern literature on the need for hospitality in our communities and in society at large.[4] Hospitality, however, is an ancient Christian value. Paul made hospitality a criterion for leadership in a Christian community (1 Tim. 3:2; Titus 1:8). St. Benedict made hospitality a central value in his monastic rule. Rule 53 states that "all guests are to be received as Christ" with a special welcome for "pilgrims," that is, strangers from outside. The need now to "welcome the other" is heightened by contemporary means of transportation, communication, and relocation. The "other," who used to be "over there," is now right next door. If our world is to live in harmony, then hospitality to strangers is more imperative than ever. This is certainly demanded by Christian faith, for which "neighbor" knows no limits and includes enemies. The etymology of "catholic" (*katha holos*) suggests that its best meaning is "all are welcome."

If such radical welcome is even to be approximated in church and society, it must surely begin in the family. The roots of discrimination against "others" most often arise from the home. If young people hear parents speak with bigotry on any basis, race or religion, economics or orientation, age or ability, gender or ethnicity, they are most likely to take on the same prejudice. Conversely, the family is the primary place to nurture welcome and respect for the "other," for people who are not the "same" as us. Vatican II made a sweeping statement in this regard: "Every type of discrimination, whether social or cultural, whether based on sex, race, color, social condition, language or religion, is to be overcome and eradicated as contrary to God's intent" (Pastoral Constitution on the Church in the Modern World, n. 29). The community and hospitality of the family are key to such eradication. Let us imagine some practical strategies to enhance family *koinonia* and thus its educating in faith.

Strategy 1: Make sure that every family member feels cherished, respected, and included. I'm the youngest of ten children, nine of whom grew into adulthood. Beyond siblings, I had copious aunts and uncles from both sides of the family, and then cousins galore and of all degrees. I learned early that every family has its "ecology"— configurations of relationships and partnerships. Even among siblings, there are various networks; this is to be expected. However, the bottom line is that every member should feel fully included and cherished for their own sake. Though not perfectly, my family of origin did well with such hospitality. My parents especially made us all feel equally loved and even favored when we needed it.

Beyond a general commitment to being a community, families need practical strategies for making all members feel cherished, included, and welcome. One can think of celebrating each person's birthdays and milestones; praising achievements; being encouraging in challenging times; spending personal one-on-one time with members; listening to one another's stories, joys, and sorrows; often asking "How are you?" and "How are things?"; thanking members for favors done and gifts shared; taking turns with domestic jobs and assignments; giving everyone a say in family discussion and decision making; and more. Different cultures and family traditions come into play in how to forge such hospitality. Regardless, Christian faith requires it; and it is a source of catechesis.

Strategy 2: Find ways to welcome "the other" with an open heart and open mind. Every family needs to imagine its own ways to achieve this strategy. In my little family now, we've gone out of our way to have Ted meet "different" people. We always speak of "others" with great reverence and respect, whether the differences between us are religious, racial, economic, ethnic, or whatever. Likewise, a family should encourage open discourse, letting every member have their word and respecting one another's opinions—even in disagreement. Though children need to be developmentally ready, there is great benefit in exposing them to religious traditions other than their own. The guiding attitude should be that of Jesus. Though Christians have a special home within God's family, yet "In my Father's house, there are many dwelling places" (John 14:2).

Strategy 3: Favor the ones who need the favor most. This strategy could well be under *diakonia* below, but my own experience leads me to place it here, under *koinonia*. Over the past twenty-five years, great clarity has emerged that Christian faith requires disciples to make a "preferential option for the poor." This phrase was first used in a letter from Fr. Pedro Arrupe S.J., the Superior General of the Society of Jesus, written in 1968 to Jesuits throughout Latin America. It was developed by one of the greatest theologians of our time, Fr. Gustavo Gutiérrez, the "father" of liberation theology.[5] However, now it is frequently repeated in official Church documents, including the *Catechism* (see, e.g., nn. 886, 1033, 1435, 2443–49). It reflects the biblical witness that God favors those who need the favor most—those to whom life is denied in some way. A people of God need to do likewise.

My way of comprehending this favor for the poor is through the image of the Good Shepherd. I'm thinking specifically of a "holy picture" I had as a child, of Jesus with a lamb across his shoulders. Of course, it was inspired by John 10:1–21, where Jesus refers to himself as the Good Shepherd, echoing a central image of Yahweh in the Hebrew scriptures. When I wonder about which lamb the Shepherd carries, I realize it is the lame one, the stray one, the sick one, in other words, the one that *needs* to be carried. Surely the family should be like a good shepherd to all its members, carrying each according to need at varied times.

We all have our poverties in life; some are economic, indeed, but there are other kinds of impoverishment as well. I propose that "favoring the poor" needs to begin in our families. If not done at home, it is not likely to be done outside of it either. Within the family, the poverties can vary from time to time and from generation to generation. Think of the loneliness that older members can experience, especially in the aftermath of losing a lifetime spouse. Then they need some special "favors"—of time, attention, listening, company. And the young can have their moments of great poverty as well.

Teddy once flew down a dangerous hill on his bicycle, with me shouting at him from behind to slow down. He didn't and crashed at the bottom, badly scraping his hands and knees, but nothing was broken. I picked up the poor little guy, howling in pain, and held him in my arms to console him. Of course I wanted to say, "I told you to slow down," but I knew that that would be better said later, if at all. He knew he had done wrong, that the fall was his own fault, and yet he was so poor for love and consolation at that moment. Thankfully I gave it to him. On a similar note, when I first went away to college, my mother wrote me the most loving letters. Why, I figured I must be her favorite. But when I went home for Christmas, I simply had to fit back in with the rest. I realized then that she favored me when I was away and feeling lonely. When I came home, I didn't need it, or at least not that favor. Like our God, parents are to favor the ones that need it most as they need it.

Strategy 4: Join a local faith community. Yes, the family is like a "domestic church," but it needs the supporting context of a parish or base faith community. Just showing up with the rest of the community at Sunday worship impresses kids and reminds the adults that "this" is important. In fact, there is no way that parents can raise their children as Christians or sustain their own faith for long except by participating regularly in a local faith community. This is a nonnegotiable. Beyond simply "showing up"—as for Sunday worship—the faith community of the family is enhanced if it participates actively in the life of its parish or congregation.

Strategy 5: Be a family of reconciliation. It is surely the rare family that doesn't have its squabbles, tensions, rivalries, and "uncivil" wars. Such troubles come from the process of human beings living together. I've heard the claim that 95 percent of our families are dysfunctional in some way or other. The key challenge for a Christian family, however, is to be one that negotiates peace, where people learn to admit mistakes, express sorrow, ask forgiveness as needed, and grant forgiveness without revenge or tit for tat. This is a tall order. It is powerful education, however, in a defining aspect of Christian faith if people can experience reconciliation and peacemaking within the home.

Christian faith should be able to unite and bond families into reconciling communities, helping members to transcend the everyday offenses that people can commit or experience within their household. St. Paul wrote to the Corinthians that God has reconciled us through Christ and "has given us the ministry of reconciliation" (2 Cor. 5:18). This ministry should surely flourish within the Christian family.

Marturia: The Family as a Community of Witness

As I said above, these functions of ministry overlap, and especially within the home. For example, I've placed the work of justice under *diakonia,* but I imagine it here as well. Under *marturia*/witness, we can summarize that a Christian household of faith is to give good example to one another and to its surrounding world by living as a base community for God's reign in Jesus Christ. As I've said many times, the fullness of God's reign will be realized only in God's time, at the *eschaton* promised at the end of history. Meanwhile, God's reign is realized now, "on earth as in heaven," as people live its truths, values, and commitments. No family is ever a perfect and totally effective symbol of God's reign, but we must try to approximate being one. By God's grace working through our own best efforts, a family can bear witness to one another and to the world with the faith it professes.

An old Christian adage says, "Charity begins at home." And, indeed, true love is most needed there, though not confined there. The greatest commandment—to love God with all our mind, heart, and strength and our neighbor as ourselves—must be realized first and foremost in the family. We can surely say that the home is where all the values of God's reign are most needed—and tested: right and loving relationships; faith in God and one another; hope that keeps hope alive for everyone; peace and patience, truth-telling and honesty, respect and responsibility; and so on. The ultimate challenge for disciples may be to live Christian faith within our own household.

I have a friend whom I would deem a radical Christian pacifist. For many years he has been involved in high-visibility protests against war and nuclear armaments and has been arrested and done jail time for his actions. I once told him of my admiration for his courage and convictions. He responded that being a pacifist "out there" is easy compared to being one at home. He then explained that he had a fifteen-year-old daughter at the time and commented, "With a teenager, you have to choose pacifism again every day."

Though challenging, our own home may be the locus where we are most in charge of lived faith, where we *can* craft an environment that witnesses to God's reign in Jesus. There is so much in the structures of society that we cannot control, that impinges on our lives with a givenness that can overwhelm. Within our household, however, we can mount a good attempt to resist and live otherwise. So even as we recognize and lament the chauvinism of the world and church around us, by God's grace we can practice real inclusion and respect for all within our family. Even when we feel overwhelmed by injustice and violence in society, we can still attempt to practice justice and peacemaking at home. We recognize the ways that society destroys the environment, but we can practice being "green" in our family. I'm not recommending that we construct the household of faith as a cocoon apart from the world. At least this is not a mainstream Christian aspiration, though I admire the witness of groups like the Amish. Instead, I'm suggesting that we have more choices regarding our households than we do in church or society. Let's make good ones.

A helpful yardstick for a family might be to ask that old youth ministry question: "If this family were put on trial for being Christian, would there be enough evidence to convict it" (originally attributed to G. K. Chesterton). Or if strangers dropped in, could they tell, before long, that this was a truly Christian family, not by outward trappings such as a cross on a wall (too easy), but because it is transparent that people here live the deep values of the gospel? Perhaps you can imagine and build upon the following strategies to encourage such witness to Christian faith in and by your family. Christian witness is crucial to the family as religious educator.

Strategy 1: Review often the atmosphere of the home to reflect Christian values. Like the air, "atmosphere" is nigh impossible to pin down. Yet every family has a distinctive one that its members create and inhale constantly. It affects whether a family functions as a Christian household and educates in faith. We can name this strategy simply by saying that Christian faith should determine a family's value system, attitudes toward people, beginning with one another, and its outlook on life in the world. It may help to think of the converse to a Christian atmosphere. If the family is a place of ridicule and fear, of negativity and criticism, of false pride and greed, of rampant consumerism, of prejudice and discrimination, it surely won't nurture Christian faith.

Everyone within a household is responsible for its atmosphere, beginning with its parents, guardians, or leaders. Thus, it is a good practice to hold all accountable for it and, as needed, to review together how things are going in their common life. The next four strategies unpack this atmosphere strategy a bit more.

Strategy 2: Use language patterns that reflect Christian values and relationships. For the longest time, we thought that our words were "innocent" in and of themselves, that they simply communicated our thoughts and feelings. In recent years, however, philosophers, linguists, and social scientists have established that the language we use has a profound effect on who we are and become. Language not only communicates our thoughts and feelings; it also shapes them. One philosopher, Martin Heidegger (1889–1976), summarizes,

"Language is the house of being."[6] In other words, our language shapes the world we live in and thus who we become. The "house" where care for language deserves first attention is the home.

Young parents quickly learn that if their children are not to pick up their inappropriate language, they'd better stop using it. Although Teddy will likely learn the vulgar terms somewhere, I didn't want him to learn them from me. Early on too our family tried to avoid using words like "stupid" and "hate" and never with regard to people. Beyond avoiding the vulgar and inappropriate, we can craft language that is life-giving or language that is deadly. The life-giving kind includes words of faith in times of worry, words of encouragement in times of challenge, words of kindness and affirmation, words that complement achievements and work well done, words that are respectful and make people feel cherished. For a long time, I used the nickname "Precious" for Teddy; I would greet him with, "Hey, Precious." Now, at ten, he prefers "Hey, Dude," but I hope the early years sank in and will remain, at least in his subconscious sense of who he is.

The deadly language includes disrespectful words and sayings that reflect prejudice (e.g., racism, anti-Semitism) and negative biases (e.g., regarding ethnicity, age, or ability). It includes gender-favoring language (more below at Strategy 5) and family myths and old stories that put people down in any way or discourage human flourishing for anyone.

Strategy 3: Craft the family's Sabbath keeping and recreation to reflect Christian values. Christian faith should teach us how to work and how to take recreation. God must have known that some of us would need *a law* to take a day of rest, so God obliged with the Third Commandment. The prophet Hosea warned the Israelites to stop saying "Our God" to "the work of [their] hands" (14:4). He meant idols in the strict sense, but surely our busy society also tempts us to idolize the work of our hands—and heads. Keeping Sabbath, both worshipping God and resting from work, is to mark the life of a Christian family. This will educate in faith if only by reminding members to place their primary trust in God instead of their own works. The coming of the kingdom in its fullness does not depend on our efforts, but on God. This is why we can take Sabbath.

Recreating together should also be the pattern of a Christian household. Shared recreation that is wholesome and healthy is surely a great way to bond family and can teach many good values. One important effort that we make toward Ted's moral formation is playing board games together after supper and insisting that everyone follow the rules. We can *tell* him not to cheat or steal, but having to follow the rules of Yahtzee is likely more effective and teaches other good facts of life besides.

Strategy 4: Practice an environmental consciousness. Again, this could be under commitment to justice; I place it here because it resonates with family *atmosphere*. We are just figuring out that our faith gives Christians great responsibility to care for the environment. Pope Benedict XVI has been relentless in trying to establish ecological responsibility as integral to Christian faith. Such a value must surely be inculcated in the family. This requires practicing a "green" consciousness, finding practical ways to help preserve the environment.

Something as simple as the three R's is a good start: reduce, reuse, recycle. Even as I write this, however, I'm conscious of how much more our own home could be doing or avoiding. I know that our house is not energy efficient, that we should have a compost bin, that we often waste food. When I come back from visiting a third-world country, I'm struck afresh with the extraordinary level of waste that pervades the American culture. Yet I have hope precisely because of our children. Little kids can really "get into" caring for the environment. We can enhance their motivation with God language and out of Christian faith. A spiritual basis is most likely to help people keep on in any such effort.

Strategy 5: Recast as needed the family's gender roles toward equality. Let's be clear. Christian faith should stand full force against gender discrimination and in favor of gender equality and inclusion. Here we're really talking about women's rights and roles within society and church, and thus within the home. One of the great insights of contemporary feminism is that "the domestic is political." How we structure gender roles and relations within the home and in society are reciprocal. The home, however, can stand for equality even when the society or church does not. To take one concrete example, young families with children in this day and age need a co-parenting partnership, unless either one is content to stay home full-time and function as the primary parent.

I re-echo here the point from above about language. One way that we perpetuate the sexism of our culture is through gender-favoring language, as in "man" or "mankind" when the referent is all people. To many, this may seem a too subtle if not insignificant issue. However, empirical studies show that such language is far from innocent and that it perpetuates the favoring of men in church and society. The family is a good place to practice an inclusive language pattern for ourselves and more expansive language for God.[7] To insist that God is only male is to break the First Commandment, which forbids "graven images" of the divine. Inclusive and expansive language takes a little effort at first, but it soon becomes natural. All the more so, if modeled in the family.

For Reflection and Conversation

- Pause here and ask, how is my family a community of Christian faith?

- How can it grow as such a family?

- In what ways does my family witness to Christian faith, within and without?

- How can we improve upon such witness?

Leitourgia: The Family as a Community of Worship

Another story from my Jewish friend. When the seminar pressed her about how Jewish families pass on their faith and identity, she named as most effective the religious rituals within the home: the Sabbath meal, celebrating Passover, Hanukah candle lighting and gifts, the Succoth tent in the backyard, and the dairy meals at Pentecost. By contrast, Christians have generally lost such family liturgy. We may have fine worship in our churches, but it largely stays there. We need to "bring liturgy home" and have worship within the household as well.

Without religious rituals, prayers, and symbols, homes are far less likely to nurture people in Christian faith. I'll wager that if you pause here and think back to childhood, you will remember a religious ritual of some kind that had profound influence on your faith formation. As we search for rituals for our family, there are many that are common to all Christians and many more that are traditions in a particular culture. Wherever we find, create, or reclaim them, Christian homes cannot be without "liturgy" if they are to nurture their members in faith. I'll make a few suggestions.

Strategy 1: Practice everyday rituals of prayer and worship. Here I'm thinking of old reliables like pausing for grace before meals. Our family does this before evening dinner. We often say the common one, especially with guests: "Bless us, O Lord, and these thy gifts, which we are about to receive from thy bounty, through Christ our Lord. Amen." Sometimes we do a spontaneous grace or follow another formula. A favorite is, "Come. Lord Jesus, be our guest; let these gifts to us be blessed." It is also a good practice to begin and end a meal with the sign of the cross, "blessing ourselves" by tracing the cross of Jesus on our bodies. Morning and night prayers should be standard as well. When it is my turn for night prayers with Teddy, I do a modified form of the *examen,* the old "examination of conscience" dressed up a bit. We review the day for things for which to thank our Loving God, things about which to say "sorry" if needed, and then some things to ask from God (Teddy has a running list of people to pray for). None of these prayer rituals need take long, some half a minute. Yet if done regularly, not only do they "raise the mind and heart (of the family) to God"; they also educate in faith.

Strategy 2: Create your own family prayer rituals. The first morning I held Teddy in my arms, when he was about four days old, I began the practice of taking him to a window, opening the blinds, looking out on the day, and, hail, rain, or shine, saying, "Thank you, Loving God, for a good night's sleep and a brand-new day." A simple little ritual, it takes about a minute. I wanted Teddy to grow up convinced of God's unconditional love, to begin each day with an attitude of gratitude, and to know that every one is a fresh start. I also wanted him to realize that we must look out on the world, which we can't do from bed, and no matter what the weather (which in Boston varies greatly) say the prayer. When he got to be two or thee, we began to do it together, and since about five, he does it himself; I join in if I'm around. The key is to create practices that suit your family and are likely to become rituals.

Strategy 3: Find rituals in the common faith and in cultural traditions. Christianity and Catholicism in particular have lots of common spiritual practices that families can do either at home or in their local parish. I'm thinking of Advent wreaths, Lenten poor boxes, Christmas crèches, Ash Wednesday ashes, Palm Sunday palms (kept throughout the year), praying before the Blessed Sacrament, the rosary, stations of the cross, *lectio divina,* centering prayer, the Jesus Prayer, retreats, spiritual companioning, the *examen,* fasting from food and abstaining from meat, praying before icons, the liturgy of the hours, devotion to Mary and the saints, praying for the departed, various forms of focused prayer (e.g., to the Child Jesus), and more. When informed by good theology (e.g., devotion to Mary should lead to Jesus and discipleship), such spiritual practices can help to nurture and sustain people's faith.

Particular cultures have lots of distinctive spiritual practices. More recently, the Church and its scholars have come to a new appreciation of "popular religion." This refers to cultural practices, some of which arose outside of the official Church, that have nurtured and sustained people's faith across the ages. Often, devotion to Mary is localized within a culture, for example, Our Lady of Guadalupe in Mexican Catholicism, Our Lady of Czestochowa among Polish people, and so on. Hispanic Catholicism is particularly rich in popular religion: the *altarcitos* ("little altars") set aside for prayer in the home, the *Dia de los Muertos* to remember and pray for the dead on November 1 and 2, *Las Posadas* leading up to Christmas and remembering Joseph and Mary's search for shelter, and many more.

My original Irish culture had all kinds of religious traditions for the home. One of my favorites is the Christmas candle. People light it throughout Advent and place it in a window toward the road to welcome every stranger, because anyone could be the Christ. Another was the holy water font by the door with which one sprinkled and blessed oneself or got sprinkled before leaving the home. Of course, we celebrated St. Patrick's Day on March 17, giving thanks for the gift of Christian faith, and St. Brigid's Day on February 1, remembering a great woman leader (some even claim a bishop) of the early Irish church.

After Vatican II, such popular practices fell off, and for some good reasons. Many had become exaggerated devotions, sometimes with a dash of superstition, there being a fine line between faith and magic. Vatican II made a successful effort to recenter what should be at the core of Catholic faith: Jesus, the Bible, Mass, the sacraments, and discipleship. Now, however, almost fifty years later, we might return to some of those old devotions, informed by better theology and without exaggerating their importance to the Faith.[8] We need some such personal and family-centered practices. They are powerful ways to nurture and sustain people in faith. They educate. The key is for families to choose ones that will be meaningful for them, so that they are likely to practice them regularly.

Strategy 4: Have religious symbols in the home. Catholic homes of a previous era were often festooned with statues and religious art, though much of it rarely deserved that designation. Again, much of this realia was swept away by the tide of Vatican II. Now, I'm proposing that some aesthetic and well-chosen religious art in the home can be a source of catechesis. When decorating Teddy's room, we came upon a lovely picture of the Good Shepherd, not with the lamb across his shoulders, but holding it at the breast. We've often paused before it and talked about how much God and Jesus always love us, no matter what! Good religious art, now more readily available if only as prints of classic pieces, can be a source of catechesis. Indeed, this is why the Church promoted the arts throughout its history—as a medium of religious education.

Strategy 5: Engage the arts and nature to nurture spirituality. Not only religious art, but all the arts can help to turn minds and hearts toward the Transcendent. The aesthetic and the spiritual are at least first cousins. Both engage the soul and raise up the human spirit.

Not only paintings but all forms of art can to do this: sculpture, music, poetry, the performing arts. Parents also have opportunities to encourage wonder and awe, especially at nature, and to foster respect and reverence for the mysteries of the human body. All such "reaches for the transcendent" nurture people's spirituality and, indirectly at least, contribute to educating in faith.

Diakonia: The Family as a Community of Well-being

Much that I've said already about the centrality of justice and peacemaking and then about *diakonia* in the parish echoes here for the family. Indeed, many of my previous strategies could be repeated here, like care with language patterns, favoring the ones who need the favor most, and protecting the environment. Simply put, the Christian family must practice justice and service both within and without, within itself and to the world at large. This is its mandate by Christian faith, and, my constant point: such work and its attendant atmosphere in the home educate its members in a faith that does justice and compassion. I offer suggestions to stimulate the imagination for *your* family or household.

Strategy 1: Often review the shared life of the family for commitment to justice, peace, and compassion—within. The old adage I cited that "charity begins at home" is surely true of justice as well. Every family can look at its own dynamics and shared life, often checking how well it is performing in its commitment to justice within itself. Every member must be treated fairly and with respect at all times, receive compassion as needed, and always feel safe within their own household. Certainly a Christian family should be free of violence and abuse, verbal and physical. The latter is a dreadful injustice. In fact, domestic abuse may well be the worst form of oppression there is. Even if people are oppressed or bullied in society, they should at least be able to return to their own home and experience justice and safety there.

Strategy 2: In matters of discipline, try to practice restorative justice. Let me be honest and say that this is the aspect of parenting that I find most difficult and do least well. Yet I know that the discipline of a Christian home should reflect both justice and compassion (I err toward the latter—even indulgence) and should be restorative, not just punitive. I offer three points that I'd like to follow myself. First, and especially for younger children, rules and expectations must be stated clearly and understood by all involved. Second, we can say likewise about the consequences for infractions. I'd also add that there needs to be fair warning and then consistent follow through. Third, if consequences must be meted out, they should be eminently fair and, if possible, restorative. By this I mean that there should be opportunity for the perpetrator to make up for the mistake. Then forgiveness and a clean slate should follow. The ideal to which I aspire is that all this be done without anger.

Strategy 3: Give everyone their voice "at the table." Even little kids need to feel that they have voice and are heard in matters of common family concern. This nurtures their sense of respect and responsibility, crucial to formation in a faith that does justice. Family consultation is great training for participation in the life of church and society. Regarding family rules and regulations, insofar as possible, all should have voice in constructing them and then in reviewing their fulfillment or discerning their breach. We've found it helpful to have a "family summit" to discuss rules and expectations. All have voice and are heard insofar as is reasonable; we don't let Teddy decide his bedtime yet.

Strategy 4: Pay attention to family finances for justice and compassion. As in a parish, a family budget can reflect commitment to justice and compassion. Every Christian family can review its finances and how it spends and holds its money. Why not give family members of age a voice in the family's stewardship, including how much it contributes to the local parish, to diocesan collections, and to other worthy causes or works of compassion. If a family has investments or retirement funds, members can monitor that their money is invested in keeping with the principles of social justice. The latter include decent wages and working conditions, fair hiring practices, good environmental policies, and honest payment for raw materials. A family might add other conditions for their investments, for example, to favor a social concern (like low-cost housing) or to avoid profiting from nuclear weapons. It could be very effective to assign older children the task of investigating family investments with such criteria. This is not as difficult as it sounds, since many investment houses can readily provide such data.

Strategy 5: Do works of justice and service as a family in the community. To do some work of justice or compassion as a family is an ideal form of faith education. What an impact it can have on children to see their parents involved in such works, and it renews the parents' commitment in giving a good example to their children. Such good works can also extend to the political arena. On occasional Sunday afternoons, Teddy and I go together to help with lunch at a local Catholic Worker Community. He loves to chop and slice the vegetables and to serve the food, but he's best of all at sitting and chatting with the guests, which they love (many would have grandkids, but they are not around). I give this example not to draw attention to my feeble efforts, but to suggest how every family can imagine joint ventures in the works of justice and compassion.

Kerygma and *Didache:* The Family as a Community of the Word

The key to this family ministry is to convince parents that they have "a rich faith worth sharing," a phrase I often use in public presentations on parents as catechists. A lot of younger parents have lost confidence in knowing their faith. They don't have the old catechism answers of their parents and don't feel confident about what they do know. The Church's eager willingness to do catechesis for them has also let parents off the hook. For most, the parish or school has become their surrogate religious educator. Another difficulty is that many parents have serious reservations about some of the policies and structures of the Church, and they allow this not only to make them critical of the institution, but also to become alienated from the life-giving waters of their Christian faith.

The key—and this may sound too simple—is to encourage alienated parents to recenter their faith in God and in Jesus, in the gospel and the Spirit's work of God's reign in the world, not in the institution that represents the Church. The Church is only a means to an end, not an end in itself. If parents can refocus onto their Christian faith and off of the church institution, they can rediscover the priceless legacy they have to hand on to their children, the greatest imaginable. Many times I've said to gatherings of young parents, "Imagine raising your children to follow the way that Jesus modeled and made possible by his life, death, and resurrection. Imagine how loving, faith filled, and hopeful they will grow up to be; and how just and peaceful, how merciful and compassionate, how open and hospitable, how respectful and responsible, how joyful and happy they will be in life. Is this what you want for your children?" Inevitably, I always hear a resounding yes. Then I add, "Well, then, share your Christian faith with your children. And remember, the Holy Spirit is always on hand to help." Here are some other strategies.

Strategy 1: Take every opportunity that comes along to share faith as a family. The great issues of life are constantly raised in families or can be raised by parents about meaning and purpose, who we are and how best to live, what to do with our time and who is our neighbor. These are always strategic opportunities for God-talk, for sharing faith. Just recently Teddy asked me the great question, "So, Dad, how do babies get into their mommy's tummies?" What an opportunity for God-talk about life and love. I began with how God is Love and totally in love with us, how we are made in God's likeness, so we too can participate in God's loving work of creation and procreation, and so on. I kept the anatomy details until the end. Afterward, I was thankful that I got to tell Teddy rather than having someone else do it and realized I should have volunteered this conversation sooner.

Of course, all the questions and issues don't need to be so ultimate or dramatic. The ordinary and everyday of life constantly bring opportunities for parents to share faith with their children about thousands of issues. Indeed, conversation about most topics can be turned to engage souls, to nurture their spirituality with the language of faith.

Let me make a particular point here about the role of grandparents in sharing faith with their grandchildren. The relationship between grandparents and grandchildren can be a very special bond. It usually has an aura of munificence, with grandparents "allowing" what parents might forbid and, conversely, children accepting counsel and direction from grandparents that they might resist—as least as teenagers—from parents. My sister Peg and her husband, Kevin, are surely two of the greatest grandparents in the whole world. Their grandchildren love to visit, and the special treat is to stay overnight. They get their favorite dishes and desserts, stay up late, and love to hear bedtime stories of when Granny was a little girl. This kind of loving bond is surely an ideal context in which to share faith. Peg and Kevin do so very well, more through their life-style patterns and conversations in the home than by formal instruction. I'm convinced that all grandparents have a great story of faith to tell; they can be confident in sharing it with their grandchildren, even if it didn't take very well with their own children.

Strategy 2: Create opportunities to break open the Word of God as a family. There are many ways that a family can share faith together around a reading of scripture. For example, read the assigned Gospel of the day at Sunday brunch and then talk about what people have heard.[9] Or read a piece of scripture as night prayer. When focusing on the scriptures, I suggest four movements: (1) a careful reading with everyone enticed to listen; (2) a question like, "So what did anyone hear for our lives?"; (3) another reading and a comment—perhaps by a parent; and then (4) another question, "So how are we to live the spiritual wisdom of this scripture?" Again, readers will recognize the *life to Faith to life* dynamic.

Strategy 3: Join in the catechetical programs of the parish. This is imperative, of course, for children and youth who are not in Catholic or denominational schools, where there is good religious education. Even those who are in such schools, however, can benefit greatly from the catechetical and youth ministry programs of their parish. Likewise, the adults of a family can enrich their faith by participating in the adult education programs of the parish and then bringing fresh spiritual wisdom back into the home. The ideal would seem to be intergenerational programs—now on the increase—where all the family can participate and the conversation can continue afterward in the household.

Strategy 4: Parents, share faith stories, including your own, with your children. What child doesn't love bedtime stories, and favorites are ones from when their parents or grandparents were children. Why not tell of your First Communion or Confirmation (if you have the pictures, they will be a humorous highlight) and other stories from your own faith journey? At bedtime, I often retell a Bible story to Teddy, with a bit of elaboration. So the guy who helped the man who got jumped by robbers on his way from Jerusalem to Jericho had promised to bring home a gift to each of his kids, and they were wondering what delayed him. When he told them the story, they were really proud of what their dad had done for the poor fellow in the ditch. The donkey that carried Mary to Bethlehem was named Danny and knew well what an important job he had. Later on, he proudly carried her and the child Jesus on their escape to Egypt. Once, when Teddy asked, "Dad, where did they get the Blarney Stone?" I ended up telling the whole story of the Exodus. You see, we don't really know where the Blarney Stone came from, but it might well be a chip off the rock that Moses struck in the desert to find water for his people. I know I'm taking liberties, but the scholars say that the original authors did too, all the better to reach their audience.

Strategy 5: Consider lacing everyday conversation with God-talk and faith language. I state this strategy tentatively, because it may sound out of kilter with our postmodern world. Also, people are usually put off by constant "Praise you, Jesus" talk or other pious platitudes. This is not what I intend.

In my Irish family of origin, there was lots of faith language woven naturally and unpretentiously into everyday patterns of speech: "It's a fine day, thank God" (or more often, "It's a grand soft day, thank God"), "I'll see you tomorrow, please God," and so on. Perhaps we can't return to this pattern, but surely we can retain remnants of it. For example, when someone sneezes, we still say, "Bless you." It is actually more theologically correct to say, "*God* bless you," since it is not we who have the power to bless, only God. And in times of trouble or worry we can remind ourselves that our

Loving God will be with us, and in times of joy we can remember to say "Thanks be to God," and so on. Why not?

To close my reflection on family ministries as catechetical, I reiterate that the home is the primary educator in faith, especially of its children, and the adult members are also enhanced in their spiritual journey by living in a household of faith. None of our families can do all of the above. Mine doesn't, and what we do is far from perfect. But our best intentions and then good efforts to share faith with our children and each other is itself an effective witness, even if never done perfectly.

For Reflection and Conversation

- What liturgy or religious symbols do you have in your home that nurture faith? How can you improve upon your present practice?

- What works of justice or compassion do you practice as a family within the family? Outside of the home? How can you enhance such practices?

- How do you share faith as a family by means of Scripture and Tradition? Are there ways you can enhance these efforts?

Nurturing the Nurturers

If parents are to fulfill their sacred function as the primary religious educators of their children, then they need help from the parish or congregation. The faith community must develop and provide ways to "nurture the nurturers," as Bushnell advised. I said at the outset that this requires intentional programming by the parish to support and engage families and households. A most helpful development since Vatican II has been the enlisting of parents in the sacramental preparation of their children. Now we must imagine well beyond such programs.

Focusing on families is an aspect of the new paradigm shift toward *total community catechesis*. The family and the parish are the foundation stones of this development. The parish needs to offer parents the resources that will enhance their parental ministry. There are lots of printed, audio, and video materials that can help parents. Likewise, family catechesis can begin with the marriage preparation offered by a parish or diocese and then be augmented by the programs for parents when they come to have their children baptized. A parish can network young parents to support each other as households of faith and draw in the help of grandparents as available. There surely needs to be as much preparation for parenting as there is for getting a driver's license.

In sum, the more a parish can invest in the pastoral care and education of its parents and guardians, the more likely it will be to have households of faith that are effective religious educators. Conversely, the more its families become households of faith, the more the parish will flourish as a sacrament of God's reign in the world. Educating for faith in our time calls for a deep partnership between parents and parish.

CHAPTER SEVEN

Catholic Schools as Educators in Faith

A New Vision for Catholic Education

I was invited to give a two-week series of workshops to Catholic school teachers in Pakistan. My host there, Sr. Katherine Prince, had told me to tell them at customs in Karachi that I was coming to Joseph and Mary Convent School. I wondered why that would be helpful in this Muslim country, but it worked like a charm. They whisked me through as if I were a celebrity. As I was to discover, the school is held in very high regard, and is much desired by the powerful families of Karachi for their children.

Besides Joseph and Mary School in Karachi, to my amazement, I found a large network of highly esteemed Catholic schools (over five hundred) throughout Pakistan. In many of these schools, the student body is over 90 percent Muslim, as is the faculty. Still, I came to recognize that they are eminently Catholic schools. In essence, they have found the universal values that are foundational to Catholic faith and have turned them into an educational philosophy that can be embraced by and will benefit any person of goodwill.

For example, the whole curriculum of these schools reflects the value of the person and emphasizes the equal dignity of boys and girls. It encourages a positive outlook on life and challenges the fatalism that often pervades the surrounding culture. It builds up a sense of school community and promotes friendship across class and ethnic divides. It encourages students to develop a personal spirituality, to commit to justice and peace, and to respect those who are different. In addition, the Pakistani Catholic schools have strong academic curricula that encourage students to think critically, to question and come to understanding, and to make personal judgments and decisions, while the government schools favor rote learning. The late Benazir Bhutto often stated that she never would have entered politics or become the first female prime minister of Pakistan, if she had not gone to Jesus and Mary School in Karachi, kindergarten through high school.

That brief experience in Pakistan has helped to shape much of my own reflection and writing about Catholic education since then. I've been particularly focused on *what it is that makes a Catholic school Catholic*. Clearly it is much more than outward symbols like crucifixes on classroom walls or a saint's statue in the foyer. In those Pakistani schools, no Christian symbols are allowed, and, well advised, they scrupulously avoid proselytizing to the Christian faith. In fact, most of the Catholic schools require students to take catechesis in Islam.

In this chapter, my local focus is the eight thousand Catholic schools in the United Sates and their role in whether *there will be faith*. They are unique within Western democracies in that they receive no government aid and depend entirely on tuition and endowments. I will always lament this state of affairs as a blind spot in the great American experiment. It is most ironic that these schools are denied public financing on the grounds that it would not serve the common good, whereas all the research indicates that Catholic schools serve it very well.[1] The renewed vision I propose for Catholic schools in this chapter highlights service to the common good, a defining aspect of Catholic social ethics.[2] Let me also add that my focus is particularly on grade and high schools, although Catholic universities, my context for the past thirty-five years of teaching and research, will be my backdrop.

I'll also be thinking of the vast network of Catholic schools throughout the world. The most recent statistics indicate that there are about 140,000 Catholic schools, serving almost 50 million students. I've personally experienced them on every continent and invariably have been inspired by their commitment to good education and the common good of society. From this, and from my close working relationship with American and Canadian Catholic schools, I'm more convinced than ever of the contribution such schools can make to persons and societies and of the vision that can sustain them.

Chapter 3 proposed that all education is to be a work of humanization. Good education enables people to make and keep life human for themselves and others or, in more spiritual terms, for all "to become fully alive to the glory of God" (St. Irenaeus). It educates people to have a life as well as to make a living. I'm convinced that Catholic schools have the philosophical and spiritual resources to epitomize this vision of humanizing education for persons and to promote the common good of their society, wherever they are located. This is to say that the universal vision for all Catholic schools, as for all ministries sponsored by the Church, is the coming of God's reign. Their vision must be God's vision, calling them to educate for the realization of God's will of fullness of life for all "on earth," regardless of the path their students take home to God.

Catholic schools are already living into this vision, and my intent in this chapter is to lay out the values that can enable them to embrace and realize it all the more. This will amount to a philosophy of Catholic education or, better still, a spirituality of it, because the sustaining values arise from faith convictions that are put to work throughout a school's whole curriculum. I call it a *renewed* vision, however, because, though present throughout church history and suggested by the deep waters of Catholic Christian faith, it was not always what originally prompted the founding of Catholic schools. At least in the English-speaking world, Catholic school systems were developed mostly for defensive reasons, some well warranted. In America, for example, the "public" schools of the 1700s and 1800s were suffused with what were perceived to be Protestant values and, at times, an overt anti-Catholicism. At the Third Plenary Council of Baltimore (1884), the assembled U.S. Catholic bishops decreed that every parish should have a parochial school, because they saw this as essential to preserving the faith of their people. The origin of Catholic schools in Canada, England, Ireland, Australia, New Zealand, and much of the English-speaking world reflects a similar defensive posture.

Presently, however, we're in a very different situation. For example, far from being infused with any values, American public education attempts to be "value free." As a system, it also has profound weaknesses. Some of American public schools are among the best in the world, but some are among the worst (at least in the democratic world). Tragically, they are worst of all where we need them to be best of all, namely, in our inner cities and poor rural areas. Because the funding of public schools is closely tied to the local tax base and because local school boards still, in large part, decide the curriculum, it is sad to say that in America today, "A child's education still depends primarily on zip code."[3] Though many inner-city and rural Catholic schools are threatened with closure, only because of finances, they continue to offer a quality education in many neighborhoods where most needed.

As America now struggles for real educational reform, one would hope that the country may notice an excellent supplemental school system already in its midst. Whether by vouchers or charter school status or by returning to parents in tax deductions the money they save the public treasury by sending their children to Catholic schools (the estimate is about $20 billion a year), the federal government and states could consider giving Catholic schools public financial aid and embracing them as serving the common good of American society.

That they serve the common good can be said of Catholic schools throughout the world. Far from being sectarian, isolationist, or proselytizing, Catholic Christian faith provides the basis of a very life-giving philosophy of education that can enrich the lives of any people, regardless of their faith identity, and make huge contributions to the common good of all. This claim is based on the two-thousand-year history of Catholic education and the fruits it has borne over time.

As I noted in Chapter 3, it was the Christian Church that sponsored and shaped the educational system of the Western world. Even the great universities were originally founded by papal charter and staffed by the then new religious orders. When national school systems began to emerge in the aftermath of the Reformation, the Catholic Church invested even more heavily in schools, both personnel and finances, at first in Europe and then in the mission lands. We can say that the Catholic Church has been by far the largest single sponsor of education in human history. In a great variety of cultures and over a long period of time, Catholic schools have provided high-quality education that has enriched the lives of millions of students, making a huge contribution to their societies. From this rich story we can weave a renewed vision to inspire the best of Catholic education for our time and after.

In particular, Catholic schools can and should provide their students with a high standard of religious education. I'm convinced that they can craft their explicit religious education curriculum to both inform and form the identity of their Catholic students. Likewise, they can provide for students from other traditions either a catechesis in their own faith as numbers warrant or, if they so desire, the opportunity to learn *from* and be enriched by access to the spiritual wisdom and moral values of Catholic Christian faith. There is every good reason, then, for a Catholic school to welcome non-Catholic students. While respecting their own religious tradition, it can provide them with a rich moral and spiritual formation, with a sense of meaning and purpose in life as well as with a good education that prepares them to live well and to be good citizens who contribute to the common good of society.

I hasten to insert a parenthetical caveat here. I am not arguing for the old stereotype that Catholic schools are inevitably more effective in religious education than parish programs. In fact, there is much to indicate that a good parish program within the life of a good parish has "religious learning outcomes" that are comparable to those of a Catholic school.[4] I surely argued for good parishes and programs and their effectiveness as faith educators in Chapter 5. As this chapter represents throughout, the purposes of Catholic schools include but are far broader than the religious education of their pupils. Their transcendent foundation—faith in God—also encourages a humanizing education, suffused with spiritual values, that is powerfully life-giving for all students, regardless of their religion, and serves the common good of all. Nor do my claims here in any way diminish the role of parents and all I've said in Chapter 6. The Catholic school that does not see its function as partnership with parents and does not actively involve them in the education of their children would be an inappropriate one.

I'd also hope that schools sponsored by other Christian traditions might be enriched by the conversation of this chapter. I'm thinking especially of schools sponsored by the Lutheran and Episcopalian Churches, both quite significant in size and influence in the United States and throughout the world.

Wherever they are and whatever their cultural location, Catholic schools should ask, be clear about, and implement "what makes a Catholic school." The Church should know why it sponsors such schools, what it expects them to be and teach as educational institutions, and to what end. I'm convinced that the more truly Catholic they are, the more likely that such schools contribute to the common good through humanizing education, that they educate their Catholic students in Catholic faith, *and* that they enrich the morality and spirituality of all who attend, regardless of faith tradition.

For Reflection and Conversation

- From your perspective, what do you expect from a Catholic school?

- What are some commitments that you would consider essential to a school's Catholic identity?

- How do you imagine Catholic schools contributing to the common good of society?

From the Deep and Fresh Waters of Catholicism

Luke's Gospel recounts an incident when it appears that Jesus simply borrowed Peter's boat for a while, in order to push back from the crowd, all the better to be heard over the water. Peter does not seem to mind; the fish aren't running anyhow. Afterward, and it would seem as recompense, Jesus tells Peter to throw in his nets again, this time into the "deep water." We presume he means a little far-ther offshore. Peter explains that he has "worked all night long and caught nothing," but agrees to do so. Not yet a disciple, Peter must have been at least impressed by Jesus's preaching. To the astonish-ment of Peter and his companions James and John, they get a huge catch. Then Jesus invites them to become disciples and to "catch people" with him through *the way* that he was teaching (5:1–11).

The Greek verb for "catch" there is *zogreo,* which also means to "take alive." Perhaps this is a helpful image for the work of Catholic educators. We are indeed to "catch" people, attracting and actively engaging them as agents of their own learning, so that they may become more fully alive for themselves and for the life of the world. If we go to the deep waters and to the "spring of water gushing up" from Jesus's gospel (John 4:14), then our educating should do as much. Luke reports that Peter and his companions "left everything and followed Jesus." May Catholic educators do likewise.

Inspired by Jesus, the deep and fresh waters of Catholic Chris-tian faith offer to educators great currents of universal values and spiritual wisdom that can satisfy the thirst of learners and inspire educators' own best efforts. The more educators draw upon these currents, the more likely they are to do both good education and good education in faith. Likewise, schools become truly "Catholic" when these currents of value from the depths of Catholicism per-meate the whole curriculum. By the *whole* curriculum, I mean *what* is taught, as in the content, *how* it is taught, as in the pedagogy, *why* it is taught, as in its purposes, *where* it is taught, as in the ethos of the school, and *to whom* it is taught, as in the anthropology that the school presumes and promotes. Like the Muslim children in Paki-stan, everyone in a Catholic school should be educated by the whole curriculum to a deep faith in God, in others, in themselves, and in life. In addition, the religion curriculum for those who choose it should educate in Catholic Christian faith.

The remainder of this chapter summarizes some of the deep and universal values that must permeate Catholic education in order to render it truly *Catholic*. I will name eight commitments around an understanding of: (1) the human person (anthropology); (2) creation and life in the world (cosmology); (3) human relationality (sociology); (4) knowledge and the ways of knowing (epistemology); (5) historicity; (6) politics; (7) spirituality; and (8) "catholicity." When we weave together the Catholic perspectives on these issues, they become a philosophy or, better still, a spirituality that can inspire educators and schools to provide a truly Catholic education, wherever it takes place. It is indeed the case that the rationale I suggest for this spirituality of education arises from the deep waters of Catholic Christian faith. I'm confident, however, that its values and the vision they suggest can be embraced by all people of goodwill, especially from other great religious traditions. Though people might have different rationales for holding them, these values are universal. I summarize here what I've written about at length elsewhere.[5]

A Catholic Anthropology: Made and Growing in the Divine Image

Chapter 2 reviewed what might be considered a classic Catholic anthropology, in other words, an understanding of the human person from the perspective of Catholic Christian faith. We saw that Catholicism represents an essentially positive understanding of the person, insisting that we are all made in God's image and ever invited to grow in divine likeness. A Catholic anthropology reflects a balance of three convictions about us, sometimes held in tension: (1) that the divine image and likeness is a permanent gift, never lost to us; (2) that we are originally capable of personal sins and social sinfulness; (3) yet that we have been "saved" and restored to our divine potential by God's abundant grace through the incarnation, life, death, and resurrection of Jesus Christ.

This positive view of our human condition constitutes what the great theologian Bernard Lonergan (1904–84) called "a realistic optimism," with *optimism* about our inner goodness and potential being the defining noun. To say that we are made in the likeness of our creator affirms the dignity, equality, and value of every person. It means that all people deserve the highest respect and possess inalienable rights and responsibilities. Beyond this, as reflections of our Creator, we have an "inner vitality" (or call it the "soul") for learning, creating, and shaping our world and who we become.[6] Likewise, we possess an innate capacity—a "natural law"—that enables us to know and disposes us to choose good more than evil, truth more than falsehood. In fact, we are capable of being partners with God within human history, of improving, by God's grace (effective love), our own and other people's lives, and of working for the coming of God's reign in the world.

For Education: Writing almost four hundred years ago, John Amos Comenius (1592–1670), the great educational reformer who influenced many reformers who came after him (Johann Pestalozzi, Friedrich Herbart, John Dewey, Maria Montessori, Jean Piaget), founded his whole educational philosophy on the conviction that all people are made in the divine image and likeness. Comenius argued that if teachers could become convinced of this, it would revolutionize education toward the great humanizing enterprise it should be.

The conviction that we are made in God's image surely calls for holistic education that engages the whole person, head, heart, and hands. It should fully develop the capacities of learners' minds for reason, memory, and imagination; the capacities of their hearts for right and loving relationships; the capacities of their wills to know, choose, and live the best of values and life-giving virtues. Given peoples' "inner vitality," they need to be active participants in the teaching/learning dynamic, agents of their own knowing and not just passive recipients. They should be empowered in their great human potential and be prepared to be makers of history toward God's reign. Called to be more than the creatures of their culture, they should be educated as its creators and re-creators as well. In the sentiment of St. Irenaeus of old, a good Catholic education is to enable its participants to become "fully alive to the glory of God."

A Catholic Cosmology: A Sacramental Outlook on Life in the World

From the Greek *cosmos,* meaning "world," and *logos,* meaning a "word about" or "understanding of," cosmology is the old philosophical term for people's outlook on life in the world. In plainer terms, we might call people's cosmology the tinted lenses through which they look at everything and in consequence what they "see." How we understand our own lives and what life is all about has a profound influence on how we live and engage in the world. It pertains to how we make meaning, whether or not we find life to be worthwhile and ourselves to have purpose within it. My grandmother would often repeat that "attitude is everything," and I think she was right—in large part.

A favorite youth ministry poster of my vintage said wisely, "God never makes junk." As with its outlook on the person, Catholic faith sees all of God's creation as essentially good and with purpose and meaning. The same is true of culture, that is, of what we humans create as participants in God's creativity. Although we can put the work of our hands toward evil and destruction, what we cultivate is never inherently evil. This is why Catholicism has never condemned

dancing, singing, celebrating, good food, or even alcohol, allowing
Catholics a little more fun at times. Although all of creation can
be abused and, now we know, destroyed, all is first and foremost a
gift of God. We are to enjoy it according to its proper ends and be
good stewards of its integrity. Our own lives in the world are to be
embraced and celebrated, cherished and defended from womb to
tomb. We are ever called to "choose life" (Deut. 30:19) and to live
life "to the full" (John 10:10, JB). We can embrace the world and our
lives within it as meaningful and worthwhile not because of our
efforts to make them so, but because the world and our lives arise
from what the theologian Paul Tillich (1886–1965) called "ultimate
meaning" and "the ultimate ground of Being"—which is God.[7]
The richest possible outlook on life in the world is that everything
arises from God who *is* Love and is *in* love with us.

This graciousness of life in the world finds its high point in the
sacramental principle that is so constitutive of a Catholic outlook.
This is the conviction that God reaches out to us, and we respond
through the ordinary and everyday of life—through nature and the
created order, through our relationships, through all our good efforts, and through the experiences that come our way. This sacramental principle is climaxed, of course, by the seven great sacraments
we celebrate in church. Even there, however, God reaches out to us
through "the ordinary"—bread and wine, oil and water, community and lovemaking in marriage. The great seven and the sacramental principle that they symbolize most effectively encourage an
outlook that views life in the world as both gift and responsibility
(as always with God's grace), that encourages us to see the more in
the midst of the ordinary and even "to see God in all things" (St.
Ignatius of Loyola).

For Education: Education inspired by such a cosmology should
nurture in people a tremendously positive outlook on their own life
in the world, on creation, and on culture. It should indeed dispose

them to "choose life" and, as I've said already, prepare them to have a life as well as to make a living. It ought to shape their imagination to see the potential and the possibilities for themselves and for society. It should educate them to pay attention to life and the world around them, to look at everything with curiosity and appreciation, and then to look through it all as well, ever alert for "the more than meets the eye." In faithfulness to such a cosmology, Catholic education should encourage the generativity of students to make their own contribution to human culture. Likewise, it should give them a deep sense of stewardship toward nature, empowering them to be partners with God in caring for creation and enabling it to flourish. In sum, it is to foster in people a sacramental outlook on themselves and on life in the world.

When I was in high school, I had the same teacher for science and religion. I'd have to say that he did more in science class to foster a sacramental outlook on life than he did in religion class. In the latter, he was "by the book"; whatever the Church taught had to be accepted without question, even if it meant little to our lives. In science class, however, he came alive as an educator and constantly called us to wonder, awe, and amazement at creation. Whether we were looking through a microscope or telescope, he would bring us beyond the immediate and obvious, and although rarely using explicit God-talk in science class, he disposed us to imagine the Creator reflected in the created order.

A Catholic Sociology: Made for Each Other

Sociology refers to our understanding (*logos*) of our human relationality, our *socius* that prompts us to associate with others. As noted before, the Catholic perspective is that the person is inherently relational. We are not "individuals" who stand alone and enter into community by choice and only when to our advantage. Instead, we become human and can live humanly only through community. We are literally "made for each other." The understanding that God made us naturally communal is the basis of our personal and social ethics. On a personal level, we *are* our brother's and sister's keeper, responsible for and to one another. Socially, our communal nature is the foundation of Catholicism's emphasis that every citizen is responsible to contribute to the common good of society. We are truest to who we are and are meant to be by God when we care for the common well-being as well as for our own.

Our communal nature reflects and shares in the inner life of God, in whose triune image of right and loving relationship we are made. This emphasis on being communal "by nature" (read, by God's design) is further highlighted by Christian faith, which makes community the context and condition for discipleship to Jesus. Christians are to function as the Body of Christ in the world, with all the members working together to continue God's saving mission in Jesus. Thus, by nature and by faith, we are encouraged to embrace and live our communality. We are ever both persons-in-community and a community-of-persons.

For Education: Such a sociology calls for education that builds up community in both society and church. To be faithful to its identity, a Catholic school would itself have to function as a life-giving community that reflects and teaches profound respect for everyone and that promotes people's rights *as* neighbor and their responsibilities *for* neighbor. Likewise, it should teach people how to work well together and prepare good citizens for society, citizens who contribute to the common good as well as to their own. The Catholic school must educate people to transcend ethnic and racial barriers, to be open to "the other," and to forge solidarity with all people.

The very pedagogy of such a school should encourage cooperative learning, collaboration and mutual support, conversation, and partnership among students within the teaching/learning dynamic. The "lone ranger" in competition with all the rest, so pervasive in our society now, is the antithesis of the communal self-understanding at the foundation of a Catholic school and education.

A Catholic Epistemology: A Reasonable Wisdom for Life

The Greek *episteme* means "knowledge," and epistemology refers to how we know and what we mean by knowledge. Clearly this is a foundational issue for schools and educators; a constitutive purpose of every school is to promote knowledge. But what do we mean by knowledge and what way of knowing is a school to favor? There is, I believe, a recognizable Catholic response to these questions that should shape the operative epistemology of Catholic schools. We find its roots in the biblical word and then in the great scholars of the tradition like Augustine and Aquinas; more recently, Bernard Lonergan has developed and clarified further what would be a "Catholic" epistemology (more in Chapter 8 under a praxis epistemology).

A Catholic epistemology honors the whole person—the mind and will, the body and emotions—in the knowing process. First, the data that is presented to the mind comes in through the senses, from people's own sensory encounters and lived experience. Then the mind reflects on the data, using its innate structures for reason, memory, and imagination. When all three capacities are in play, people can think critically, historically, and creatively. Then people's minds and emotions work together when they are invited beyond paying attention to data and understanding it to making judgments and decisions about what they understand. It is people's emotions and their experiences from life that dispose their wills to make wise judgments and good decisions. Without engaging the affective and experiential, people are likely to stop at understanding, at the purely theoretical, and not move on to judgments and decisions. In moving beyond understanding to judgments and decisions, however, they can hold theoretical and practical knowledge in a fruitful tension; in other words, what they know can shape how they live and who they become.

Because it engages and unites both intellect and will, intelligence and emotions, ideas and experience and encourages understanding, judgments, and decision, such an epistemology invites people beyond knowledge toward wisdom for life. Wisdom arises as people make good judgments and wise decisions out of what they experience and understand. A wisdom way of knowing encourages people to take on the responsibilities of knowledge, to put what they know to good use *for fullness of life for all.*

I highlight that such an epistemology engages the agency of the knowers in the knowing/wisdom process. It draws upon their own experience and encourages them to "think for themselves." However, it also emphasizes community and conversation as the best context for knowing and gaining knowledge. In other words, we are to think *for* ourselves, but not just *by* ourselves. Further, such reflection should be absolutely unfettered and free. As St. Augustine insisted, all truth is of God. Probing and questioning leads to the truth, and there must be total academic freedom in its pursuit.

For Education: In describing the epistemology we have already indicated the implications for education. Clearly, a Catholic education should encourage people to draw upon their own experience and to probe it for its wisdom *from* and *for* life. Likewise, it should promote critical and creative thinking, an open pursuit of knowledge and wisdom, and help people to realize and embrace the responsibilities of their knowledge. It champions probing, questioning, and free inquiry, confident that all answers will lead to more questions and eventually into Mystery, not mystery that we cannot explain, but mystery that explains everything, namely, a God who loves us. The Catholic school is to create an ethos of scholarship that pursues academic excellence as both theoretical knowledge and practical wisdom.

Catholic education should give people a passion for pursuing the truth—cognitive, relational, and moral—wherever it can be found. It should teach people how to learn, giving them the tools and disposition to go on learning all their lives. Indeed, the ancient monastic tradition was convinced that the love for learning was symbiotic with the desire for God.[8] The great philosopher Alfred North Whitehead (1861–1947) claimed that "the essence of education is that it be religious" in that it is to inculcate both "duty and reverence," the latter being the human reach for "eternity."[9] Surely all Catholic education can become "religious" as Whitehead intends it.

For Reflection and Conversation

- As you embrace a positive outlook on the person and on life in the world, what practical differences might this make to your educating?

- Do you agree with the Catholic emphasis on community and on educating for spiritual wisdom? Why or why not?

- If so, what might be some implications for your own work as educator?

A Catholic Historicity: The Wisdom of the Ages

What about the knowledge, wisdom, and arts that have arisen from the experiences and experimentation of those who went before us? Is it imperative that we learn from the legacy of history, or is that all "outdated" now by our present discoveries, insights, and creations? The great Protestant theologian Langdon Gilkey claimed that one of Catholicism's great strengths is that it appreciates "the reality, importance, and 'weight' of tradition and history."[10] Indeed, this is true.

A Catholic historicity reflects the conviction that the traditions from the past, however they are carried (the sciences, humanities, and arts, the Scripture and Tradition of Christian faith), are a rich legacy for our time, a source of knowledge and wisdom. As mentioned earlier, John Dewey described this historical resource as "the funded capital of civilization."[11] We deserve to inherit this great humanizing "capital." Without it, we'd be greatly impoverished. This appreciation and respect for past "capital" does not mean that we are to passively inherit and simply repeat it. Life is always an open horizon. Our present and future are not reruns and should not be held captive by the past. This being said, we need to appropriate reflectively and creatively the legacy of the past, appreciating its knowledge and wisdom, questioning its shortcomings and limitations, and building upon it to create what is life-giving in our present and future.

Following on, Catholicism is convinced that there are great universal truths and time-tested values, things that have always and will always be true, everywhere and for all time. For example, justice may vary in application from one circumstance to another, but it is a universal value that is true and demanded in every time and place. Likewise, it will always be true that God loves all people, equally.

This pushes back against the current of postmodern sentiments that everything is relative and contextual, depending on whatever time and place we're in, as if history and its legacy have little value.

In the context of Christian faith, this valuing of history and what has been handed on to us calls for a deep commitment to and appreciation of Scripture and Tradition as sources of God's ongoing revelation to people's lives today. Our "pilgrim's progress" toward the ongoing/coming of God's reign goes on unabated, and the Holy Spirit continues to guide the Church in interpreting for each time in history how to faithfully live the truths handed down to us through Scripture and Tradition. As Vatican II reminds, Scripture, Tradition, and the Church "are so linked and joined together that one cannot stand without the others"; they "all work together . . . under the action of the Holy Spirit" for "the salvation of souls" (Dogmatic Constitution on Divine Revelation, nn. 9, 10).

For Education: Given the above, a Catholic school needs to provide a strong curriculum that teaches the humanities, sciences, and arts. It should enable people to inherit the "funded capital of civilization" and to draw new life from it for the present and future. Such rigorous scholarship, however, need not be simply learning *about* the resources of the past, but learning *from* them for our time and in ways that enable the present to make its unique contribution and leave its own legacy to the future. The word "liberal" in what was traditionally called the "liberal arts" signified "liberating." Catholic education should be freeing for persons and societies, indeed a source of liberating salvation.

For the explicit religious education curriculum of a Catholic school, this aspect requires a thoroughgoing and comprehensive study of Scripture and Christian Tradition according to learners' developmental readiness and abilities. At every grade level, however, what is taught to represent Catholic faith should reflect the teaching of the Church's magisterium and the best of contemporary

biblical and theological scholarship. It should be taught with peda-
gogies that enable students to bring their lives to their Faith and
their Faith to their lives with personal conviction and commitment.
People from other religious traditions who attend Catholic schools
should have the option to be exposed to Christian faith and morals
so as to learn *from* them or, when feasible according to numbers and
budget, to receive catechesis in their own tradition.

A Catholic Politics: Justice for All

Previous chapters have well reviewed why a commitment to social
justice is a mandate of Christian faith. Here I simply note again that
all education is a political activity of sorts in that it shapes the lives
of people and how they participate in the public realm. It is amply
clear that the Catholic school is to promote a politics of justice for
all, a commitment to educate people both to live justly in their own
lives and to work for justice and peace in the world. This justice
must be for all levels of life, personal, communal, and societal, and
be of all kinds, commutative, distributive, social, and restorative.
It must encourage people to be like our compassionate God, going
beyond giving "everyone their due" to favor the ones who need the
favor most, the poor of any and every kind.

For Education: A Catholic education should encourage people to
think contextually, in other words, to be able to analyze how systems work, to uncover the ideologies that legitimate them, and to
recognize how culture and location shape their own thinking and
outlook. These abilities are often described as social analysis, their
intent being to raise people's "social consciousness." In the Gospels,
Jesus often blesses those who have "the eyes to see" and "the ears to
hear" what should be seen and heard in life. At the final judgment,

Jesus portrays the damned as saying, "We never saw"—the poor, the needy, and so forth. He makes clear, however, that such a defense will not be acceptable.

Our injustices are often hidden or made to seem legitimate, as if this is the way things should be. Catholic education must enable people to see what should be seen in society. And beyond seeing what should be seen, Catholic education is to empower people to redress situations of injustice and dispose them to work for change toward justice for all.

Every graduate of a Catholic school should emerge with a deep commitment to promoting the quality of life, to justice as a seamless garment, and to protecting the integrity of creation. Graduates should have a fire in the belly for justice at every level in church and in society. They ought to come out committed to oppose all sinful social structures and to help reform them or create new ones. In Catholic schools, justice and peace—the coming of God's reign—should be a standard guideline for what and how to teach across all subjects. Conversely, if graduates of Catholic schools emerge with social biases and prejudices, if they come out sexist, racist, elitist, ageist, homophobic, or biased in any other way, we have not given them a truly Catholic education. To practice what it preaches, a Catholic school should have a special favor for the "poor" students, the ones who need some added tutorial and attention.

A Catholic Spirituality: A God-Shaped Hollow in the Human Heart

The very foundation of Catholic education is faith in God as revealed in Jesus Christ, with the intent of being an instrument to continue God's saving work in the world through the power of the Holy Spirit. As such, the whole curriculum of Catholic schools should be suffused with spirituality. In contrast to some very privatized understandings in New Age spirituality—a warm, fuzzy feeling between "me and God"—a Catholic spirituality means to bring a God-consciousness to all of life and to live the divine-human partnership. In other words, spirituality is living as if one really believes in and relates to God, which amounts to "putting faith to work" in the everyday of life. For educators, this will amount to letting their faith suffuse the whole curriculum—the *what, why, how, where,* and *who* of their educating.

It is worth noting again that the biblical sense of both justice and holiness of life are the same, namely, right relationship with God, self, others, and creation. Thus, our commitment to justice needs to be sustained by our spirituality, and our spirituality must express itself in the works of justice and compassion. Add to this the fact that a specifically Christian spirituality calls people to discipleship to Jesus, to follow *the way* that he modeled and made possible. This is marked most eminently by the radical law of love of God, self, and neighbor, with no limits to who is neighbor. Beyond justice, peace, and compassion, however, a Catholic spirituality should also bring the fruits of gratitude, joy, and celebration to people's lives. Growth into such holiness is a lifelong journey; it is sustained by community and conversation, by good spiritual practices, by personal prayer and communal worship.

Catholic faith also reflects the conviction that all people are inherently spiritual. Alive by God's own life (Gen. 2:7), we are endowed with a natural affinity or, better still, an "original grace" that sparks the spiritual in us. God's desire for us prompts our desire for God. Thus, "care of soul" becomes a key requirement for living humanly. I cite him again, because the great French philosopher Blaise Pascal said it well, "There's a God-shaped hollow in the human heart that nothing else can fill."

For Education: Simply stated, a Catholic school is to nurture the spirituality of its students, inculcating in them a "care of soul" that will be lifelong. It should give them access to the great spiritual wisdom of Catholic Christian faith. Indeed, one of Catholicism's richest resources is the extraordinary spiritual charisms that have arisen throughout its history (Ignatian, Benedictine, Franciscan, Carmelite, Mercy, Celtic, etc.) and continue to be vibrant today. Catholic schools can educate people to bring their lives to their faith (whatever their faith may be) and their faith to their lives. This is the kind of education that nurtures people's spirituality. It should encourage people to join with a faith community and to be in conversation with fellow pilgrims on the spiritual journey. In fact, the school itself should offer spiritual opportunities for both faith community and conversation.

In addition, the whole curriculum and pedagogy of a Catholic school should reflect the spiritual nature of its students. Plato described the function of the teacher as "turning the soul" of students toward the true, the good, and the beautiful. Well, to "turn the soul" one must engage it. In other words, Catholic education should often get down into "the deep heart's core" (Yeats) of people, into their interiority and personhood—the soul. There they will engage what Augustine called "the teacher within," by which he meant their own spiritual vitality for learning and knowing.[12]

A Catholic Universality: People Without Borders

We like to say that "catholic" means universal, and indeed it does. But that was Aristotle's favored meaning of the word. Its roots are the Greek *katha holos,* which literally means "to include everyone." This was likely why early Christian authors like St. Ignatius of Antioch (d. 107) began to use it to describe the Christian community. The first Christians were keenly aware of and committed to welcoming all comers and to reaching out to all in need—regardless of their religion. However, James Joyce may have said it best (in *Finnegans Wake*): "Catholic means here comes everybody."

To be "catholic" calls a community to include all people in its hospitality and care. It demands that we reach out with love for everyone, the neighbors next door and those on the far side of the world. It means to care without borders. Though such education is to ground its Catholic students in the particulars of Catholic Christian faith, it should open them to the universal as well, to the universality of God's love, saving intent, and self-disclosure among all people. A truly "catholic" attitude requires respect for people and religions that are different and being open to learn from them as well as to share with them.[13]

St. Augustine's favored use of "catholic" means to be open to the truth, wherever it can be found. Parochialism and closed-mindedness are antithetical to Catholic faith and thus to Catholic education. Likewise, authors often point to Catholicism's disposition to embrace what are seeming paradoxes, to say "both . . . and" instead of "either . . . or" to many of the tensions of life and faith. So Catholics affirm both nature and grace, reason and revelation, Scripture and Tradition, Good Friday and Easter Sunday, personal and communal prayer, marriage and celibacy, and the list goes on.

For Education: A truly Catholic education ought to nurture in people an inclusive and universal consciousness, enabling them to welcome in and reach out to all comers. It should encourage a deep respect and appreciation for—not just toleration of—every "other." As a result, it is to forge in people an openness of mind, heart, and hands that will prepare them to learn from, relate with, and reach out to anyone and everyone of goodwill. A Catholic education should open people in their quest for truth, wherever it can be found. While giving people a sense of identity within their own particular faith and culture, it should open them to the universal as well, instilling and reflecting the conviction of God's love for all people.

Catholic education is to prepare people to live with, even to embrace, the paradoxes of life. Life in Christian faith is full of them. An either-or stance is what most often leads to war and violence, injustice and oppression. Again, to highlight the opposite, if students come out of Catholic schools with attitudes that reflect sectarianism, parochialism, and closed-mindedness, we have not given them a Catholic education.

Weaving a Vision for Catholic Education:

As throughout *Will There Be Faith?* the guiding vision of Catholic education here—as a ministry of the Church—is the reign of God. This amounts to the realization by God's grace in Jesus Christ of God's vision of fullness of life for all humankind and the good stewardship of creation. For Catholic education this vision translates into commitment to a humanizing education for persons and serving the common good of society. Catholic educators are called to stretch into this vision by implementing the following values throughout the whole school curriculum:

1. A positive understanding of the human person and the great potential of every student;
2. A sacramental outlook on life in the world, seeing "the more than meets the eye";
3. A commitment to community that is all for one and one for all;

4. A participative and holistic way of knowing that is likely to lead people to wisdom and responsibility;

5. An appreciation and reclaiming of the "funded capital of civilization" bequeathed from our foreparents, with central emphasis on accessing the spiritual wisdom of Scripture and Tradition;

6. A politics that is deeply committed to justice for all;

7. A spirituality that puts faith to work in the everyday;

8. A "catholicity" that has no borders to its welcome and outreach.

Many of these commitments overlap, and none can stand alone. When woven together, however, they amount to a Catholic philosophy and spirituality of education.

For Reflection and Conversation

- In conversation with the proposals made in this chapter, imagine you are explaining to someone the value of a Catholic education. What would you be sure to highlight?

- Whatever your context might be, how might you practice the deep values of a "Catholic" education?

The Whole Curriculum

Some years ago, Eliot Eisner insightfully distinguished between the explicit, the implicit, and the null curriculum; the last constitutes what schools choose not to teach.[14] In many ways we have already reviewed what should be the *explicit* curriculum of a Catholic school.

In this closing section I encourage schools to look at their *implicit* curriculum as well. To this end, it may help to use the schema of ministries from the two previous chapters. My intent is to sharpen the intentionality of a Catholic school to educate in faith. Although a school is not a parish, yet, in its own way, a Catholic school can reflect all the functions of Catholic ministry. Let's see!

Kerygma *and* Didache: *The School as a Community of the Word:* By way of religious education, this is clearly the primary function of a Catholic school, which is why I list it first. All that I've said above and in the previous chapter about the need to offer comprehensive and ready access to the whole Story and Vision of Christian faith by an engaging and reflective pedagogy echoes again here.

For American Catholic high schools, the *Doctrinal Elements of a Curriculum Framework for the Development of Catechetical Materials for Young People of High School Age,* issued by the U.S. Conference of Catholic Bishops (November 2007) can be helpful. Though reflecting a very traditionalist reading of the *Catechism of the Catholic Church,* its primary source of content, this document can ensure that young people of high-school age will be taught a comprehensive and age-appropriate review of Catholic Christian faith. Of course, any such curricula need to be taught with a pedagogy that actively engages students and gives them access to the teachings and wisdom of Christian faith in ways that both reflect good theology and are meaningful to their lives. To reiterate, religious education should always be good education.

Koinonia: *The School as a Community of Welcome:* In a truly "catholic" school, all should feel welcome and included, regardless of their talents, religious background, ability to pay, and all other false criteria. Clearly, many of our schools have miles to travel before we can claim to be truly "catholic." Likewise, all students should be nurtured in genuine hospitality and in openness of mind, heart, and hands. A Catholic school is also to encourage its students to participate in their neighboring parish or congregation, working in partnership with its local faith communities.

Marturia: The School as a Community of Witness: All that a school represents by its ethos and atmosphere, explicitly or implicitly, should bear witness to the truths and values of Catholic Christian faith. This pertains to everything about the school: its mission statement, its objectives, its budget, the causes it supports, the modes of discipline it mediates, where it places its priorities, and so on. All should be distinctly Christian in their basis and implementation.

Leitourgia: The School as a Community of Worship: The Catholic school need not try to replace or replicate the local parish. Yet it should provide opportunities for communal worship, at least on occasion (e.g., feast days, anniversaries, graduations). Some of the most meaningful liturgies I've participated in have been in some context of a Catholic school. Likewise, a Catholic school needs to have a chaplaincy that nurtures the spiritual growth of the community through retreats, opportunities for shared prayer, and spiritual mentoring.

Diakonia: The School as a Community of Well-being: What a Catholic school teaches in its explicit curriculum should encourage a faith that does justice for peace. It can also provide service learning programs as an integral aspect of its curriculum, both teaching the rationale for such works of justice and compassion and encouraging students to reflect critically upon their actual praxis of social service.

Now, regardless of the context, whether it is in the home, the parish, the program, or a church-sponsored school, I have a distinctive approach to recommend for the pedagogy of educating in Christian faith. With the building blocks now in place, I'm ready to explain it in detail. How to go about a *life to Faith to life* approach will occupy us in Chapters 8 and 9.

CHAPTER EIGHT

Life to Faith to Life: The Foundations

An Approach of Shared Christian Praxis

I've been looking forward to this moment. I hope you have too. I'm eager to explain, in a user-friendly way, what I've referred to repeatedly throughout as a *life to Faith to life* approach to religious education and catechesis. In this chapter, I set out its rationale. In Chapter 9, I review the pedagogical movements by which a parent, teacher, or pastoral leader can put it to work in any event of faith education.

I began teaching and writing about this approach to religious education some thirty-five years ago, and I called it *a shared Christian praxis approach*. That is still a good name for it, but takes a lot of explaining. Then one day in 1992 I was presenting the approach in Vilnius, Lithuania. I was working with an interpreter, which made it all the more challenging, although I had a fine one. I could tell from people's faces that I wasn't being successful. At the first break time, my interpreter, Birute, asked, "Tom, what do you really mean by a shared Christian praxis approach?" I responded, "It's alarmingly simple. It is a pedagogy that encourages people to bring their lives to their Faith and their Faith to their lives." Birute broke into a smile and said, "Why don't I tell them so." When she did, there was ready recognition, as if we'd all come to see something obvious. The value is that *life to Faith to life* states precisely and patently the dynamics involved, allowing people to begin to imagine how to implement such a pedagogy or conversation.

After writing some big books about it and many years of trying to teach and model the approach—never perfectly—I'm happy to describe it now with this pithy and simple phrase. I hasten to add that it is far from a simplistic or fail-safe approach. Like all effective teaching, it requires intentionality, preparation, and some deep convictions on the part of the religious educator (summarized at the end of this chapter). Much of the rationale is already woven throughout the previous chapters of this book. I collect and amplify it here.

Bringing *life to Faith and Faith to life* recommends a pattern that religious educators can follow in a teaching/learning event. It suggests the pedagogical moves to make at the beginning, the middle, and the end. Yet, as I elaborate in Chapter 9, the sequencing of its movements has great flexibility, with many possible variations and combinations. Even more important than the pedagogical moves are the commitments and attitudes that undergird them and, indeed, the approach in general.

So anyone aspiring to take this approach must commit to creating a community of conversation among participants; to actively engage them as agents of their own and one another's learning; to invite them to express and reflect critically on their lives in dialogue with each other; to lend them ready, persuasive, and meaningful (connecting with their lives) access to Christian Story and Vision; to encourage them to appropriate its teachings and spiritual wisdom as their own; and to invite them to make decisions for lived Christian faith. Or, in nonconfessional contexts, the intent must be that participants at least learn *from* it for their lives.

The approach becomes almost instinctive as teachers, parents, and pastoral leaders make it their own. Yet it is much more than a skill. It requires intentionality throughout every event: being conscious of the participants and theme of the occasion; keeping them actively engaged; devising effective questions and questioning activities; imagining how best to access Christian Story and Vision, so that it resonates and connects in meaningful ways with these participants' lives; ever encouraging and moving the conversation toward the hoped-for learning outcomes. Regardless of the approach, good pedagogy is always a challenge and demands such intentionality throughout every teaching/learning event. There is no "surefire" formula or way to educate well. After some thirty-five years of trying to model this approach in my own work and ministry, I still consider myself a novice. I marvel at how often I do it poorly and am ever learning how to do it better.

I stumbled into this approach myself, beginning with a high-school religion class I tried to teach in 1968—I was just a few years older than the students—and from many other experiences and influences since then. Let me name two that were most significant. One is the statement in Vatican II's Pastoral Constitution on the Church in the Modern World (*Gaudium et Spes*): "They [are] wide of the mark who think that religion consists in acts of worship alone . . . and who imagine they can plunge themselves into earthly affairs in such a way as to imply that these are altogether divorced from the religious life. *This split between the faith which many Christians profess and their daily lives deserves to be counted among the more serious errors of our age*" (n. 43, emphasis added).

I remember being totally taken with this statement when I read it as a young college student, shortly after it appeared. Writing in 1965, one might expect that the Council would name the most "serious error of our age" as Communism, materialism, individualism, or a host of other candidates. Instead, it names the divide that we Christians maintain between the faith we profess and our daily lives in the world. It rang so true to me, and still does. Even then I began to imagine how we might educate so that we Christians, by God's grace, might be a little more likely to integrate our lives and Faith into a lived, living, and life-giving faith.

While this may sound as though I'm loading the dice, the second great influence was paying attention to the pedagogy of Jesus throughout the Gospels, in particular as epitomized by the Stranger on the road to Emmaus. We reviewed this in Chapter 1. Here I simply urge readers to revisit that text (Luke 24:13–34) and to note again Jesus's pedagogy. First, the Stranger joins the disciples' company and walks *with* them. Then, instead of telling them what to see, the Risen Christ invites the two lost disciples to turn to their own lives, to reflect upon them by sharing the "story and vision" of their most recent experience. This they do, recounting their confused version of what had happened and what they *were* hoping" the Messiah would achieve, namely, that he would be "the one who would set Israel free." Only then does he lead them into the Faith tradition. Beginning with Moses and all the prophets, he interprets for them every passage of scripture that referred to himself and explains that the Messiah had to suffer in order to enter into his glory. This sets up a dialectic between the disciples' image of the hoped-for Messiah and the one who actually came—a suffering servant, not a political liberator.

Now their own *life* and the Story and Vision of their Faith tradition are on the table. Amazingly, however, the Stranger still doesn't tell them what to see, but waits for them to come to see for themselves. And they do, in the breaking of the bread, always a privileged locus for "seeing" what should be seen. The disciples are now ready to return to life again with renewed and deepened faith. So they turn around and head back to Jerusalem. This would have been a hazardous journey late at night. But when people come to see for themselves (recognition as much as cognition), they feel compelled to go share it, preach it, teach it, live it. That Emmaus road story will always be a paradigmatic example for me of mentoring people from *life to Faith to life.*

Throughout this chapter I take the instance of teaching *Christian* faith, which makes it a *life to Christian faith to life* approach. However, from the good work of friends and former students, I know that this approach can be effective in teaching many of the great religious traditions. Likewise, it is ideal for teaching religion in nonconfessional contexts, so that participants may learn *from* it for their lives. Before we go any further, pause for your own reflections on life.

For Reflection and Conversation

- Describe your own approach to doing religious education— very broadly defined.

- How did you develop this approach? Trace some of the influences that shaped it.

- What aspects are you happy about? Name the positives you recognize in your approach.

- What might you want to improve or do differently?

From the Wisdom of the Ages and the Mind of the Church

A challenge for religious education today is recognizing that all of our churches have gotten a long way away from the pedagogy of Jesus. Until quite recently, the typical mode of religious education was a very didactic process of a teacher *telling* (usually children) what to believe and how to live. It did little to actively engage participants or to draw upon their own lives—their experiences, or what I will call here their praxis. The dominant pedagogy was memorizing catechism questions and answers (Catholic) or Bible verses and stories (Protestant).

Great improvements have been made in recent years, and the *life to Faith to life* approach stands on sound shoulders. At the beginning of the twentieth century, education was becoming a formal science of study, as were its related disciplines, such as the psychology of learning. Religious educators, both Catholic and Protestant, began to turn to these sciences for guidance and improved teaching methods, realizing that religious education should also be good education. A major breakthrough for Catholic catechesis was a movement called the Munich Method.

Initiated within the archdiocese of Munich, Germany, around 1900, it was a significant departure from memorizing a catechism. Its pedagogical movements were *preparation* (getting students interested), *presentation* (clear and sequential), *explanation* (for understanding), *association* (within the broader scheme of Faith), and *application* (to life). This sequence actively engaged students in the teaching/learning dynamic and encouraged them to correlate the instruction in Christian faith with their everyday lives.

A similar pedagogy emerged in the Sunday schools of Protestant churches. In the United States, leading Protestant religious educators like George Albert Coe (1862–1951) were much influenced by the pedagogy of John Dewey, with its emphasis on "reconstructing experience" as an entrée into learning the "funded capital of civilization." The stated purpose of the Religious Education Association, founded in 1903, was "to bring education to religion and religion to education."

By the mid-twentieth century, two dominant and sometimes competing approaches to religious education were evident. Though known by different titles, again they were parallel movements in Catholic and Protestant contexts. Among Catholics, they were distinguished as the "kerygmatic" and "experiential" approaches. The first was launched by the Austrian Jesuit Fr. Josef Jungmann (1889–1975) and carried on, after the Vatican silenced Jungmann, by the latter's student, Johannes Hoffinger S.J. (1905–86). Kerygmatic catechesis centered on the scriptures and the "story of salvation," a major shift for Catholics. Jungmann championed bringing the gospel into people's lives as good news.[1] However, another group of scholars (Alfonse Nebreda, Pierre Babin, Marcel Van Caster, Gabriel Moran) recognized that people must first be "readied" to receive the gospel message, that is, preevangelized. This requires turning students first to their own experience and then using a more inductive approach to teaching the Faith.

In Protestant circles, a strong sentiment continued that religious education (the favored term) should be primarily inductive, beginning with human experience. Religious education should engage students to reflect on their own lives, build up community, and ready them to "change the world" (a George A. Coe slogan). On the other hand, the influence of Karl Barth (1886–1968) and his neoorthodoxy movement encouraged a group of *Christian* educators (their preferred title) to favor a more didactic approach, with renewed emphasis on teaching "the Bible and sound doctrine."

Here I make a parenthetical note. I understand the *life to Faith to life* approach as bringing together both kerygmatic and experiential catechesis, both religious education and Christian education.[2] It is *inductive* in that it engages people to reflect on their own lives and *deductive* in that it is committed to thorough instruction in Christian faith, albeit in ways that echo as meaningful into people's lives. It also intentionally correlates these two sources—life and Faith—and encourages people to integrate them into lived, living, and life-giving faith. In fairness, the leaders of both kerygmatic and experiential catechesis intended as much, but they did not propose a clear and usable pedagogy to promote the desired outcome, namely, people's integration of life and Christian faith.

The roots of a *life to Faith to life* approach, however, reach down much deeper than the twentieth century. An emphasis of my own research throughout the years has been the history of the Church's educational ministry. Much of what I now propose reflects the insights that I've found there. Here I can only mention a few tidbits that I subsume into this approach.[3] My point is that a *life to Faith to life* approach is not a peculiar new invention, but reflects the wisdom of the ages in religious education.

For example, Plato championed a dialogical approach, in which the teacher asks students the kinds of questions that would engage their personal reflections and draw out "the truth within" them. Known as the Socratic method (after Socrates, the philosopher-hero in Plato's dialogues), questioning for reflection and not just for recall has endured throughout the ages as a powerful way of activating the agency of learners in the process of knowing. It is not surprising, then, that Aristotle, Plato's most renowned student, argued that a praxis-based way of knowing (i.e., reflection on experience) is most likely to lead beyond knowledge to wisdom for life. Such a way of knowing promotes knowledge that is both reasonable and practical and helps to form people in virtue, surely an intent of education in faith.

In Chapter 4 we noted that the great apologists for Christian faith like Justin Martyr proposed a rhetoric of persuasion that was both reasoned and appealing to people's deepest desires for a good life. Clement of Alexandria, one of the first Christian authors to reflect on *how* to teach Christian faith, insisted that the educator must always begin by engaging people's real lives and affections, by getting their interest. This is how Christian faith can be persuasive and form people in the "path of virtue," said Clement. He added that when instruction follows after such personal engagement, knowledge of Christ is likely to "set free" and lead to spiritual wisdom.[4]

St. Augustine echoed this sentiment, emphasizing the importance of getting to know one's students and teaching everything "according to the mode of the receiver." A *life to Faith to life* approach finds a deep echo in Augustine, because he emphasized both engaging "the teacher within" students (their own reflection) *and* teaching them the "story of salvation."[5] They were to correlate the two, the wisdom from within and the wisdom from without, in order to know deeply God's love and respond to it in life. Likewise, Thomas Aquinas was a great advocate of "learning from experience." He was adamant that everything in our mind comes in through the senses from life; we then reflect on this data to understand and make judgments. Likewise, he also championed a systematic and well-reasoned presentation of Christian faith.[6] So we can say that Aquinas was determined to hold together the work of theoretical and practical reason, so that what people understand well *from* life becomes the resource for making good judgments and wise choices *for* life.

The last I'll highlight in passing is John Amos Comenius, the grandfather of modern education. Gathering up insights from the philosophers of education who came before him, Comenius insisted that people must "learn by doing" and yet must also be taught the "pansophia," the "wisdom of the ages" as assembled in the sciences, arts, and humanities, all to form them in living good lives.[7] As I noted earlier, Comenius influenced many of the great reformers

who came after him; here I just mention a few. Jean Piaget (1896–
1980) wrote his dissertation on Comenius and the latter's incipi-
ent sense of developmental stages of cognition; Friedrich Herbart
(1776–1841), who inspired the Munich Method, learned from
Comenius to first get students "interested" by connecting with
their lives; John Dewey echoed Comenius's stress on learning from
experience *and* on teaching the "funded capital of civilization"; and
Maria Montessori (1870–1952) picked up on Comenius's emphasis
on direct sensory learning.

I reiterate too that a *life to Faith to life* approach promotes what
Bernard Lonergan called "authentic cognition." Lonergan, likewise,
was drawing together some of the best insights from the history of
epistemology (especially from Aristotle and Thomas Aquinas) and
attempting to unite theory and practice, knowledge and wisdom.
As explained before and as will be more evident when I describe its
movements (Chapter 9), a *life to Faith to life* approach encourages
participants to personally attend to and understand the data under
study both from their own lives and from Christian faith. If they
are to truly "know" their faith, however, learners must move beyond
understanding to appropriate its wisdom into their lives and make

decisions in its light. This dynamic reflects Lonergan's schema of
the dynamics of cognition, namely, *attending, understanding, judging,* and *deciding.*[8]

Note that this cumulative process of "knowing" also reflects
what I interpret to be Jesus's intent in the parable of the Sower
and his subsequent explanation of it. This is his classic elaboration
of what people are to "do" with the word of God (the seed of the
Sower) that comes into their lives (the ground). Matthew (13:18–
23), Mark (4:13–20), and Luke (8:11–15) vary slightly in their accounts, but all portray the Sower as munificent, even profligate in
throwing the seed, not choosing the ground carefully but scattering
it everywhere. As Jesus elaborates later, however, all who receive it

must come to "understand" (Matt. 13:23) the word of God. Then they must take it to heart, make it their own, in order to bear good fruit. They must "hear the word and accept it" (Mark 4:20), which is a matter of judgment and decision. Only when it takes root (Luke 8:15), in other words, connects with people's lives in meaningful ways, can they bring forth the fruit of Christian discipleship.

This cursory sweep of some of the best philosophers of education offers rationale for an approach to faith education that: (1) engages people's interests and what is meaningful for them; (2) has them reflect upon their own lives in the world—call it praxis, experience, or whatever; (3) gives them persuasive and ready access to Christian faith as meaningful to their lives; (4) prompts them to correlate and integrate these two sources of truth and spiritual wisdom—life and Faith; and (5) invites them to decide for lived Christian faith. This is precisely what the *life to Faith to life* approach can achieve in a systematic way.

For Catholic polity, it is important to highlight here that the *General Directory for Catechesis* champions a pedagogy that draws upon people's life "experience" *and* teaches clearly "the Faith handed down." As noted earlier, the *GDC* is the most recent comprehensive statement from the magisterium, so it well represents the official mind of the Catholic Church on catechesis. It opens with a resounding affirmation of Vatican II as "the great catechism of modern times" (n. 3) and then celebrates that "the catechetical renewal developed in the Church over the past decades continues to bear very welcome fruit" (n. 24). The *GDC* then reviews those fruits, summarizing much of the ground gained since the early twentieth century. I already cited its emphasis on the centrality of Jesus and discipleship to him, the role of parents and parish, and so on. When it speaks precisely of pedagogy, the *GDC* repeatedly makes clear that catechesis must engage both "life" and "Faith" and enable people to correlate them as lived Faith.

For example, catechesis must promote "a correct . . . correlation and interaction between profound human experiences and the revealed message" (n. 153), for it is by "correlating faith and life" (n. 207) that "catechesis . . . bridges the gap between belief and life, between the Christian message and the cultural context" (n. 205). Religious educators must engage people's lives in the world precisely in order to teach the Faith in meaningful ways, because "experience is a necessary medium for exploring and assimilating the truths which constitute the objective content of Revelation" (n. 152). Effective catechetical education presents every aspect of the faith tradition "to refer clearly to the fundamental experiences of people's lives" (n. 133). To encourage lived faith, religious educators must make participants' own lives in the world integral to the curriculum. "One must start with praxis to be able to arrive at praxis" (n. 245). The citations could go on.

For Reflection and Conversation

- Think back over your own experience of being educated in faith. How would you describe that approach?

- What were some of its strengths? Its weaknesses?

- What wisdom can you learn from that experience for how to educate well in faith now?

Unpacking *Life to Faith to Life*

A *life to Faith to life* approach to religious education and catechesis encourages a teaching/learning community of active participation, conversation, and presentation, in which people share their reflections upon their own lives in the world around a generative theme of life or of life in faith, are given persuasive and meaningful access to the truths and spiritual wisdom of Christian Story and Vision regarding the theme, are encouraged to integrate their lives and their Faith and to make decisions for lived, living, and life-giving faith as disciples of Jesus for God's reign in the world. Some aspects I've already explained in previous chapters, and some will become more evident as I describe its typical pedagogical movements in Chapter 9. A few I will clarify here.

An Approach to Religious Education and Catechesis

I deliberately refer to *life to Faith to life* as *an approach* rather than a method; many teaching methods can be used within its ambit. Still, it is an intentional and reflective way of educating in faith. As such, and after a person has appropriated its convictions and commitments, it becomes one's style or, better still, one's overall *approach* as a religious educator. I've used it at literally every grade level of education from kindergarten to doctoral students. In fact, some of the best catechetical curricula I've written are for kindergarten.[9] Likewise, I and many others have used this approach to youth ministry, in adult faith education and Bible study, in RCIA programs, and in every conceivable situation of educating in faith. Further, I and others have developed it as an approach to preaching, to pastoral counseling, to spiritual direction, and as a general style of ministry.[10] The approach has been used and proved effective in diverse cultures and with people of all ages across the life span. I'm also convinced that there is something "natural" about a *life to Faith to life* approach. It is not contrived, but reflects how we learn much of what matters most in our lives, namely, by correlating experience with broader resources of knowledge to reach new positions and insights. It can be used in any and all efforts by educators to mediate between life and a faith tradition.

The *life to Faith to life* approach is effective both for religious education and for catechesis. In religious education, the approach puts more stress on scholarly study. In catechesis, the emphasis is more on faith formation. Educators can readily adjust questions and questioning activities, so that religious education can enable people to learn *from* a tradition and catechesis can invite people to embrace a tradition as their identity in faith. For example, in a lesson on Jesus, a religious education context might come back to life with a question like, "What can you learn for your own life from this study of Jesus?" A catechetical context would more likely ask, "Do you want to become a disciple of Jesus? If so, what practical difference might this make for your life?"

To move beyond learning *about* to learning *from* or *becoming* within a religious tradition requires some such approach. Yet for all contexts both personal engagement and great freedom are built into the very dynamics of this pedagogy. In every context it encourages people to name and reflect upon the generative themes of their lives, to seek out the spiritual wisdom of religious tradition(s) regarding those themes, and then to discern and decide for themselves about such wisdom. It gives people meaningful access to religious tradition(s) and actively engages them in the process; this is crucial for both learning *from* and *becoming* according to a tradition Then, it honors, even encourages, the freedom of choice of participants in how they appropriate and integrate what they're learning into their lives.

What Life?

In a *life to Faith to life* approach, we must be clear about what "life" we're bringing to "the Faith" *and* returning to with its truths and spiritual wisdom. In addition, it helps to be convinced of why we turn to life at all. Why not simply teach clearly the revelation of God as mediated through Scripture and Tradition and taught by the Church—"teaching as telling." First, then, *what* life?

The simplest answer is *all of it*. By "life" here, I mean anything and everything we do and what gets done or goes on within the ambit of our lives in the world. Life, then, is what we are doing, thinking, and feeling. It is our relationships, experiences, and lived responses; it is our personal knowledge, insights, and wisdom; it is what we initiate and what comes our way from the world around us; it is whatever we make happen or that happens to us personally and within our social context. To "do" this life justice and to learn from doing it, we must both name it for ourselves—express it somehow—and reflect upon it critically and in an informed way. Here is where the more philosophical word "praxis" is still helpful. Remember, my more technical title for this whole approach is "shared Christian *praxis*." The term "praxis" highlights that to learn from life we must reflect on it with discernment (engaging reason, memory, and imagination), and this includes being informed by broader theoretical resources as well. We always reflect on life from what we already know.

"Praxis" is a term from ancient Greek philosophy that goes back at least to Pythagoras, some five hundred years BCE. It is difficult to pin down its meaning with a precise definition. Yet we experience a praxis way of knowing every day as what we learn from life, correlating it with what we already know and with what other people have learned from life before us.

To begin with, praxis refers to purposeful human activity, what we do reflectively as deliberate and imaginative—toward some desired end. Praxis infers that we both intend what we are doing and can learn from what we are doing. It is neither abstract theory nor a technical skill or know-how. Instead, praxis is something in between, namely, reflective and informed action toward desired and practical outcomes. As I said above, we always bring to the praxis of life what we already know and have learned—our own "theory"; we never reflect on life as if we're a *tabula rasa,* a blank slate. True, then, to our existential situation, praxis combines what we usually mean colloquially by the terms "theory" and "practice." It is reflective and informed, theoretical we might say, and yet the intent is to put ideas and insights to work toward good and practical ends, with further learning and formation from the very process along the way. In other words, the reflection and theory involved in a praxis way of knowing has practical intent from the beginning, throughout, and in the end.

Take, now, the instance of educating in Christian faith. Here a praxis way of knowing and teaching will first invite people to reflect upon their own lives in order to discern what they already know and can learn, thus recognizing their knowledge and wisdom from their lives in the world. Then, as religious education lends access to Christian faith, a praxis way of knowing encourages educators to explain even the most abstract dogmas of the Faith with practical intent. In other words, the educator should re-present the systematic teaching of the Faith so it will resonate in people's lives, so that it may be meaningful and livable. The intent is precisely that participants may embrace such "theory" as their own, subsuming it as an aspect of their ongoing reflection on and learning from life. In other words, in a praxis way of knowing, concern for the practical—for everyday living—suffuses the theoretical, and the theoretical is deliberately cast so as to inform the practical. This is how people can learn both from reflecting on their own lives and from "the funded capital" of Christian faith and then correlate and integrate these sources—life and Faith—into a renewed praxis of Christian living.

Below I emphasize teaching Christian Story *and* Vision, in other words, both what Christians believe and what the Faith means for everyday life. Commitment to raising up the Vision as well as accessing the Story helps to ensure that the latter gets "told" with practical intent for people's lives. Then, as people try to live their faith, try to live the theory, the ongoing praxis of it becomes its own source of spiritual wisdom and deepened faith. In other words, praxis and theory can partner in an endless cycle, each renewing the other, each an entrée into the other.

I note, again, that we can recognize this dynamic of "from praxis to theory to praxis" in the teaching style of Jesus. He constantly made people pay attention to and reflect upon their own lives. He wanted them to read the "signs of the times" (Matt. 16:3). Then in their everyday lives he taught his gospel "as one having authority" as well (Mark 1:22). Clearly, however, in turning them toward both life and faith, Jesus always had the practical intent that people integrate the two and become disciples.

Again, I contend that this *praxis to theory to praxis* dynamic is not something that we need to contrive, but is, rather, the dominant epistemology of the everyday, especially for matters that shape and affect our lives. For example, before Teddy came home to us, my spouse and I, being good academics, read a number of books about parenting. Indeed, we read them with "practical interest"— we'd have to care for a newborn very soon. "Theoretically," I'd say that we became something of experts. Oh, but what a difference it made to our learning to be suddenly thrown into the deep end of the parenting pool. Now, some of what we'd read in those books was indeed helpful and made our approach a little more reflective and informed. But the actual praxis of parenting, our trying to do it in a reflective way and our learning from doing it (still, every day) has dramatically increased what we now "know" of parenting and has formed our identity as parents as well. If we'd only read books and then never had the great privilege of parental praxis, we'd have forgotten most of the theory and would never know what we *really* know now. On the other hand, as we encounter the daily issues of parenting and as the newborn becomes a fifth-grader (seems like overnight), we often go back to the books with new questions and look for what might be helpful. We seek theory for practice rather than theory for its own sake, and our practice has greatly clarified our theory. Such is the power of praxis as a source of knowledge and wisdom. Imagine bringing this mode of knowing to teaching/learning Christian faith.

As noted previously, Aristotle developed a praxis way of knowing as the most fitting to educate for practical wisdom and the formation of people in virtue. Of late, many educators (e.g., Paulo Freire) and theologians (e.g., Gustavo Gutiérrez) have revived the term precisely because it unites theory and practice, too often separated in Western society's dominant epistemology, to the debility of both. Praxis combines theory and practice through informed reflection, action, and the imagination that can correlate and unite them. So a praxis or life-based approach to education encourages people to intentionally *reflect* on and be informed in what they are *doing* in order to *imagine* consequences and forge renewed praxis.

A praxis or life-centered way of knowing echoes John Dewey's emphasis on learning from experience and this serving as an entrée into what has arisen from the experience and experimentation of people before us, what he called the "funded capital of civilization" (the humanities, arts, and sciences). Dewey's intended learning outcome, pragmatist that he was, was ultimately to grow in living well and renewing society. Readers will note from the quotations above that the *GDC* also favors the term "experience" for learning from life. In the same vein, Dewey says, "We have to understand the significance of what we see, hear and touch."[11] This takes "critical intelligence" to probe the sources, causes, and likely consequences of present experience. Dewey called this the "reconstruction of experience," what I'd call reflection on life. This led Dewey to his key proposal: "Education is that reconstruction or reorganization of experience which adds to the meaning of experience and which increases the ability to direct the course of subsequent experience."[12]

For Dewey, then, my approach could well be called an "experience to Faith to experience" pedagogy. I think he'd like it. However, I prefer the terms "life" and "praxis" over "experience," because they highlight the personal agency and activity of the knower. By contrast, experience has the connotation of whatever comes our way, something that we "have" or "undergo" or is foisted on us rather than something that we initiate. Still, whether we use "life-centered," "experience," or "praxis," they all name a way of knowing that arises from and returns to shape our everyday lives and identity. This makes for an ideal epistemology for educating in Christian faith. If Christian faith is to be meaningful to people's lives, then it must echo into and integrate with their reflective way of being in the world.

Let us look a little deeper into the reflective aspect of praxis, or of learning from life. Since the educator is to encourage such reflection, it is imperative to be clear about what it entails. The *reflective* aspect of praxis involves the whole human capacity for thought, reaching to our thinking about our thinking. So it engages reason, memory, and imagination, which are all used to interpret and understand our lives in the world. Critical reflection looks inward to the depths of personal awareness and outward at the whole public world through social analysis. By critical reflection we discern what we think, and then why we think we think that. In this second level of reflection, we can probe our own biases and personal blind spots. Likewise, critical reflection pushes us to ask how our context and culture are shaping our reflections. Such considerations of our historical situation and of ourselves within it is at the heart of critical reflection.

Precisely because critical reflection is upon one's own life in the world, it is never dispassionate. Though it can sound heady, the reflective element of praxis is deeply intertwined with emotion. Our desires always shape our intended action, and our action reflects our desires. Or speaking metaphorically, to reflect on our own lives in the world is to know our own story and vision, and it is impossible to do so dispassionately; to know and direct our lives always engages emotion.

In religious education, then, the reflective element is also in play as we encounter the "practical theory" of Christian Story and Vision, enabling us to understand what it means and what it means for *our* lives. Reflection combined with emotion to shape renewed praxis is at work again as people make judgments and decisions, as they take Christian faith to heart and decide how to live it. In sum, critical reflection combined with emotion is essential to noticing and understanding the data of life, to knowing and understanding the data of Christian faith in a practical way, and then to making judgments and decisions that integrate the two—life and Faith—into the praxis of lived Christian faith.

When I lay out the pedagogical movements in Chapter 9, I make clear that we might not use reason, memory, and imagination, both personal and social, for every instance of critical reflection. We are to engage whatever seems most appropriate in the context and to the theme. But these mental functions, suffused with emotion, can often roll together; in fact, we constantly and quickly combine them in everyday life. For example, on a recent visit I made to New York City, a friend there asked my opinion of the current Boston Red Sox. In the blink of an eye and reflecting on how they're doing, I used informed reason ("Well, they're playing well right now"), memory ("But they regularly break our hearts near season's end"), and imagination ("Yet we still have hope at this time of year"). I also recognized that my own opinion is nigh determined by my sociocultural context; to be other than a Red Sox fan in Boston is tantamount to treason. Yet I chose to respond with what I feigned was an objective response, "Oh, the best team in baseball right now." My New York friend, a Yankee fan, promptly contradicted. Of course, unlike me, he was biased. Whoops, might that be a lack of *critical* reflection on my part?

I reiterate that I do not use "critical" here in its colloquial negative sense, that is, of finding fault or highlighting what is wrong. Instead, faithful to its Greek roots in *krinein,* it means "to carefully discern," as in figuring out what's what. It means coming to understand, weighing evidence, making judgments, reaching decisions. Such good discernment looks at what "is" and why it is, and then imagines what might be and should be, and what causes us to think and imagine so. This makes it a very positive exercise rather than a negative one. In a praxis way of knowing, imagination is the linchpin that links the active and reflective, the practical and theoretical, the heart and head. When combined with emotion, imagination disposes the will to choose ongoing and responsible praxis in the world.

I'm often asked, "When are children ready for a praxis epistemology in religious education?" One response I make is that I have helped to write two very effective kindergarten religion books using a praxis approach.[13] This is a reasonable question, however, in light of developmental theory. Jean Piaget would say that abstract thinking doesn't begin until the teen years at the earliest. Research by Laurence Kohlberg, Robert Kegan, and other developmentalists indicates that a high percentage of adults often fall short of in-depth critical reflection on their personal and social praxis. On the other hand, a praxis way of knowing is the one that is most natural for us, as it begins from the very beginning of life. Just imagine the vast world of knowledge—for instance, spoken language—that a five-year-old has already "learned from life." Further, "the tree is in the seed." In other words, and as Piaget advised, good education encourages concrete reflection in the very early years, that is, on observable things or examples, so that full-blown critical reflection becomes more likely in adulthood. The journey into maturity of faith is aided and abetted by good discernment all along the way.

Why Turn to Life?

Now, to the question, *"Why* turn to life?" In a teaching/learning event of Christian religious education, why should the educator engage people in reflecting on and integrating faith with their own lives in the world? I will suggest one great pedagogical reason and then some good theological ones for doing so. First, I note parenthetically, after all that I've written here already, raising this question may surprise readers. There are still sentiments abroad, however, even among church leaders, that the best way to teach Christian Faith is by what John Dewey characterized as "abundant lecturing." This is to assume that the "funded capital" is simply "predigested knowledge" and that the educators job is to "ladle it out in easy doses."[14]

Perhaps there are some disciplines of learning that can be taught that way, for example, quantum physics, although a good physics teacher would likely contest. Indeed, if the intent of religious education were that people only learn *about* a religion, then abundant lecturing might be sufficient. However, if a faith tradition is presented to people simply as information to be learned, with no echo or sense of meaning for their lives, it will remain as "inert ideas." They may learn *about* it, but they're not likely to learn *from* it. And it would truly be a miracle of God's grace if such a pedagogy led them to embrace it as their religious identity with commitment to living its truths and teachings.

For religious education, the quotes from the *GDC* above state well the pedagogical reason for turning to life in order to educate in faith. In sum, "Experience is a necessary medium for exploring and assimilating the truths which constitute the objective content of Revelation" (n. 152). Catechetical education must help to bridge the gap that Christians maintain between their lives and their faith and that Vatican II lamented as the "most serious error of our age." The *only* way to do so is to pedagogically engage both "life" and "Faith" in order to "correlate" them to each other (see *GDC*, nn. 205–7). I prefer the even stronger term "integrate." Religious educators must encourage people to reflect on their own lives in order to find echoes with and entrée into the wisdom of Christian faith and then give them access to Christian faith as meaningful to their lives. The more a teaching/learning event brings both into play, life and Faith, the more likely are participants to integrate the two into lived faith. Even to learn *from* their encounter with Christian faith (or with any religious tradition), educators must present it as having potential meaning for life. This is all the more true if we want people to integrate Christian faith as their own identity with commitment to living as disciples of Jesus.

The sentiments of the *GDC* only reflect what has been the better philosophy of education across the ages. As I've noted repeatedly, all the great exponents and philosophers of education have insisted, in one way or another, that all knowledge arises originally from human experience and experimentation. Therefore, to inherit the legacy of knowledge from previous generations, a passive "handing on" is not sufficient. This leads at best to what the great twentieth-century scholar Alfred North Whitehead called "inert ideas" in people's heads, to "ideas that are merely received into the mind without being utilized, or tested, or thrown into fresh combinations."[15] (Note that Whitehead's primary expertise was in mathematics; even math cannot be simply "lectured.") Life-giving and humanizing education of any kind cannot be achieved by what Paulo Freire called "banking education," in other words, "a depositing of information in passive receptacles."[16] Instead of a "jug to mug" pedagogy, people in every generation need to come to their own cognition and recognition—re-cognition (to know again)—of established knowledge and especially of the truths and values discovered by those before us. Piaget summarized this well when he proposed, out of his research with children, that "to understand is to reinvent."[17] And if "seeing for oneself" is imperative for understanding, it is surely necessary for judging and deciding, the latter two being essential to education in faith.

So, for good pedagogical reasons, religious education must lead people to reflect on their own lives, as both a point of departure and a point of arrival in coming to "know" their faith. There are good theological reasons as well. Engaging people with what matters to their lives is not simply an effective teaching ploy. It also reflects the conviction that our lives in the world are a locus of God's revelation and grace.

We already reviewed the sacramental principle, which is central to Catholic faith. Although God's grace or effective love in our lives is mediated in a primary way through the seven sacraments, it also comes to us through the ordinary and everyday. We can say something similar about divine revelation. While the Bible and Tradition are the normative sources of God's revelation, the Holy Spirit ever moves in our ordinary and everyday lives, inspiring, prompting, and guiding us in how to live Christian faith. So the *life to Faith to life* approach reflects the conviction that the Spirit is ever revealing God's will for us in daily life and likewise mediating God's grace to enable us to discern and respond faithfully.

The Bible also reflects that God reveals in the ordinary and the extraordinary events of human history. The Israelites and first Christians recognized God's self-disclosure and loving presence in their lives, in their own experiences, we might say. For the Israelites the high point of God's revelation was in their experience of slavery and then liberation in the Exodus event. For Christians, the apex of divine self-revelation was in the direct experience that the first disciples had of Jesus—God's Word made flesh within time and place. God's revelation through Scripture and Tradition is complete in that we await no further normative revelation, and what is already revealed can never be withdrawn. The "greatest commandment," that we love God with all our mind, heart, and strength and our neighbors as ourselves, will remain forever so, no matter what experiences we may have to the contrary (e.g., encountering people who might seem unlovable).

Still, what this normative revelation means for us and how to live it in daily life continues to unfold, and God's grace is present to help us discern and to sustain our efforts to respond. For example, we need to be constantly figuring out who are the neighbors most in need, how best to care for them, and so on. It was precisely such "critical reflection on life" that prompted the Church to call Christians beyond personal one-on-one charity to the works of social justice. We Christians must ever reflect on our lives in the world if we are to recognize "what God is up to" and how God is inviting us to respond by living as a people of God. Only thus can we bring the spiritual wisdom of Christian faith back to life again as renewed and deepened faith.

To invite people to reflect critically on their lives in the world, therefore, is not simply a pedagogical move to get their attention before accessing "the real stuff," namely, the truths and spiritual wisdom that are mediated by Scripture and Tradition. Instead, having people pay attention to their present praxis is to honor and draw upon how God is present, revealing God's will and mediating God's grace in the ordinary and everyday of their lives. Then after encountering the Story and Vision of Christian faith, it is necessary to bring people back to life again if their faith is to become lived, living, and life-giving, *for fullness of life for all.*

Focusing on a Generative Theme

I said in the opening summary that a teaching/learning event using a *life to Faith to life* approach needs to focus its curriculum *around a generative theme.* Let me explain. First, as both educators and learners we know well from experience that it is nearly impossible to teach or learn anything if there isn't real interest. Of course, we can learn things just for an exam, but even then there must be a motive (good grades), and such "stuff" is soon forgotten after the exam is over. The things we learn in life that remain, that make a difference in who we are, in our outlook, our ethic, and our way of being in the world are seldom learned without our active interest. Such interest arises around a topic that arouses curiosity and/or that really matters, so that it's in our "best interest" to know it. In other words, we are most likely to learn whatever seems meaningful to our lives.

Paulo Freire, the contemporary educator who coined the phrase "generative theme" for what is of real interest to people and thus a starting point for education, proposed that such themes always arise from life, from present praxis. For example, when we raise up a great question, issue, challenge, problem, fear, hope, threat, or desire from people's lives, this is most likely to be generative and to actively engage their interest.

I recently experienced two very different sermons on the same weekend based on the Gospel text, "Come to me all you who labor and are burdened, and I will give you rest. Take my yoke upon you . . ." (Matt. 11:25–30, NAB). The first sermon began with a scholarly exegesis of the Gospel reading, explaining what a "yoke" meant in the world of the time, that here the passage likely refers to the "yoke of the law" being imposed by scribes and Pharisees, and that Jesus would relieve people of this burden by teaching the spirit rather than the letter of the law. The homilist ended with some spiritual exhortations. I call this the "salad time" in a sermon: "Let us be nice, let us be good, lettuce and tomato."

The second preacher began, instead, by asking the congregation, "Did anyone come here today carrying a burden, a worry, a concern? Hands up." Every hand in the church went up (he had already made a helpful point). Then he went on to talk about burdens, that we take them on or have them put upon us, that some are real and some are self-made, and so on. After such reflections, all ringing true to people's lives and obviously engaging their interest, he turned to the spiritual wisdom of the Gospel reading and to what it might mean for the burdens we carry now. He ended with good questions about what it might mean to place such trust in Jesus and an invitation to decision. There was a marked difference in the congregation's attention to the two sermons; with the second being visibly far higher. Yet both preached on the Gospel of the day. The difference, I discerned, was that the first did not engage a "generative theme" in people's lives, whereas the second did so very effectively.

As might be expected, establishing the generative theme needs to come at the beginning of a teaching/learning event. In Chapter 9, I describe it as the *Focusing Act.* Although it is the opening pedagogical move, of course, the "interest" must continue and be maintained throughout the whole event.

Although the generative theme may focus on something of life in general, in religious education the focus may also be on *life in faith,* that is, on an explicitly religious praxis from the beginning. Both must be of real interest to the lives of the participants, the difference being that the focus on life usually doesn't employ religious language, whereas the focus on *life in faith* does.

Let's imagine a high-school religious education class on the theme "Who is Jesus?" On the one hand, using a generative theme just from life, it could begin with a reflective exercise on "Who's the real you?" and invite young people to name and reflect upon their own emerging identity (an intense issue for youth). Then, the explicit Faith moment would enable them to encounter the identity of Jesus, highlighting how who he was might enhance and inspire who they can become. On the other hand, I've also drawn upon a life in faith theme for such a lesson, focusing from the outset on "Who is Jesus *for you*?" I've begun such a class with a meditative exercise that placed students on the road to Caesarea Philippi when Jesus asked the disciples, "Who do people say that I am?" After hearing the latest rumors, Jesus asks, "But you, who do you say that I am?" (from Matt. 16:13–20). I then invited students to respond personally to Jesus's question as if it were put directly to them, to name and reflect upon their own image of him and where they got it, what difference he makes to daily life and why, in other words, on their "praxis" of Jesus, not their theory. So the generative theme can be from life or from life in faith. The key is to enable participants to recognize and begin to reflect upon a theme of real interest to their lives.

Sometimes, the themes to be taught are suggested or even required by an official curriculum. This is often true in Catholic contexts. For example, *Doctrinal Elements of a Curriculum Framework for the Development of Catechetical Materials for Young People of High School Age,* now mandated by the U.S. Conference of Catholic Bishops, gives precisely and in great detail the "doctrinal elements" to be taught. Likewise, grade-school catechetical curricula have a detailed scope and a particular sequence that are aimed to teach, comprehensively and at ever deepening levels, the core doctrines, worship, and ethics of Christian faith. In such cases, the challenge is to look at the faith topic to be taught, to review the age level and context of the participants, and then to devise a "generative theme" that will be a praxis-based entrée for these participants into the assigned aspect of Christian Story and Vision.

For example, in teaching the story of creation to high-school students, the generative theme might be their own attitude toward and appreciation of nature, their praxis of environmental stewardship, or—a life in faith theme—what they really believe about the source of creation and how this shapes their outlook on life in the world. Then, the Focusing Act establishing the generative theme might be asking them to pause and look at some aspect of creation around them (I've done this by having students really examine a leaf), showing a movie clip of its beauty, or taking them for a nature walk.

The generative theme chosen for any occasion, whether a prescribed curriculum of Christian faith is being followed or topics are being allowed to emerge from the community or occasion, should be something that is of real interest and meaningful to these participants' lives. Also, the theme must be likely to be enlightened by the spiritual wisdom of Christian faith. But this is true of all the generative themes of life. They all find resonance and wisdom in Christian Story and Vision. It always takes preparation and imagination, however, to find an engaging theme for any given group's context, background, age, and so on. Actually, good religious education always requires as much, regardless of the approach being used.

Persuasive and Meaningful Access to Christian Story and Vision

In the context of *Christian* religious education, the Faith tradition to be re-presented in the midst of life is primarily Christian. In a *Jewish* religious education context, it would be the Jewish faith, and so on. Public-school religion curricula (e.g., in Sweden and England) will attend to a variety of religious traditions; all, however, should be accessed as sources of spiritual wisdom *from* which people can appropriate some wisdom for life. Here, however, I'm taking it that the defining spiritual resource is Christian faith and that typically the intent is to shape people's identity in this faith or at least that they learn *from* it for their lives.

I say that the access is to be *persuasive* and *meaningful*. In many ways, these are two sides of the same coin. In Chapter 4, I laid out the need for a "new apologetics" of Christian faith. Instead of using fear, coercion, or authoritarianism, we must present Christian faith in a manner that appeals to people's desires, their reason, and highlighting the potential good fruits of such faith in everyday life. Such persuasion can be mounted without manipulating the discernment of learners, especially as the very pedagogy encourages freedom of choice—the antithesis of coercion (Movement 4 of a *life to Faith to life* approach does so explicitly, as I explain in the next chapter). Meanwhile, Christian Story and Vision should be presented in meaningful ways so that it connects with, resonates with, and seems relevant to people's lives.

For example, we could present the Exodus as an old story from long ago and have people learn the names of the characters involved, maybe memorize the various plagues sent upon the Egyptians, learn the data about the Passover night and meal, the parting of the sea, and the escape into the desert, and then have a quiz on these "facts." Or we could present the details of the Exodus story (to learn about *is* a beginning), then hold up the event as an extraordinary source of hope in the context of people's oppressions and slaveries today, pointing out that God can intervene in human history to set people free, and then move on to what this might mean for us now. The first is simply informative; the second should also be informative and then meaningful to people's lives as well.

Let me now clarify what I intend by Christian "Story and Vision." Of course, I cherish the more traditional language for the media of Christian faith as "Scripture and Tradition." I see a peda-gogical value, however, in naming and accessing their revelation as "Story and Vision." For a secure identity, everyone needs a narrative that makes sense of their lives and a vision of hope for the future.

"Story and Vision" suggest a narrative of faith that is ongoing, that reaches into our own time and will continue after us. They can be engaging for people, as all stories and hopes are, and can invite participants to step inside them, to find echoes and hori-zons for themselves and their lives. We may be a little more likely to lend persuasive and meaningful access to Scripture and Tradi-tion when we present their revelation as the narrative that makes the most sense out of life and offers the best outlook from here. So I use "Story and Vision" to symbolize the whole historical real-ity and spiritual wisdom of Christian revelation and the demands and promises that this faith makes upon the lives of its adherents and communities. I capitalize the terms to signal their primordial and normative status apropos of our own story and vision.

Christian Story is realized and expressed in myriad forms: texts, traditions, and liturgies; creeds, dogmas, doctrines, and theologies; sacraments and rituals, symbols and myths; values, virtues, and ethics; commandments, laws, and mandates; spiritualities and ex-pected lifestyles; songs and music, dance and drama; art, artifacts, and architectures; gestures and religious language; memories of holy people, celebrations of holy times, and reverence for holy places; community structures and forms of governance; and more. Accord-ing to age and developmental readiness, all Christians deserve to have access to the "whole Story" of Christian faith, to be educated in its comprehensive sources of spiritual wisdom for life. This must be done in ways that are faithful to its constitutive truths, worship, and ethics.

The Vision prompted by Christian Story is ultimately the reign of God, the realization of God's intentions of peace and justice, love and freedom, holiness and wholeness, and fullness of life for all humankind, here and hereafter. Practically, the Vision reflects the invitations and implications that Christian Story has for people's lives. It is the meaning in front of the Story, its gifts and demands, its hopes and promises for persons and societies today. The Vision is what guides people in living their faith in their present time and place. And every aspect of Christian Story has a Vision to it: as God loves us, we must love each other; as God forgives us, we must forgive those who trespass against us; the Exodus *then* is about setting free the oppressed *now*.

Sometimes the Vision is self-evident if the Story is represented well, yet I've found it important over the years to deliberately catechize for the Vision. If you're teaching children that Jesus is their friend, lay out as well what it means to be a friend of Jesus. If you are teaching that we can receive the Real Presence of the Risen Christ in Eucharist, lay out as well that this expects the living of Eucharist in daily life. In sum, laying out the Vision is precisely what makes the Story meaningful and persuasive to participants' lives. As I noted above, the Vision helps to ensure that the Story is accessed with practical intent, toward lived, living, and life-giving faith.

Recently, I was crafting a sophomore-level lesson on the Blessed Trinity. Such a lesson should indeed teach the dogma of the Trinity, the oneness of God in three Divine Persons, distinct and equal, the dynamic love and perichoresis of their relationships (i.e., the interdependence between the three Divine Persons), and so on. But more than this, and honoring the Vision, catechesis of the Blessed Trinity should lay out what it means for us. For example, a God of right and loving relationship, both within Godself and always toward us, surely calls a people of God to so live—in right and loving relationship. Made in the divine image, right and loving relationships are our greatest potential, our highest calling. Also, the Trinity reminds us that the works of justice are a mandate of our faith in such a God; the biblical definition of justice is "right relationships." In other words, the Trinity explains not only who our God is, but who we are and how we are to live as a people of God. Laying out the Vision of a dogma as "abstract" and mysterious as the Blessed Trinity is precisely how it can take on powerful meaning and relevance to people's lives.

A Teaching/Learning Community of Participation, Conversation, and Presentation

I say "teaching/learning community," because the intent is a leveling of roles, so that all participants are both teachers and learners together. In this I see the educator's role (whether this is teacher, parent, or group leader) as that of *leading learner.* The word "educator" comes from the Latin *educare,* meaning "to lead out." Religious educators have the designated function of leading out the community and in the process must be open to learning themselves. The more everyone in the group is actively engaged in the teaching/learning dynamic, the more they will both learn from and teach each other.

To encourage a community of teaching/learning calls for a pedagogy of *participation, conversation,* and *presentation. Participation* requires the active engagement of all according to their learning style. It asks the educator to activate and draw upon people's own agency for knowing and creating knowledge, to encourage participants to reason, remember, and imagine, to probe, question, and analyze (self and society), to discover and see for themselves. The educator must prompt participants to pay attention to data—from life and from Christian faith—to understand them and then to make judgments and decisions about them. Such active participation in the teaching/learning dynamic seems all the more imperative for educating contemporary people in faith. Without their active participation in coming to "know" it, it does not seem likely that people's faith will endure and mature amid the exclusive humanism of our postmodern world. Although a socialized faith from family or village or one embraced out of obedience to authority appears to have been effective in a more enchanted era, the disenchantment of our time makes unlikely that a passively accepted faith will endure.

Then the *conversation* is to welcome the contributions of all. It asks participants to commit to listening and sharing, to being respectful and honest, to agreeing and disagreeing as appropriate, to cherishing one's own truth while being open to the truth of others and to the possibility of being changed by the exchange. So this is not chitchat, a trading of pleasantries, or a waiting for one's turn while ignoring what others are saying. Plato and the ancient philosophers named the engagement of real conversation as "dialectics." The Greek *dialektos* had the sense of an intense exchange of different viewpoints, a good argument between varied positions. Since no two human lives are the same, great diversity of opinions is to be expected within any group. Some later interpreters of Plato, however, presumed that such conversation inevitably becomes conflictual. I disagree and note that this has not been my experience in a pedagogy of *life to Faith to life*. Indeed, there can be disagreements and good arguments, but usually without conflict. I think the key is that people are sharing their reflections on their own lives, their own story and vision. This makes other members more likely to listen respectfully, even if theirs are quite different. It is hard to simply reject or "disagree" with a person's life and hopes.

The educator or anchor person has a responsibility to encourage all members to participate in the conversation. The substance of the conversation is first about issues in people's own lives called up by a generative theme, what I've been calling metaphorically their own stories and visions. I say "metaphorically" because the discourse here is not exclusively narrative, and yet it brings to expression people's reflection on their lives in the world. As a result, the more they can share their "real story" as appropriate—their most honest reflections—the better for their own knowing and for the group's.

Then the conversation is also between people's lives in the world and the truths and spiritual wisdom of Christian faith, metaphorically again, between participants' own stories and visions and Christian Story and Vision. Bringing such "exchange" to expression within the community has a great power to it. The group dynamic lends momentum to participants to appropriate Christian faith into their lives and to make it their own through personal decision.

Regarding the *presentation* aspect within the teaching/learning community, I'm using this term to signify that participants need to have ready access to the resources of Christian Story and Vision. As I will outline in Chapter 9, such access can be mediated in myriad ways, not only by formal "presentation" per se. In fact, the Latin root of "presentation" means to "make present." So the better term here may be "re-presentation" in the sense of making present again as well as signaling the educator's responsibility to represent the truths and wisdom of Christian faith.

The presentation or re-presentation of the Faith is the designated service of educators to the faith community. They must see to it that Christian Story and Vision are "made present" to participants and that they have ready and persuasive access to its truths and spiritual wisdom. Further, the Faith must be made present with coherence, so that it makes sense, rings true to participants lives, and is likely to resonate in their souls. The re-presentation is to reflect the persuasive apologetics on behalf of Christian faith that I outlined in Chapter 4.

In fulfilling their responsibility to re-present Christian faith, educators might even be didactic at times. The imperative, however, is that they do so in ways that invite conversation to follow on, that prompt rather than discourage reflection; they should not tell participants what to think, but invite them to think for themselves and to make this faith their own or at least to learn *from* it. Beyond the standard presentation, educators can employ a great variety of teaching methods for "making present." Educators can access Christian Story and Vision through textbooks that students study together, through directed research, and through all the more contemporary media of re-presentation: movies, tapes, blogs, the Internet, and so on. Educators can send students to original texts to interpret them with guidance. They can organize direct experiences like field trips, and the list for re-presenting goes on. The key always is that people have ready and persuasive access to the teachings and spiritual wisdom of Christian faith and in ways that dispose them to at least learn *from* it for their lives and perhaps to commit to living it.

For Reflection and Conversation

- What are your own thoughts, feelings, and wisdom now about a *life to Faith to life* approach to education in Christian faith?

- What are you coming to see for yourself as its assets and liabilities?

- How would you imagine implementing it in your own praxis as a religious educator, whether you are a parent, teacher, or group leader?

Convictions Needed on the Part of Educators

Here we can be brief and summarize many points already implied in passing. The *life to Faith to life* approach calls for some key convictions or "trusts" on the part of educators. Though I've offered theological and pedagogical reasons for all of them, they are, in fact, spiritual convictions. In no particular order, the *life to Faith to life* approach invites educators:

1. To trust that people can be agents of their own knowing in Christian faith; that they are not only recipients, but agents as well. This asks educators to let go of "teaching as telling" and to invite real conversation among participants.
2. To trust that community is the best paradigm for educating in Christian faith and to build up community within the teaching/learning event.
3. To trust that people can learn from one another and that their own stories and visions can be a source of God's present revelation in their lives.
4. To trust that the Holy Spirit continues to be present to people, revealing God's will and mediating grace in the ordinary and everyday of life.
5. To trust in the Story and Vision of Christian faith as the normative and life-giving source of spiritual truths and wisdom for life—for all Christians.
6. To trust that people can discern how to take Christian Story and Vision "to heart" and to appropriate such spiritual wisdom into their lives.
7. To trust that the Holy Spirit can work through such a process and that people have the ability, by God's grace, to come to their own decisions for lived, living, and life-giving faith.
8. To trust that all people of goodwill can learn *from* religious education in the rich treasury for being human and religious that is Christian faith.

With the components of a *life to Faith to life* approach well in place, our next step is to outline the precise pedagogical movements for its implementation. Such is our topic in Chapter 9.

CHAPTER NINE

Life to Faith to Life: The Movements

Putting the Approach to Work

The agenda of this chapter is to review the Focusing Act and then the five pedagogical Movements that implement a *life to Faith to life* approach. Let me name them here at the outset in a more active and user-friendly form. They are:

Focusing Act (FA): Engage people with a real life or faith theme.

LIFE *Movement 1* (M 1): Have people respond to the theme as it pertains to their lives.

Movement 2 (M 2): Encourage them to reflect critically on the theme in conversation together.

FAITH *Movement 3* (M 3): Share the Story and Vision of Christian faith in ways that are pertinent to the theme and meaningful for this group, context, and occasion.

to

LIFE *Movement 4* (M 4): Encourage participants to appropriate and integrate Christian faith with life.

Movement 5 (M 5): Invite people to make a decision—cognitive, affective, or behavioral in response to the whole process.

The listing of the moves and even my explanation that follows here can make them seem so complicated, whereas, as I've contended throughout, this is a natural approach to take. In fact, we often use it in the pedagogy of daily life—outside of schools and belying the stereotype of teaching as telling.

Life to wisdom (or Faith) to life is, in fact, the approach that most parents take in dealing with substantive issues with a child, at least on a good day. We typically begin by listening to what's going on in the child's life, then offer words drawn from some broader wisdom—perhaps from Christian faith, but at least from some source of wisdom greater than the child's experience—and then try to move back to life again, encouraging the child to see new possibilities. So here's a story to bring with you throughout this chapter, especially if I'm making things sound too complicated.

Shortly after Teddy turned nine, he approached me with one of those developmental milestones. "Hey, Dad, I think I don't believe in Santa Claus anymore." Teddy had put our generative theme right on the table. His momentous statement was our Focusing Act. No doubt about our curriculum from here. For Movement 1, I began with, "What do you mean you don't believe in Santa Claus anymore?" It turned out that his first doubts were more about the reindeer flying through the air than about Santa himself. I asked how he felt about not believing. He felt sad for the loss of toys, but he also wondered whether we'd simply lied to him, a more important issue. Then for Movement 2, I asked "Why stop believing in Santa Claus now?" He replied, "Nearly no one in third grade believes it anymore." I asked if that was a good reason and where his closest friends stood on the matter, whereupon he posed the direct question, "There really isn't a Santa Claus, right?" I knew it was time to share the true Santa story and the wisdom of it.

So, for Movement 3, I told the story of how Santa Claus got started with the great St. Nicholas, who used to secretly leave toys for children at Christmastime to help them celebrate the joy at the birth of Jesus. After he died, many parents continued this practice for the same reason. I assured Teddy that we weren't really lying, but only helping little kids realize what a wonderful celebration Christmas should be. On the Internet I found the famous *New York Sun* editorial of September 21, 1897, "Yes Virginia, There Is a Santa Claus." We read it together and talked about what the author was trying to convey, namely, that Santa Claus is really about all the love—from God and parents—that is the true spirit of Christmas.

Moving back to Teddy's life again (M 4), I asked questions like, "So what do you think? Is Santa a good idea? Are you sorry or happy we did it? Were we lying or being loving to you?" Gradually Teddy came to see and agree that Santa Claus is a great idea, but then, thinking practically (M 5), he inquired if he'd still get presents at Christmastime. I assured him that of course he would and that the spirit of Santa will always live on, even if not as a fat old man with a white beard and a red suit. Teddy agreed with, "That's cool, Dad"; it sounded like a cognitive and affective decision. We had quite naturally gone through all the movements of a *life to Faith to life* approach.

The flow of "bringing life to Faith and Faith to life" suggests a pattern of teaching moves or movements. I used to call them "steps," but that put people in too "lockstep" a mind-set. Instead, these movements are analogous to those of a symphony, with the (generative) theme carried throughout and the movements occurring, recurring, and blending together into one grand opus. I lay out the movements here in their logical sequence, but, as I make clear later, they can take place in many different patterns and combinations. They are symphonic more than sequential.

As mentioned, I outline them as a Focusing Act and then five Movements. The Focusing Act and Movements 1 and 2 pertain to "life" as a source of God's revelation in people's own lives and an entrée into the revelation of Christian faith. Movement 3 pertains to "Faith" as the truth and wisdom of Christian Story and Vision (or whatever tradition is being studied). Movements 4 and 5 mark the return to "life" again, in which people are prompted to make connections and decisions in the light of Christian faith.

I note again that in nonconfessional contexts of religious education, educators will encourage appropriations and decisions about what people can learn *from* their reflections and encounter with the Story and Vision of Christian faith or from whatever tradition they may be studying. Here, however, my focus and examples will be from the context of Christian religious education, where the intent is to have people both learn *from* and take on Christian faith as their religious identity.

As I describe each movement I will give examples at the grade-school, high-school, and university levels as well as from family conversations, parish Bible study, youth ministry, and adult education. Let me set out a "bird's-eye view" of them again, this time with a more formal description of the curriculum intent of each movement. In a community of participation, conversation, and re-presentation, the tasks are:

Focusing Act: Establishing the curriculum
around a life or faith generative theme

LIFE *Movement 1* (M 1): Expressing the theme in present praxis

Movement 2 (M 2): Reflecting critically on the life or faith theme

to

FAITH *Movement 3* (M 3): Re-presenting Christian Story and Vision with meaning and persuasion

to

LIFE *Movement 4* (M 4): Appropriating the truths and wisdom of Christian faith into life

Movement 5 (M 5): Making decisions in light of Christian faith

For Reflection and Conversation

• Even before a detailed explanation, can you imagine yourself laying out a "lesson plan" using this *life to Faith to life* approach?

• What theme would you use? How would you focus on it and actively engage people with it?

• What might be your M 1 and M 2 questions or questioning activities (naming and reflecting on present praxis of theme)?

• How might you do M 3 (accessing Christian Story and Vision)?

• How might you facilitate M 4 and M 5 (encouraging people to see for themselves and make decisions)?

The Focusing Act: Establishing the Curriculum
Around a Life or Faith Generative Theme

Good teaching typically begins by giving participants a sense of "what this is about." We can call it establishing the curriculum, although this occasionally emerges later or may shift along the way. Even if it is only a third-grade teacher saying, "Okay, children, take out your math books," the students know that now is math time. In a participative process like *life to Faith to life,* people need to know "what we're talking about here" in order to feel secure enough to participate.

The Focusing Act should give people a sense of the curriculum topic and establish it as a generative theme for the teaching/learning event. Doing so makes it more likely that people will actively engage as co-learners. In sum, the intent of the FA is to: (1) engage these participants with a generative theme for this teaching/learning event; (2) lend all present a shared sense of the curriculum—"what we're talking about"; and (3) draw them into active participation and conversation by having them recognize the theme in their lives and be disposed to express their sense of it.

As I said in Chapter 8, the generative theme can be from life or explicitly from life in faith. The key is that it be something of real interest to these participants, meaningful to them as people, and that it serve as an entrée into the aspect of Christian faith to be taught at M 3. The generative theme established in the Focusing Act typically remains the organizing theme for the whole event and is to echo throughout all the movements.

As you can imagine, the Focusing Act can be done in myriad ways. First, it can be an overt activity—a joint praxis—either outside or within the teaching/ learning event. (Then it is literally a Focusing *Activity.*) For many years I took undergraduates in my theology course at Boston College to cook Thursday morning breakfast at a local Catholic Worker community house. Back in the classroom, I would often invite them to name and critically reflect upon this experience or praxis. For youth ministry programs, a joint project of compassion or justice can be an ideal Focusing Activity. To really learn from their service, however, participants need later to name and to reflect on it, to encounter Christian Story and Vision around it, and to draw out the wisdom for their ongoing discipleship.

The FA can also be achieved by a symbol, which when raised up before participants, enables them to begin to recognize the generative theme in their own lives. Such a symbol (as something to look through into life) can be a poem or puzzle, a song or movie, a game or role-play, a demonstration or case study, a picture or artifact, a scripture story or ritual, a descriptive or evocative statement, an instance or example, or a good question, as in "Did anyone bring a burden to church today?" (my sermon example in Chapter 8). We can also add a group project, a nature walk, a field trip, a liturgical celebration, and so on. The key for the FA is to do or raise up something that gets people engaged and recognizing the theme as present in and meaningful to their lives.

In this day and age, let me highlight how the Internet and other communications media can readily provide "virtual" experiences and symbols of life and faith to engage people. We have only just begun to take advantage of these new technologies to enhance religious education. Indeed, the modern media of communication can be used throughout all the movements to help establish the generative theme, to prompt people to expression and reflection, to access Christian Story and Vision, and finally to help participants imagine how to bring the wisdom of their faith back to life again.

In an event with first-year high-school students, I used the U2 song (they watched it on YouTube) "I Still Haven't Found What I'm Looking For" to raise up the generative theme of "God's desire for our lives." This then served as an entrée into the topic of God's deepest desires for us as expressed in the symbol of God's reign in Jesus (M 3). After the students heard the song, they first responded to questions like, "What do you think the singer is looking for?" and then, "What are you most looking for in life?" This flowed into M 2 as, "Who or what is shaping your desires?" "How do you hope to fulfill them?" "Do you ever imagine God having a role in fulfilling your desires?" Likewise, I've often begun a graduate course in religious education with a movie clip of a stereotypical Sunday school class and then invited people to recognize and describe their own praxis of religious education as compared to the stereotype (M 1).

With younger children and a limited time frame (e.g., in a fifty-minute parish program class), it may be enough to begin with a bold and engaging opening statement. I've begun a third-grade lesson on "Jesus is our friend" by simply saying, "Today we're going to talk about the best friend you'll ever have in life, the one who will always be your friend." This got their interest. After another sentence or two, I began to elicit from them what it means to have a best friend. I invited them to draw themselves with a friend, to talk about their drawing and their friendships (M 1), and the movements flowed on from there.

In Chapter 8, I said that *life to Faith to life* is tantamount to combining the experiential and kerygmatic approaches to catechesis. Recently I was asked the question, "Can you begin with the kerygma?" My response is yes, when it helps to establish the generative theme. In fact, with youth and adult groups, I often begin by "borrowing" from M 3 (Christian Story and Vision) a brief summary crafted to highlight how vital a theme is to our lives and why it is in our own best interest to pay attention to it.

For example, I've begun an undergraduate class on God with a summary such as: "The most foundational aspect of our lives in faith is our image or understanding of God." I went on to say a little more with regard to how we all have our own image and why our "God" is so vital. I offered examples of the effects of both life-giving and debilitating images of God. Having established the theme and the centrality of it to the students' lives, I then posed a question or questioning activity that invited them to express their own image, understanding, or felt sense of who God is in their lives (M 1), flowing on into where or who or what had shaped their God image (M 2). If "borrowing" from M 3 as a FA, the key is not to fall back into the old pattern of a lot of presentation first and then, "Are there any questions?"

When this approach is used across a number of meetings (e.g., my undergraduate theology course could take a month for a full unit on God), some meetings might be more presentation than conversation. Yet each class would require a Focusing Act to revive people's interest or to establish a subtheme. Also, on a day of heavy presentation, there should be frequent pauses for M 4 and M 5 questions to dip in regularly for appropriation and decision.

In a scripture study group with adults, the FA is often simply to have participants pause, center, and prepare themselves to listen with hearts open to the possibility that there might be a word of God for their lives through this reading. Oftentimes the facilitator explicitly invites participants to recall and, as comfortable, to voice the events and issues of the past week, the life that they are bringing to hear the text. Then someone reads the assigned scripture in a style likely to be listened to and "taken in" by the participants. M 1 follows with questions like, "What aspect of your life came into view as you listened?" "What rang true to your life now?" "What might be a word of God to your life, and why?" (M 2 dipping in).

Sometimes, however, that scripture group focuses on a common life theme first, something suggested by the text that echoes in their lives. Then, after naming and reflecting on the theme, they hold it in mind while listening to the text chosen. For example, in a recent session on the miracle of the loaves and fishes, the group leader read the text and then suggested that the group focus first on the "hungers" they experience at this time. Participants proceeded to identify the hungers in their own lives (M 1) and why they have such hungers (M 2), before moving back to the scripture reading and the wisdom it might hold in response to their hungers (M 3). They concluded by identifying the small supply of "loaves and fishes" that they can personally draw upon (M 4—suggested by a participant) and then how they might maximize them *for life for all* (M 5).

In parenting, the Focusing Act can be a question or issue that a child poses to us, as in the Santa Claus conversation with Teddy. Often we know exactly what to talk about, because the child has raised the topic with urgency, signaling that it is indeed "generative." Or the FA can be one that we raise in response to a discipline situation. "So it looks like you're having a hard time going to bed tonight. What's up?" Indeed, "What's up?" can often be enough to get kids to "name their present praxis." Everyday conversations can also offer generative themes from life or faith, which when pursued (and no parent can take on all of them all the time) can lead from life into sharing Christian faith and back to life again with renewed faith.

I've also participated in events in which a group assembled and began a conversation, and the generative theme emerged as we went along. This can happen in scripture study groups where the chosen text reflects many generative topics and one gradually rises to the top from the group conversation. There, the text itself is "generative" for people and keeps the conversation focused. In youth ministry sessions, participants themselves often want to come up with the generative theme—"What will we talk about tonight?"—and this should be honored. However, in faith discussions with adolescents, and actually with all groups, we often need some dialectic between participants' *felt* interests and what they actually should learn—what is in their *best* interest. Let me explain.

In Chapter 8, I described *interest* as both what people are personally interested in and what they should be interested in or need to know according to an acceptable standard. I think of a friend who teaches music in a junior high school. She begins in September by asking her students, "So what kind of music are you interested in?" She gets the current list: hard rock, rap, funk, heavy metal, and so on. By Halloween, however, she has them listening to Mozart and Beethoven as well. In other words, she honors their interests, but also gets them interested. The religious educator or pastoral minister has a similar responsibility to honor the interests of participants and to stimulate and deepen their interests in Christian faith.

Movement 1: Expressing the Theme in Present Praxis

The intent of Movement 1 is to enable participants to express themselves in response to the generative theme as they encounter it in their present lives. They can express what they do themselves or what they see others doing, their own praxis of the theme or what is going on around them in their sociocultural context. The key is that people "pay attention" to the theme as they recognize it in their lives and then that they bring to expression their own description and consciousness of it. Their expression of their "present praxis" of the theme can be how they do it, engage it, or observe it in their "life-world," what it means for them, their feelings about it, or their attitudes toward it. They can express their descriptions, perceptions, and assessments of it, what they know about it, or their commitments and values regarding it. In other words, the key here is to elicit from participants whatever their own praxis of the theme may be—as seems likely to be effective.

People's expressions can be spoken, written, drawn, constructed, or mediated by any means of human communication. The most obvious mode of expression is the spoken or written word. People can respond verbally to a question or engaging activity, and their response can be a statement, an analogy, an association of ideas, an opinion, a description, and so on.

In a sense, the dynamic of M 1 is always a question or a questioning activity of some sort, inviting participants to stop, think, and "name" somehow the generative theme as operative in their own lives. By a "questioning activity," I mean any exercise that draws people out in response to the theme, that gets them thinking and expressing themselves, sharing their opinions or feelings. In sum, then, the dynamic of M 1 is a question or questioning activity that invites participants to stop, think, recognize, and "name" (bring to expression) the generative theme as operative in their lives or situation.

For example, with adolescents in a session on Jesus the Liberator (M 3), M 1 simply asked, "When you hear the word *freedom,* what are some of your immediate associations? Let's make a list." Educators who are more creative and artistic may employ mime, drawing, painting, making a symbol, drama, dancing, or movement. I have some friends in Hawaii who have used this approach in Bible study. When the FA is the reading of a text, M 1 often invites participants to express what the text means for their lives through movement and gesture. Wonderful! I've never been this creative myself.

If using this approach to Bible study and beginning with a particular text as the focus, it is important to make the shift from a theoretical to a praxis way of knowing here at M 1. At times, this can be quite subtle. For example, "What does this text mean" is a more theoretical question. "What do *you* hear this text saying to *your life* at this time" is a more praxislike one.

It can be effective to have high-school or youth ministry groups "think, pair, and share" at M 1. This means first to assemble one's own thoughts in response to the question or questioning activity and then to pair with another person to share them. Even when adolescents don't gather into smaller groups, I've found it important to have a "wait" time (if only a minute) before having them respond to an M 1 question. This makes for more considered responses. Though I usually don't do so myself, I have teacher friends who like to call randomly on students. This move certainly keeps everyone on their toes and thinking, rather than sitting back and letting the extroverts carry the conversation. However, people should always have the right to pass if they are not ready to share.

M 1 can also be a group activity; for example, adolescents creating a collage or graphic expression of "the Church" that represents their own functioning ecclesiology. Then, as they explain their graphic, M 2 readily follows, inviting them to reflect critically upon their ecclesiology. What has shaped their sense of Church? Why do they see it as they do? What are some possible consequences for their lives?

Journaling can also be effective with adolescents, especially for more personal themes. Even if they don't share their journal entries, the conversation has begun at least with themselves (and perhaps God), and they know better what they think from writing it down. Then, as they listen, they will inevitably be in conversation with other stories and perspectives. Indeed, the student journal can be employed in all of the movements. It lends a sense of safety as needed, especially around sensitive issues.

With older students and adults, I've found it helpful to allow some writing time after the opening invitation for them to name or express their present praxis. The writing allows for clarification and is less threatening than immediately launching into conversation. Then, when thoughts are better assembled through the writing process, I invite them to join with a neighbor and to share their reflections. In large gatherings where people are new to each other and perhaps sitting with strangers, I often add (the first time), "Feel free not to *talk* to your neighbor; but I do request that you be willing to *listen*." This takes the pressure off of people feeling compelled to have something to say and having to say it. It even gives them permission not to join in at all. Most times, however, everyone does.

In parenting, M 1 is often simply, "Tell me about it." A child comes to you with a problem or issue. Rather than presuming to know well what it is, even if you do, it is better to have the child "name" it. So when Teddy says, "Dad, James and I are not friends anymore," rather than saying, "Oh, you will be tomorrow," because I've heard this before, or, "I think you should make up," it is better to say, "Tell me about what happened," and take it from there.

Typically it is the educator's function to pose the M 1 questions or questioning activities. I've also been in events, however, where the focusing prompted people to volunteer their own responses to the theme. Likewise, groups accustomed to this approach often begin to put M 1 and M 2 and M 4 and M 5 questions to one another.

In larger groups, everyone may not get to share at every movement. I've found that a few representative offerings are sufficient to get the general sentiments of the community into conversation. I've also learned the hard way never to force people to share. Even in situations where I might call on someone, I establish the guideline that all can feel free to pass.

Movement 2: Reflecting Critically on the Life or Faith Theme

The intent of M 2 is to have participants reflect critically together on the theme in their lives, on their own expressions about it, and to share this in conversation. As noted, critical reflection can engage reason, memory, or imagination and is often a combination of all three. People's reflections can be both personal and social, but again, all of our thinking is always a little of both. What we think is always much influenced by our sociocultural context.

Reason questions would ask people why things are the way they are, what causes them to be this way, what they think their meaning might be, why they think their own expressions are as they are, and so on. In short, any question or activity that encourages people to reason and probe more deeply into their present praxis around the theme is appropriate here. For example (and I will bring this through all three functions of reflection), in the lesson on "Jesus is our friend" with third-graders, in M 2 I've asked children, "Why do we need friends?" "How do we know when someone is a good friend?" "What are some things in us or around us (i.e., in the society or culture) that make it easy or difficult to be friends?"

Memory questions or questioning activities might ask participants to recall their experiences regarding the theme, to consider the origins of their present sense of it in their lives, or to recognize how their own social location or biography may be shaping the theme and/or their responses to it. So here, re-membering includes uncovering how people's various "memberships"—in different groups and situations—influence their praxis of the theme and their interpretation of it. I've used probing questions like, "Why do you think you think that?" "Where does that thinking come from?" and "Who or what influences your opinion?"

For example, with children and "Jesus is our friend," I've asked them to remember how they became friends with some best friend, to recall a good experience of friendship or one in which they were disappointed and what made the difference, and finally to share some of the traditions of their families with regard to friendship. Reason and memory reflections are akin to people coming to share their own *stories,* that is, what arises from their own biography in the world.

Imagination questions or activities invite people to recognize the likely consequences of the particular theme as it unfolds in their lives, to imagine what could be or should be done regarding it, and to consider how to work toward a desired outcome. Imagination also encourages participants to recognize their best hopes in connection with this theme and what they might do to achieve them. The key pedagogical task here is to have people imagine beyond present praxis, to recognize the likely consequences of their praxis and the possibilities it holds for them.

To this end, I often ask questions that begin with, "What do you imagine . . . ? What if . . . ? How can we . . . ? What are the likely . . . ? What needs to be changed . . . ?" In other words, whatever stimulates participants to think about the consequences—likely, preferred, or demanded—of their own lives in the world in connection with the theme is effective for imagination in M 2. Such expressions from people's imaginations are akin to their coming to recognize and express their own *visions.*

I asked the children, "What would life be like without friends?" or, moving toward faith language, "Do you ever imagine Jesus as your friend?" With this age level too, I often use an imagination question or activity to transition between M 2 and M 3 (Christian Story and Vision). On the other hand, I've often done M 2 with this age group simply by asking them to "tell a story" about the theme in their lives and then to imagine what lies ahead.

As an example of reason, memory, and imagination working together, I cite a class with first-grade children focused on the theme of forgiveness. M 2 was built around questions like:

> Tell about a time when you felt hurt by someone. How did you feel? (memory)

> Why do we sometimes need to say, "I'm sorry" to other people? (reason)

> How might people feel when we hurt them? How might they feel when we say, "I'm sorry"? (imagination)

So, depending on readiness, the key task at M 2 is to stimulate critical and creative reflection to help people come to understand and discern what is "going on" in their lives around the generative theme. Anything that encourages this honors the intent of M 2.

On occasion, I've prompted arguments and sponsored debates to encourage critical reflection. For the latter, it is helpful to put people in pairs, give them opposing positions on the same topic, and allow time for them to argue for one position. After a while, have the partners switch and take the opposing view. Finally, allow them to take their real position on the issue. I've done this with adolescents and young adults on controversial topics. This kind of "switch sides" debate can be done with a whole class as well; divide it into two groups, each with a position, reverse positions midway through, and finally have the groups decide on their preferred position. Such debating is also effective in M 4, after the encounter with Christian Story and Vision and at the beginning of integrating life and faith as lived faith.

In adult Bible study, I've often encouraged M 2 reflections with questions like the following: "Why do you think you're hearing what you hear from this text?" "What does it help you to remem-

ber?" "What invitations do you find here?" "What is your initial
sense of how it calls you to respond?"

Once participants have attained the cognitive ability to engage
in abstract thinking, we can encourage social as well as personal
reflection. For example, to encourage sociocultural analysis in Bible
study, we could ask about the social or cultural influences that are
shaping participants' interpretation of the text and what social consequences their interpretation might have. With such social analysis,
we're trying to uncover the assumptions, ideologies, and interests
that shape our public world and how they are influencing our understanding of present praxis—even our interpretation of the Bible.
Though it can sound complicated, sociocultural analysis of any
present praxis can be prompted by three simple questions regarding
the generative theme: "Who's making the decisions here?" "Who's
benefiting?" "Who's suffering?"[1]

With adolescents and young adults, I've found that insights or
statistics from the social sciences can also prompt social analysis.
Just to know how many people are homeless in Boston this winter
or how many people die every day from hunger or malnutrition
in our world can bring people to question what is going on and to
imagine what we might do to change things.

So critical reflection can look inward to probe the depths of one's
own consciousness and outward to uncover the systemic nature of
our public world and its vested interests. Also, in any group, the
dynamic of good conversation prompts further critical and creative
reflection. For one person to break through into critical reflection
can be a catalyst that moves the community conversation to a deeper
level.

Young children cannot do abstract thinking. Yet, as I said in
Chapter 8, "The tree is in the seed." In other words, the sooner
they start to reflect about concrete operational issues, the better. So,
although young children cannot really understand the universal law

of love for all people, they can readily learn how to respect other kids in their class or neighborhood who are different from them in religion, ethnicity, race, and so on.

In parenting, M 2 often calls for a bit of probing regarding what is said in M 1. The intent here is not just for me to understand whatever is going on, but for Teddy to recognize this as well. "So how did the fight get started?" (memory). "Why would you be so mad at James that you don't want to be friends anymore?" (reason). "What would you like to do about this tomorrow?" (imagination).

It would be very unusual for a teaching/learning community to pay equal attention to reason, memory, and imagination, both personal and social, on all occasions and for every theme. It is more appropriate that the group focus on whichever function seems most salient to critical reflection on the particular generative theme and occasion.

By the end of M 2, participants will have expressed and reflected upon what we might call their own stories and visions. They will have looked at their lives in the world with regard to the theme and their personal sentiments about it, remembered some of the sources and influences on their present praxis of the theme, both positive and negative, reasoned about their present praxis, and imagined some consequences and hopes. With this understanding of and wisdom from their own lives (their own stories and visions) in conscious view, participants are all the more ready to encounter and take to heart the spiritual wisdom of Christian Story and Vision pertaining to the theme and thereafter to integrate the two—life and Faith—into lives of deepened faith (M 4 and M 5).

For Reflection and Conversation

- What might be a generative theme in your own faith life at this time?

- How might you name it?

- As you reflect on it more deeply, what do you see as some of its sources or causes?

- What memories does it resurrect?

- What likely consequences or hopes does it engender?

- How might you bring this theme and your reflections on it to the wisdom of Christian faith?

- What might you find there? So what?

Movement 3: Re-presenting Christian Story and Vision with Meaning and Persuasion

The task in M 3 is to re-present to people's lives the teachings and spiritual wisdom of Christian Story and Vision around the theme. I reiterate that the Story and Vision are to be made present in a persuasive way and as meaningful to participants. The Faith should connect with their souls, make sense to their minds, ring true to their experience, and be an enticing way to make meaning out of life.

Whatever the symbol might be from Christian Scripture and Tradition—a dogma, doctrine, scripture text, sacrament, and so on—the intent is to teach it clearly, highlighting the truth and spiritual wisdom it reflects for our lives and the response it invites. As I mentioned in Chapter 8, sometimes in re-presenting the Story well, we also raise up the Vision. I've become convinced, however, of the importance of explicitly teaching the Vision. Christian religious educators know that they are always under mandate to faithfully re-present Christian Story around the theme. It may be our raising up the Vision, however, that helps to "connect" Christian faith with people's lives, that makes it meaningful and persuasive. As the Bible says, "Where there is no vision, the people perish" (Prov. 29:18, KJV).

Echoing examples I gave in Chapter 8, yes, teachers must teach the dogma of the Blessed Trinity, being faithful to its tenets, according to age and background. Then they must also raise up what it means *for us* and for our relationships that we are made in the image and likeness of God, who even within Godself and always toward us is a God of right and loving relationship. Again, while it is imperative to teach the story of Exodus, it is also crucial to make explicit the God of freedom revealed in that story, the liberation God intends for all who are oppressed, and the responsibilities that a people of God have for promoting justice and freedom. It is the Story and Vision combined that can bring people to recognize the great spiritual wisdom of Christian faith and its life-giving possibilities, far beyond anything that an exclusive humanism can offer. By teaching both Story and Vision we can educate in faith for its ultimate learning outcome—spiritual wisdom for life.

I reiterate that every Christian is entitled to have access to the whole Story and Vision of Christian faith. This requires a comprehensive and thorough re-presenting of its scriptures and traditions. For a comprehensive curriculum, we need to craft a scope and sequence that lends children and adults ready access to Story and Vision according to developmental readiness across the age span. This suggests a spiral curriculum, ever repeating while expanding and building upon what went before. Further, even at the kindergarten level, the Story and Vision that we teach should reflect the best of biblical and theological scholarship. We should never teach anything of Christian faith in ways that make it necessary for someone coming after us to deny it. So don't teach the accounts of creation to children as literally true, but rather as great stories that teach wonderful truths about who we are and who our God is.

I use the term "re-presenting" to highlight that M 3 first entails making present to participants the teachings and wisdom of Christian faith. The more ready, direct, and user-friendly access they can have to Scripture and Tradition, the better. Re-presenting also reminds us as educators that we must try to be "representatives" of the Story and Vision that we teach, walking the walk as well as talking the talk. I don't often use the term "presenting" Story and Vision, because this could imply that M 3 is always some kind of presentation—by didaction or lecture. Like every aspect of this approach, accessing Christian Story and Vision can be done in myriad ways.

In point of fact (honesty time), in my own teaching style, so verbally laden, I tend to teach directly whatever I think is to be taught at M 3. I do try to honor the canons of good presentation, namely, *engagement of interest, clarity of expression, logical sequence,* and *overall coherence* (making sense). I also try to use a pattern of speech that encourages dialogue within participants, inviting them to think about what I'm proposing and to discern their own positions and responses, often pausing to hear their answers and questions (M 4 dipping in). I often use phrases such as, "I'll be happy to hear what you think of this," or "I'm wondering if this makes sense to you," or "You'll have your own opinions about this, which we'll hear in a while."

In the example "Jesus is our friend," at M 3 I shared with the children how the disciples tried to keep little children away from Jesus, but Jesus welcomed, embraced, and blessed them. In fact, he explained to the disciples that they must become as children in order to belong to the reign of God (see, e.g., Mark 10:13–16). For Vision, I offered some suggestions for what it might mean for children their age to live as friends of Jesus, what concretely this would ask of their lives, the joy it would bring, and how people might recognize them as Jesus's friends.

In my public presentations and university teaching, I always have a summary handout of what I'm likely to say that I typically put up on PowerPoint. The latter keeps people looking up rather than down. The handout frees participants up from trying to write down what I'm saying. In these days of copying machines, transcribing teacher talk does not seem like a good use of people's time. I often tell them, "Take your own notes, not mine; I'll give you mine." Then people are more likely to write down what they're thinking and coming to see for themselves. Those are the most important notes of all.

At M 3, I also invite my university students to turn to the assigned readings of the day and often have them work in pairs, helping each other to uncover and highlight the summary points of the reading. I've found it helpful to have them read and explain to each other, taking a text section by section, and then reversing roles. In other words, one person says what she or he thinks the first page or section is about, and the other person checks the text for accuracy. Then they reverse roles for the next section, and so on. This can be used with high-school students as well.

People more imaginative than I have used a great variety of teaching methods to re-present Christian Story and Vision around a particular theme. I've seen demonstrations (in a fifth-grade class on baptism, they simulated one), panel discussions, actual experiences (e.g., of centering prayer), storytelling, dramatic presentations, audio, video, and ICT resources, and the still and performing arts. I've seen a powerful sermon on the Gospel story of the woman bent over (Luke 13:10–17) presented as a dance. With younger children using an assigned text, peer teaching can be done by having them "read along," taking turns, and then pausing regularly to talk about and highlight the meaning of the text, helping each other to understand what is being taught and what it might mean for their lives.

We should encourage peer teaching and collaborative work

among students in any way possible. This can be done through the assigned texts or by sending people to the Internet or library to do individual or joint research on the Christian Story and Vision germane to the generative theme, and then asking them to share their research with the whole group.

Students also find *graphic organizers* and *mind maps* very helpful at M 3. The first offers a visual outline of the sequential ideas within an overarching theme, and the second, a clustering of ideas around a general theme. For example, a visual display of the whole paschal mystery—Jesus's passion, death, resurrection, and ascension, culminating in the sending of the Holy Spirit—can be a powerful graphic organizer. Likewise, when teaching "the Church," it can help to visually connect it to its associated ideas: Jesus, the Holy Spirit, the members, the leadership, the sacraments, and its role as a sacrament of God's reign in the world. Such a mind map can help people to see the big picture.

At M 3, it can be fun to do "jigsaw learning," especially with adolescents and young adults. This means assigning each group just a "piece of the puzzle" as its responsibility to figure out and re-present. Each group must then make its contribution to assembling "the whole story" for the wider group. Again, the faith narrative that runs from Palm Sunday to Pentecost is a great candidate for such an exercise. Teachers can also use jigsaw learning with a Bible story that has different characters and scenes, for example, the parable of the prodigal son. It can also be fun with both younger children and adolescents to present M 3 as a role-play, for example, a Bible story with people playing the different characters. A fine M 4, then, can be to pose the actors some questions about how they felt or what they learned from "inside" their character.

M 3 is an ideal moment for parents to share their faith. The key is not to be concerned about having all the answers to all the great ultimate questions that come your way (nobody has). As Jesus recognized, quoting Psalm 8:2, "Out of the mouth of babes" God brings forth amazing things (Matt. 21:16, kjv). This reminds that we can also *learn* wonderful spiritual wisdom and truths of faith from our children. Be open to receive from them. Meanwhile, it is fine to say, "I don't know, but let's look that up or ask someone." You can, however, always witness to your own faith; this is what most effectively evangelizes your children.

Parents need to be on the lookout for how to draw a faith perspective into both the great and everyday conversations. I recall again when Teddy asked that momentous question, "Daddy, how do babies get into a mommy's tummy?" I asked some M 1 and M 2 questions to make sure that he was really asking *the* question; he was. Then I first dwelt at length on a faith response. I talked about God as our loving Creator, who makes us in God's own image and likeness, and then takes us into partnership to create all kinds of things, even to procreate new people. I went on to say that this is why procreation takes place between people who love each other. Our God is love and people are the result of God's love working through human love. Only then did we get to the anatomy bits.

Regarding M 3, let me reiterate that I use the term "educator" with great breadth of meaning. First, the educator is the faith community, the Church. The term then includes parents with a primary role, followed by teachers, pastors, and pastoral ministers, volunteer catechists, and all who take seriously the baptismal responsibility to share their Christian faith. So, although it is the responsibility of the educator in M 3 to see to it that the Christian Story is re-presented and its Vision proposed, this can be the responsibility of any Christian. Every group and gathering for religious education, however, needs a person or people who see to it that the learning community has ready access to Christian Story and Vision. Likewise, the

Church is required to provide the educators it commissions in its name with good curriculum resources and the needed training to fulfill their catechetical responsibility.

Movement 4: Appropriating the Truths and Wisdom of Christian Faith into Life

A number of times I've referred to Bernard Lonergan's description of the dynamics of cognition, that is, what we *do* when we truly know something: we (1) pay *attention* to the data; (2) come to *understand* it; (3) reach *judgments* about it; and (4) make *decisions* in its light. Though Lonergan was building upon and could cite the work of many philosophers before him (e.g., Aristotle, Aquinas, Immanuel Kant), he insisted that we can find the proof of this dynamic within our own consciousness. In other words, think about it and you'll recognize that these are precisely the functions you perform when you really know something and especially as wisdom for life.

In Lonergan's terms, then, the Focusing Act with M 1 and M 2 invites people to pay *attention* to and begin to *understand* some data from their lives in the world. M 3 has them pay *attention* to and *understand* Christian Story and Vision as relevant to the theme. M 4 and M 5, respectively, complete what Lonergan would call the functions of *judgment* and *decision*. However, I prefer to describe the combined dynamic of these two movements (back *to life* again) as the integration of life and Faith into lived Christian faith. Such integration has two self-evident and symbiotic aspects: (a) to recognize and see for oneself what this Faith might mean for one's life (judgment), and (b) to make choices accordingly (decision). These are the sequential tasks of M 4 and M 5.

The intent of M 4, then, is that participants come to see for themselves what the teachings and wisdom of Christian faith might mean for their everyday lives. That wonderful moment on the road to Emmaus when the two disciples finally recognized Jesus captures perfectly the intent of M 4. Although it entails *cognition* (M 3, the instruction upon the road made their hearts "burn"), it is even more of a *recognition,* as when participants personally appropriate the spiritual wisdom of Christian faith and "see for themselves."

The pedagogy here is to stimulate and draw out what is really going on inside of people now—in response to the conversation and presentation of the previous movements. Can you remember a time coming home from a good lecture, seminar, or learning experience when your head and heart were spinning with thoughts, feelings, insights, connections, discernments, perceptions, recognitions, and dawning wisdom for life, and you couldn't wait to share this with family, friends, or colleagues? This is the "stuff" to be brought to recognition and conversation at M 4. It all comes down to asking participants, in one way or another, "In light of the conversation and presentation thus far, what are you doing now to Christian Story and Vision as you take them into your life, and what are they doing to you?" The key is to help participants recognize how they can take and make the M 3 presentation of Christian faith their own, appropriating it into their lives as spiritual wisdom and with personal conviction.

Again, M 4 can be crafted in myriad ways, as long as the questions and questioning activities encourage and draw out people's own appropriation of the teachings and spiritual wisdom of Christian faith around the theme. I've often done this simply by asking, "So what do you think now?" or "What are you coming to see for yourself?" or "So what's becoming clear for you?" and humorously, "So what did you learn in school today?" Responses to all such questions will often merge into M 5 as well; it is not easy or necessary to keep M 4 and M 5 apart.

In the *life to Faith to life* approach, we should not pose the same kinds of questions at the end—after the encounter with Christian Story and Vision—that we posed at the beginning. Although M 1 and M 2 questions and activities draw out people's praxis and have them reflect on their lives apropos the generative theme, M 4 and M 5 questions and activities are meant to bring people back to life again. Now, however, this is after their encounter with Christian Story and Vision, and the learning task is that they make it their own and put it to work in their lives. Where the distinction between the opening (M 1 and M 2) and closing (M 4 and M 5) movements can be a bit subtle is when an explicit faith theme is engaged from the beginning.

In the example I used in Chapter 8 of adolescents in a unit on "Who is Jesus?" recall that I brought them to expression by having them imagine themselves on the road to Caesarea Philippi and being asked personally by Jesus, "Who do you say that I am?" In response, they expressed their *present* praxis of Jesus. Then, after a theologically informed study of Jesus—his divinity and humanity, his preaching of God's reign and its radical law of love, his call to justice and compassion and what it means to be a disciple, his paschal mystery, which makes discipleship possible—the M 4 questions must ask, in one way or another, whether anything has shifted or broadened or deepened in their understanding of Jesus. For example, in a religious education context, "What's the best thing that you have learned or clarified from this study of Jesus?" or in a more catechetical or youth ministry context, "After this study, what might it ask of you to become a disciple of Jesus?"

Likewise, in a Bible study where the initial movements center on what the participants heard from a text for their lives, after the community conversation and deeper study of the text in M 3, M 4 has to ask, in one way or another, "So what is emerging for you *now* from this text?" "What has shifted or deepened for you?" "What response might it really invite if you take it to heart?"

In the example I've used throughout the movements, the children with "Jesus is our friend," M 4 could have them draw themselves with their friend Jesus, act out the gospel story they've heard, or imagine being among the children who went to Jesus and what he might say to them personally and what they'd say back, plus umpteen other possibilities. In my own praxis, and ever running short on time, I've asked questions like: "Do you *really* think of Jesus as your friend?" "How does that make you feel?" "What kind of a friend will Jesus be?" "What does that tell you about Jesus?" "What kind of friend might you be to him?"

Note well that this *is* different than simply asking, "Children, who is your friend?" They'd likely shout out, "Jesus is our friend," because this is what I just taught them. But M 4 does more than asking people to repeat what the teacher has said. It pushes beyond simple recall and invites them to see for themselves, to make it their own, and to appropriate into their lives whatever they've learned.

After a public lecture, I typically ask, "Now, have you any answers or wisdom emerging in response to my presentation?" I often add, "If you have questions, fine, but I'd prefer to hear your answers." I do this to avoid the usual format of lecture followed by "questions." Notice in such contexts how most respondents don't really ask a question; they have something to say, but craft their statement as a question, because the pedagogy has been so announced: "But don't you think that . . ." Though this may seem subtle, I think there is a significant difference and certainly different underlying assumptions between asking a group, "What are you thinking now?" and asking them, "Are there any questions?" In my undergraduate and graduate teaching over the years, I've fallen into a pattern at M 4 of inviting: "Write down something you agree with, something you disagree with perhaps, and something that you recognize as of value for your life or work" (again, with a shade of M 5).

In parenting, even when M 3 amounts to laying down the law,

it's important to allow children to respond, to ask what they think or feel about the stipulation, to let them have their word, and to take it seriously. In matters of discipline, we should check in with what they think of the consequences, to see if they recognize a correlation between the "crime" and the "punishment." We often ask Teddy to suggest what a "good" consequence might be for a particular infraction of rules. Of course, the best hope is to find a restorative one.

It is also important for catechists with younger children to check in at M 4 on what they heard in M 3. A friend teaching first-grade Sunday school thought she'd done a great job on the story of the Prodigal Son, but when she asked an M 4 question, "So what do you think of that Loving Father?" her kids said he wasn't loving at all, because he shouldn't have let the young boy go away from home in the first place. Good thing she checked!

Earlier I referred to conversation as what Plato called dialectics. By this he meant the give and take among people with various opinions that entails agreements, disagreements, and changing perspectives. This is very appropriate at M 4 and especially for controversial topics. To this end, it may help to have a debate as an appropriating activity, particularly with adolescents. Recall that this can be done with the whole group or in pairs, perhaps with the sides switching halfway through to argue the other way, and finally pausing for participants to decide their real positions (merging into M 5).

With adults, it can help at times to have designated respondents or panelists lead off an M 4 type response (*not,* however, to give a new presentation). When I've had teaching assistants in graduate courses over the years, I've asked them to be ready to lead off at M 4 and to model its intent. I instruct them to look out for the best wisdom they discern in that day's conversation and begin to suggest what it might mean for people's lives. This prompts others to follow in a similar vein of appropriation and recognition.

With regard to the intent of M 4 and M 5, I'm often asked, "What if someone rejects something that is integral to Christian faith?" First, people reject aspects of Christian faith all the time, regardless of the pedagogical approach. Second, there must be great freedom in people's coming to Christian faith; anything less is unworthy of the gospel and the example of Jesus himself. In his public ministry, Jesus called people to discipleship, but always with the right of refusal. In Chapter 1 we reviewed some explicit instances of Jesus's giving people the freedom to choose in their response to his invitation to become disciples. Some two thousand years later, Vatican II declared: "In spreading religious faith and in introducing religious practices, everyone ought at all times to refrain from any . . . kind of coercion or persuasion that would be dishonorable or unworthy" (Declaration on Religious Freedom, n. 4).

This being said, when people of sufficient age and with serious reflection clearly reject something that is central to the beliefs and ethic of Christian faith (e.g., the divinity and humanity of Jesus Christ or the call to social justice), then the designated educator has the responsibility to point out that they are placing themselves outside of this faith community. Assure them, of course, that they are still loved by God; that's our Christian faith.

Movement 5: Making Decisions in Light of Christian Faith

Movement 5 gives people an opportunity to choose and decide how they might live in response to the teachings and spiritual wisdom they have encountered in Christian Story and Vision (or from whatever tradition is being taught). As with all human decisions, they can be *cognitive, affective,* or *behavioral,* or—most likely—combinations thereof. *Cognitive:* participants can decide about their beliefs or convictions and how what they have learned is helping them to make meaning out of life. *Affective:* participants can decide about their relationship with God, especially their worship and prayer life, about their relationships with other people, and indeed about their relationships with themselves and with God's creation. *Behavioral:* participants can make choices about the morals and ethics, values and virtues by which to live their lives.

Even in situations where participants are not Christian (e.g., in many Catholic high-school religion classes), let all be invited to decide at least about what they can learn *from* the wisdom of Christian faith. In teaching undergraduate theology at Boston College for many years to religiously diverse classes, I'd often phrase the M 5 questions as, "What have *you* learned from this that you can take seriously in your life?" or "If someone embraced this position or practice, what would it mean for their lives?"

In all situations, M 5 must be an invitation; it should never compromise people's freedom or invade their privacy. As always, the invitation is to be scaled according to developmental readiness and the contexts and backgrounds of participants. Although third-graders cannot lobby Congress on global warming, they can practice and encourage their families to practice the ecological three R's, *reduce, reuse, recycle.* Likewise, the dynamic here must never force anyone to make or express a decision on cue! When I speak at conventions and large gatherings, I often simply end with an M 5 question that participants can take with them and decide about later. "So, over the next twenty-four hours, I invite you to decide . . ."

Every teaching/learning event should surely have a "takeaway." M 5 makes this an explicit aspect of the pedagogy. There is a certain momentum for it coming out of M 4 and, indeed, the two movements often combine or overlap, as I said earlier. As with all of the movements, the learning potential is enhanced by the conversation of the group; likewise here in M 5 participants will inspire each other by their decisions. Even when I work with young children, my own faith has been enriched by the decisions they can make.

Given the decision-making intent of this movement, the questions and questioning activities can be readily imagined. Educators can ask participants about their new or renewed convictions regarding the theme and teachings of Christian faith, how they might live its wisdom in everyday life, what practical commitments it invites from their lives or the concrete implications if they take it seriously, and so on. With third-graders and "Jesus is our friend," children can be asked how they will try to live and grow as friends of Jesus, what they will do because they are his friends, or to make up a prayer thanking Jesus for being their friend and asking to grow in the friendship.

Any question or questioning activity that is likely to encourage participants to make decisions is appropriate here at M 5. What people share as decisions should usually emerge from the conversation and presentation of the previous movements. So the questions or activities can invite participants to express their deepened convictions, renewed beliefs, new insights, best intentions and resolves, expanded commitments, possible strategies, concrete plans, and so on. And they can share them through any medium of human expression.

M 5 decisions are always personal in some way, made by each individual participant for their own lives. However, I've also been part of groups that have made communal decisions. Just as the Focusing Act can be an overt praxis, like a work of justice or compassion, so here the decision can be a personal or communal one for some particular Christian action. What an appropriate response to Christian Story and Vision. What begins with overt Christian praxis can end with explicit and renewed Christian praxis. As the *GDC* states well: "One must start with praxis to be able to arrive at praxis" (n. 245). Indeed, the intent of bringing *life to Faith* is always to bring *Faith to life* with deepened commitment to lived faith.

M 5 can also be realized by an activity within the teaching/
learning community itself. A powerful form of this is a shared
prayer or ritual. This can be crafted to remind of the generative
theme and to echo the previous movements, for example, repeating
a central scripture text from M 3, and then inviting and celebrating the decisions that people are making, with prayer for the graces
needed to carry them out.

With younger children in catechetical education, I believe there
is a place for memorizing the core symbols of Christian faith. I have
in mind the traditional creeds, the commandments, the sacraments,
the key doctrinal formulas (e.g., the Blessed Trinity), prayer forms
(e.g., the Lord's Prayer), moral codes (e.g., a consistent ethic for life),
and then some select scripture quotes (e.g., John 3:16, "God so loved
the world . . ."). Being able to call to mind such symbols can enhance people's personal prayer and their participation in communal
worship. It can also enable them to share their faith with others if
called upon or challenged.

The old language of "learning by heart" is still very helpful here.
The ideal is to know such symbols "by heart" and not simply "by
rote." Young people are likely to take these symbols to heart if their
memorizing comes at the end of a *life to Faith to life* process. Thus,
when something in the Christian Story and Vision of M 3 suggests
a symbol to memorize, M 5 is the ideal moment for doing so. Once
the symbol is well understood and its meaning appropriated into
life, students may actually come to know it "by heart."

For Reflection and Conversation

- What are some of the best insights or wisdoms you have come
  to see for yourself in this review of the movements of a *life to
  Faith to life* approach?

- What are some decisions emerging for your own faith life?

- Decisions for your function as an educator in faith?

Other Features of a *Life to Faith to Life* Approach

Flexibility: Although the sequence I've followed in this chapter is suggested by a *life to Faith to life* dynamic, it should never be a lock-step process. As I've said already, the movements have great flexibility and many possible combinations and variations. In practice, and depending on the topic, the distinction between M 1 and M 2 and again between M 4 and M 5 can be quite subtle. Oftentimes, to do one is to flow on into the other.

So I frequently combine the FA with M 1, engaging people with a generative theme and bringing them to some expression in connection with it. I've often combined M 1 with M 2. In fact, participants will often move instinctively to reflect critically on whatever they express or hear others express from present praxis. When this happens, welcome it rather than telling participants to hold off until later. Especially with youth and adults, I often briefly borrow from M 3 as a Focusing Act to engage people's interests, raising up the aspect of Story and Vision to be taught as of vital importance and consequence for their lives. Likewise, I often share from M 3 as the conversation of M 1 and M 2 unfolds. Oftentimes, the early conversation presents a compelling teachable moment for some aspect of Christian Story and Vision. When this happens, why wait!

I often do some of M 3 and then invite M 4 reflections, only to go back to M 3 again and then to M 4 again, many times over. I frequently combine M 4 and M 5, or they inevitably flow together. Sometimes the group conversation can bring participants back again from the closing movements to M 3 to review some teaching or wisdom from the faith tradition. Then implementing the decisions made in M 5 can become the FA for the next gathering of the same group. Depending on the theme, the process can become quite cyclical.

The approach is also very *flexible* in its time frames and locations. I've found myself honoring the commitments of all five movements within a five-minute conversation. This is often the case in parenting. In fact, five minutes is good with a fast moving ten-year-old boy. In undergraduate theology courses, however, I've also spread the movements across a number of weeks when the overarching theme (e.g., Jesus) warrants. In such cases, each of the movements will occur many times over; they go back and forth, seldom in sequence, and rarely do all five appear in every class.

Let me reiterate that I've used *life to Faith to life* in formal teaching settings from kindergarten to doctoral seminars, in adult Bible study and youth ministry events, in retreat weekends and faith-sharing groups, in preaching, and on trains and planes with strangers along the way. Even when making a public presentation at a conference, I attempt to honor the basic commitments of this approach, creating a conversation with and among participants.

Educator Commitments: The whole *life to Faith to life* approach and each of its movements asks some foundational pedagogical commitments of educators who would employ it appropriately and effectively. The commitments matter most and are needed throughout all the movements, rather than being limited to a particular one. For example, while actively engaging people is an *opening* commitment in the FA, the educator must maintain that engagement and interest *throughout* the movements.

The overarching pedagogical commitments are as follows: to create a teaching/learning *community* of *participation* and *conversation,* to give people *persuasive* and *meaningful* access to a *faithful*

re-presentation of Christian Story and Vision, and to enable participants *to integrate* their lives and their faith into a *faith that is lived,
living, and life-giving* for themselves and for the life of the word.
After that, each movement reflects its own particular commitment,
which frequently reaches into other movements as well. These commitments are asked first of the educator, but as groups become accustomed to such a process, participants can also take them on.

- The Focusing Act reflects a commitment *to actively engage* participants in the teaching/learning dynamic and to have them
  turn to something generative for their lives—of real interest—
  that can find echo in and be enlightened by the teachings and
  spiritual wisdom of Christian faith.

- Movement 1 reflects a commitment to have people *pay attention*
  to their own lives in the world and to *express* their present praxis
  with regard to the generative theme.

- Movement 2 reflects the commitment to promote *critical reflection,* encouraging people to think for themselves, personally and
  socially, to question and probe, and to reason, remember, and
  imagine about the theme as reflected in their present praxis.

- Movement 3 requires commitment to give people persuasive,
  meaningful, and faithful *access to the Story and Vision* of Christian faith, highlighting its wisdom for life for all.

- Movement 4 asks the educator's commitment to push beyond
  understanding and encourage people *to appropriate* as their
  own the teachings and wisdom of Christian faith and to recognize how they can bring them to bear upon and be integrated
  into their everyday lives and world.

- Movement 5 asks the educator's commitment to invite people *to
  decision*—cognitive, affective, or behavioral—to choose a lived

response to the teachings and spiritual wisdom they have encountered in the teaching/learning community and through Christian Story and Vision.

I say that the commitments outrank the movements because, in varied ways, they need to be present throughout the whole process as well as in their particular moves. So, as noted above, getting and keeping people engaged does not cease with the Focusing Act, but must be maintained throughout the movements. Likewise, having people pay attention and express themselves about their lives in the world does not cease at M 1, but must echo throughout, and groups will often go back again to or recall later what was said at M 1. Critical reflection is not limited to M 2. Clearly M 4 and M 5 require it, and participants need to do lots of critical reflection regarding the version of Christian Story and Vision that they encounter in M 3. The accessing of Christian faith at M 3 should be shaped by the conversation of the opening movements and with a view to appropriation and decision in M 4 and M 5.

Regarding the commitments of M 4 and M 5, although appropriation and decision making emerge explicitly in the return *to life,* their intent is present from the beginning of the process, at least in the educator's head and heart. The challenge is to craft from the beginning what can be an entrée into the wisdom of Christian faith and then to re-present that faith in ways that make it more conducive for participants to take it back into their lives.

The Role of Questions: Over the years, it has become clear to me that the *life to Faith to life* approach rises or falls on the questions and questioning activities throughout. This is because the pedagogy attempts to draw out from participants their own reflection on praxis around a theme, to give them personal access to Christian Story and Vision apropos the theme, and then to enable them to integrate its truths and spiritual wisdom into their lives as renewed faith. Such is required if they are to become agents of their faith rather than simply its recipients, thus making them all the more likely to live it. In this light, to be clear about the intent of each movement can help the educator and the participants to imagine effective questions or questioning activities to pose in any given movement.

- The Focusing Act needs questions that engage people and stimulate their interest, turning them to pay attention to their own lives in the world.

- Movement 1 questions are to encourage people to express and converse about the theme as they encounter it in their present praxis.

- Movement 2 questions are to invite participants to go deeper into their present praxis, to analyze it, personally and/or socially, and to reason, remember, or imagine about it.

- Though Movement 3 is often more re-presentation than conversation, the presenter should pose questions to maintain attention and let the conversation of the opening movements shape the re-presenting of Christian Story and Vision here.

- Movement 4 is effected by questions and activities that invite people to recognize and see for themselves what this faith might mean for their lives.

- Finally, Movement 5 calls for questions that invite people to decide in light of all that has gone before, choosing how to respond—cognitively, affectively, or behaviorally—to the teachings and spiritual wisdom of Christian faith.

Postscript

Over the past thirty-five years, I have tried to do, develop, and describe a *life to Faith to life* approach to educating in faith. I'm still honing my art to do it well in the everyday challenges of parenting and as I continue to teach graduate students in religious education and pastoral ministry at Boston College.

We must never forget that our efforts to promote "faith on earth" succeed only by the grace of God. And yet, though it is always God who gives the "growth" (1 Cor. 3:6), we remember that God's grace works through nature—here, through the good efforts of religious educators. I ask no more for this approach than that it may enable teachers, parents, and catechists to make good efforts, indeed our best efforts in this great work.

If it does as much, then I make bold to hope that the fruits of this approach will remain, making a contribution that there may be faith on earth in our time and, thus, toward the time when the "Son of Man" comes again (Luke 18:8). If that prove true, then, according to the Gamaliel principle (see Acts 5:33–39), these good efforts will have been an instrument of God's grace, which cannot be contained or defeated. To God be the glory.

ACKNOWLEDGMENTS

It is my happy duty to thank Jim Bitney, who lent his invaluable editing skills to an early draft of this manuscript. I thank Roger Freet, my editor at HarperOne, for his initial suggestion that I write *Will There Be Faith?* and for bringing it to publication. I thank Ann Moru, who did an excellent job of copyediting. I thank my spouse, Colleen Griffith, for her unfailing love and partnership in life. I thank our beloved little Teddy, the joy of our lives, who has occasioned many of the parenting examples that I share here. He has also kept me humble about my own expertise and lack thereof as a religious educator where it matters most—in our home.

NOTES

Introduction: Will There Be Faith?

1. My title echoes a fine book by my colleague John Westerhoff, *Will Our Children Have Faith?* (New York: Seabury, 1975). Almost forty years later, the question now pertains not just to "our children," but to the whole Church and society.

2. Part III of my book *Sharing Faith: A Comprehensive Approach to Religious Education and Pastoral Ministry* (San Francisco: HarperSanFrancisco, 1991) reflects on the possibilities of this approach for different functions of ministry, including preaching, liturgy, and pastoral counseling.

3. I've written about this *life to Faith to life* approach more technically as "shared Christian praxis," beginning with *Christian Religious Education: Sharing Our Story and Vision* (San Francisco: Harper & Row, 1981). I expanded and gave a more in-depth description in *Sharing Faith* (1991). Readers interested in greater philosophical and theological underpinnings of this approach will find those texts still helpful. Here, however, I offer a more usable description of a shared Christian praxis approach, beginning with the shift in title—*life to Faith to life*. I also take into account the changes that have taken place in church and society during the past two decades and draw upon my deepened understanding of this approach, which has matured, I hope, with the years.

4. The research of Robert Wuthnow of Princeton University establishes that there is a growing religious illiteracy in America; see his *America and the Challenge of Religious Diversity* (Princeton, NJ: Princeton Univ. Press, 2005). Diane L. Moore of Harvard Divinity School echoes Wuthnow's findings and con-

cerns; see her *Overcoming Religious Illiteracy* (New York: Palgrave Macmillan, 2007).

5. Christian Smith with Melinda Lundquist Denton, *Soul Searching: The Religious and Spiritual Lives of American Teenagers* (New York: Oxford Univ. Press, 2005), 162.

6. See the Pew Report, *U.S. Religious Landscape Survey,* April 2009; available online at http//religions.pewforum.org/.

7. Charles Taylor's most complete analysis can be found in *A Secular Age* (Cambridge, MA: Harvard Univ. Press, 2007). His description of "exclusive humanism" begins on p. 19 and runs throughout. Taylor says that "disenchantment" began around 1500, and perhaps this is true in the history of ideas. For most of the population, however, my sense is that the watershed came much later, around 1800 and with the advent of the industrial revolution. Even since then, the conditions for belief have varied greatly from one context to another. I grew up in a 1950s Irish village, where an "enchanted world" certainly still prevailed.

8. There were some local catechisms throughout the Middle Ages. However, the first question-and-answer, easy-to-memorize summary of Christian faith was the *Small Catechism* written by Martin Luther and published in 1529. The phenomenal success of Luther's catechism prompted Catholics to turn to this tool as well. Thus, the "catechism era" for Catholics began during the Council of Trent (1545–63) with the publication of a series of age-appropriate catechisms written by St. Peter Canisius. The First Vatican Council (1869–70) encouraged "national" catechisms, which led to the publication by the American Catholic bishops of the *Baltimore Catechism* in 1885. The "catechism era," then, lasted at least into the aftermath of Vatican II (1962–65).

9. See my essay "Questions and Answers—Again—from the *Baltimore Catechism,*" in Thomas Groome and Michael Daley, eds., *Reclaiming Catholicism: Treasures Old and New* (Maryknoll, NY: Orbis Books, 2010), 163–68.

10. See Diana Eck, *A New Religious America: How a "Christian Country" Has Become the World's Most Religiously Diverse Nation* (San Francisco: HarperSanFrancisco, 2001).

Chapter One: To Teach (and Learn) as Jesus Did

1. The title of this chapter echoes the fine pastoral letter issued by the U.S. Catholic bishops; see *To Teach as Jesus Did* (Washington, DC: USCCB, 1973).

2. See Daniel J. Harrington, *Jesus: The Revelation of the Father's Love* (Huntington, IN: Our Sunday Visitor, 2010).

3. Congregation for the Clergy, *General Directory for Catechesis* (Washington, DC: USCCB, 1998).

Chapter Two: Who Is Involved Here? Great People, Every One

1. It is significant that the Lutheran and Catholic Churches have officially reached theological agreement on this issue; see the "Joint Declaration on Justification," *Origins* 28 (July 14, 1998): 120–32.
2. Daniel Harrington, *Jesus as the Revelation of the Father's Love* (Huntington, IN: Our Sunday Visitor, 2010), 9.
3. This contemporary scholarship has been spearheaded, in large part, by women theologians. See, for example, Catherine Mowry LaCugna, *God for Us: The Trinity in Christian Life* (San Francisco: HarperSanFrancisco, 1992); and Elizabeth A Johnson, *She Who Is: The Mystery of God in Feminist Theological Discourse* (New York: Crossroad, 1992).
4. See Charles Taylor, *A Secular Age* (Cambridge, MA: Harvard Univ. Press, 2007), 37–42 and passim. Taylor contrasts the "buffered self" with a "porous self," the latter being open to relationships and their influence, including with the spiritual realm.
5. Horace Bushnell, *Christian Nurture* (New Haven, CT: Yale Univ. Press, 1967), 4.
6. Quotations from the documents of Vatican II are taken from Walter M. Abbott, ed., *Documents of Vatican II* (New York: America Press, 1966).
7. See James Fowler, *Stages of Faith* (San Francisco: Harper & Row, 1981).
8. See Thomas Groome, *Sharing Faith* (San Francisco: HarperSanFrancisco, 1991), especially chap. 12, for harnessing the faith education potential of liturgy.
9. We find evidence of this in the *Didache,* a first-century document and one of the first on catechesis—outside of the New Testament—in the history of the Church. See *The Didache,* trans. James A. Kleist, in *Ancient Christian Writers,* vol. 6 (Westminster, MD: Newman, 1948).

Chapter Three: What Faith and Why Educate?

1. I first found these helpful categories in the work of Michael Grimmitt; see *Religious Education and Human Development* (Great Wakering, UK: McCrimmon, 1987).
2. John Dewey, "My Pedagogical Creed," in *Dewey on Education,* compiled by Martin S. Dworkin (New York: Teachers College Press, 1971), 19.
3. For a short summary of Dewey's philosophy of education, see John Dewey, *Experience and Education* (New York: Collier, 1938). For the core of Paulo Freire's approach, see his *Pedagogy of the Oppressed* (New York: Seabury, 1970).
4. See Confucius, *The Analects* (New York: Dover, 1995), e.g., bk. 2, chap. 21; bk. 12, chap. 5.

5. Vatican I, "Constitution on Faith," *The Church Teaches* (Rockford, IL: Tan, 1973), 34.

Chapter Four: Liberating Salvation with Justice for All
 1. Charles Taylor, *A Secular Age* (Cambridge, MA: Harvard Univ. Press, 2007), 26; see pp. 25–28 for Taylor's summary of why "exclusive humanism" has emerged.
 2. Taylor, *Secular Age,* 18.
 3. Athanasius, *On the Incarnation,* chap. 54, par 3.
 4. See Grace Jantzen, *Becoming Divine: Towards a Feminist Philosophy of Religion* (Bloomingdale, IN: Indiana Univ. Press, 1998).
 5. "Justice in the World," statement from the International Synod of Bishops, 1971, in Joseph Gremillion, ed., *The Gospel of Peace and Justice* (Maryknoll, NY: Orbis Books, 1976), 514.
 6. See Joseph Cardinal Bernardin, *The Seamless Garment: Writings on the Consistent Ethic of Life,* ed. Thomas A. Nairn (Maryknoll, NY: Orbis Books, 2008).
 7. For a good introduction, see Howard Zehr, *The Little Book of Restorative Justice* (Intercourse, PA: Good Books, 2002). See also Stephen Pope, "Restorative Justice as a Prophetic Path to Peace," in *CTSA Proceedings* 65 (2010): 1–16.
 8. *Catechism of the Council of Trent,* ed. John McHugh (New York: Wagner, 1923), 11, 15.
 9. Avery Cardinal Dulles, *A History of Apologetics* (San Francisco: Ignatius, 2005), 33. I highly recommend this masterful and scholarly account of apologetics throughout the history of the Church.
10. *The Works of Saint Cyril of Jerusalem,* trans Leo P. McCauley (Washington, DC: Catholic Univ. Press, 1969), 153, 159.

Chapter Five: Faith on Earth Requires a Village
 1. For an overview of Charles Taylor's threefold description of secularization, see *A Secular Age* (Cambridge, MA: Harvard Univ. Press, 2007), 1–20.
 2. Taylor, *Secular Age,* 530.
 3. Taylor, *Secular Age,* 38.
 4. Taylor, *Secular Age,* 299, 473.
 5. See Thomas Groome, "Parish as Catechist" in *Church* 6, no. 3 (Fall 1990). The other popular name for this movement is "whole community catechesis."
 6. See, for example, Dennis M. Doyle, *Communion Ecclesiology* (Maryknoll, NY: Orbis Books, 2000).
 7. See Clifford Geertz, "Religion as a Cultural System," in Michael Banton, ed., *Anthropological Approaches to the Study of Religion* (London: Tavistock, 1966).

8. The Rite of Christian Initiation of Adults is, in fact, much more a liturgical than an educational document. It outlines the steps to be taken in the process of Christian initiation and the "rites" of passage along the way. It offers no suggested pedagogy. The great leaders who launched the RCIA in the English-speaking world, people like Christiane Brusselmans and Fr. James Dunning, recognized the need for a participatory pedagogy to implement it. My own work on a "shared Christian praxis approach" (described here as *life to Faith to life*) was just being published (1978). They embraced this approach and recommended it throughout the RCIA movement. Thus, the *life to Faith to life* approach is well reflected in the way many parishes conduct their RCIA program today. See James Dunning, "Method Is the Medium Is the Message," in *Christian Initiation Resources Reader,* vol. 1 (New York: Sadlier, 1984).

9. Geertz, "Religion as a Cultural System."

10. For example, "Lord, receive our gifts in this wonderful exchange: from all you have given us we bring you these gifts, and in return, you give us yourself." *The Sacramentary,* "Prayer over the Gifts," fifth day in the Octave of Christmas.

11. I'm convinced that we must reclaim the sacrament of Reconciliation with some imagination (the Church has done so a number of times throughout its history). It has great potential in the work of peacemaking and reconciliation, not only within a person's life, but among families and communities. Every parish has its tensions and disagreements. An occasional communal celebration of Reconciliation could encourage all to reach for the "higher ground" of unity and peace—beyond the conflicts and tensions that beset the Catholic Church today.

12. For example, the *Little Rock Scripture Study,* now published by Liturgical Press (Collegeville, MN), is a very effective program with an engaging pedagogy and materials graded from beginners to advanced.

13. *Lectio divina,* literally "divine reading," is an ancient monastic approach that enables the word of God through scripture to gradually "sink in" to people's hearts and lives. It can unfold as follows. Choose a text of scripture, something fairly brief and engaging. *Lectio* ("reading"): slowly read the text; notice what stands out for you or seems significant. *Meditatio* ("meditation"): read it again; now pause and talk to God about what you are hearing. *Contemplatio* ("contemplation"): read it again; now listen to and receive what God may be saying to you. *Oratio* ("praying"): recognize and pray the deep desire of your heart. Some traditions add *actio* ("action"): ask what this study and prayer time calls you to do.

14. See James Fowler, *Stages of Faith* (San Francisco: Harper & Row, 1981). I summarize Fowler's stages of faith development in my book *Christian Religious Education* (San Francisco: Harper & Row, 1981), 69–73.

15. Training for implementing *Generations of Faith* is sponsored by the Center for Ministry Development, Gig Harbor, Washington. See its website, www .cmdnet.org.

Chapter Six: It's (Almost) All in the Family—With Help

1. Sunday school is usually dated from around 1750 and the efforts of one Robert Raikes in Nottingham, England, to establish a "school" of Bible instruction on Sunday mornings. It was aimed especially at slum children to prevent them from falling into lives of crime. Raikes began a movement that continues to bear great fruit in moral formation and religious education to this day. For a good history of the Sunday school movement, see Robert Lynn and Elliott Wright, *The Big Little School* (New York: Harper & Row, 1971).

2. The Confraternity of Christian Doctrine (CCD) was begun in Rome around 1560 by a Milanese nobleman named Marco de Sadis-Cusani. It did not become widespread throughout the Catholic Church, however, until Pope Pius X decreed in 1895 that it be established in every parish.

3. Horace Bushnell, *Christian Nurture* (New Haven, CT: Yale Univ. Press, 1967), 50, 4.

4. For an excellent work on the subject, see Richard Kearney, *Strangers, Gods and Monsters: Interpreting Otherness* (New York: Rutledge, 2003).

5. See Gustavo Gutiérrez, *A Theology of Liberation* (Maryknoll, NY: Orbis Books, 1973).

6. Heidegger introduced this notion in his "Letter on Humanism" of 1945. See Martin Heidegger, *On the Way to Language* (New York: Harper & Row, 1971).

7. See my little book *Language for a "Catholic" Church* (Kansas City, MO: Sheed and Ward, 1995).

8. See Thomas Groome and Michael Daley, eds., *Reclaiming Catholicism: Treasures Old and New* (Maryknoll, NY: Orbis Books, 2010).

9. The daily lectionary readings are readily available at http://USCCB.org. They can also be purchased in a monthly booklet called *Living with Christ,* from Twenty-Third Publications, Mystic, CT.

Chapter Seven: Catholic Schools as Educators in Faith

1. See Anthony Bryke et al., *Catholic Schools and the Common Good* (Cambridge, MA: Harvard Univ. Press, 1993).

2. See David Hollenbach, *The Common Good and Christian Ethics* (New York: Cambridge Univ. Press, 2002).

3. *New York Times,* editorial, Sunday, March 14, 2010.

4. This seems to be a consistent finding based on the results of the Assessment of Catechesis/Religious Education tests (ACRE), sponsored by the National Catholic Educational Association. See "Toward Effective Parish Religious Education for Children and Young People," a report from the NCEA (Washington, DC: 1986).

5. See Thomas Groome, *Educating for Life: A Spiritual Vision for Every Teacher and Parent* (New York: Crossroad, 2001).

6. The great twentieth-century philosopher Jacques Maritain wrote an educational philosophy grounded in a Catholic anthropology. One of his conclusions was that our very personhood gives us "an inner vitality" that enables us to be active agents in our own learning. See *Education at the Crossroads* (New Haven, CT: Yale Univ. Press, 1960).

7. Paul Tillich's work can be daunting for beginners. However, he develops these concepts in the very readable *The Courage to Be* (New Haven, CT: Yale Univ. Press, 1950).

8. See Jean Lechers, *The Love of Learning and the Desire for God* (New York: Fordham Univ. Press, 1974).

9. Alfred North Whitehead, *The Aims of Education and Other Essays* (New York: Free Press, 1929), 3, 14.

10. Langdon Gilkey, *Catholicism Confronts Modernity* (New York: Seabury, 1975), 17.

11. John Dewey, "My Pedagogical Creed," in *Dewey on Education,* compiled by Martin S. Dworkin (New York: Teachers College Press, 1971), 19.

12. See Augustine, "The Teacher," in J. Quasten and J. C. Plumpe, eds., *Ancient Christian Writers,* vol. 9 (Westminster, MD: Newman, 1949), passim.

13. See "Declaration on the Relationship of the Church to Non-Christian Religions," n. 2, in Walter M. Abbott, ed., *Documents of Vatican II* (New York: America Press, 1966), 662–63.

14. See Eliot Eisner, *The Educational Imagination* (New York: Macmillan, 1979).

Chapter Eight: Life to Faith to Life: The Foundations

1. Josef Jungmann's major work was translated into English as *The Good News: Yesterday and Today* (New York: Herder and Herder, 1959).

2. Note that my first book was entitled *Christian Religious Education* (San Francisco: Harper & Row, 1981). Even the title reflects my efforts to bring together both religious education and Christian education.

3. For a more in-depth review, see my *Sharing Faith* (San Francisco: HarperSanFrancisco, 1991), esp. chap. 2.

4. My quoted phrases here are taken from Clement of Alexandria, "Christ the Educator," in Kendig Cully, ed., *Basic Writings in Christian Education* (Philadelphia: Westminster, 1960).

5. Two of Augustine's writings combine to make these points. His essay "The Teacher" emphasizes engaging "the teacher within" the students. This can be found in *Ancient Christian Writers,* vol. 9 (Westminster, MD: Newman, 1949). His emphasis on sharing "the story of salvation" is a common theme, epitomized in his *City of God.* However, Augustine deals with it as an approach to catechesis in "The First Catechetical Instruction," in *Ancient Christian Writers,* vol. 2 (Westminster, MD: Newman, 1962).

6. Again, these are common themes in the writings of Thomas Aquinas. However, his short treatise "The Teacher" is a good summary. This can be found in Kendig Cully, ed., *Basic Writings in Christian Education* (Philadelphia: Westminster, 1960).

7. Comenius's classic work was *The Great Didactic* (New York: Russell and Russell), 1967).

8. For Lonergan, "authentic cognition" requires the knower to consciously perform all four activities of the dynamics of cognition. He describes them as *attending* to data, *understanding,* making *judgments,* and coming to *decision.* For a summary, see Bernard Lonergan, *Method in Theology* (New York: Seabury Press, 1972), chap. 1.

9. See my *God with Us* text for kindergarten (New York: Sadlier, 1982) and *Coming to God's World* (New York: Sadlier, 1988).

10. Its potential for other functions of ministry is well reviewed in Part III of my *Sharing Faith* (San Francisco: HarperSanFrancisco, 1991), chaps. 11–15.

11. John Dewey, *Experience and Education* (New York: Collier, 1938), 68.

12. John Dewey, *Democracy and Education* (New York: Macmillan, 1916), 89.

13. See n. 9.

14. Dewey, *Experience and Education,* 46, 82.

15. Alfred North Whitehead, *The Aims of Education and Other Essays* (New York: Free Press, 1929), 9, 1.

16. Paulo Freire, *Pedagogy of the Oppressed* (New York: Seabury, 1970), passim.

17. See Jean Piaget, *To Understand Is to Reinvent* (New York: Penguin, 1973).

Chapter Nine: Life to Faith to Life: The Movements

1. For this insight, I'm indebted to the work of Joseph Holland and Peter Henriot; see *Social Analysis: Linking Faith and Justice* (Maryknoll, NY: Orbis Books, 1983).

INDEX

abdad ("to cultivate and develop"), 58
Adam and Eve story, 57–60
afterlife, belief in, 125
American public education: Protestant values perceived in, 234; struggle with reform by, 235; "value free" attempts by, 234. *See also* Catholic schools
Amish, 136
Analects (Confucius), 96
Anointed One, 134
Anselm, 129
apologetics. *See* Christian apologetics
Apostles' Creed, 116
Aquinas. *See* Thomas Aquinas
Aristotle, 96, 268, 278, 324
arts (religious), 221–22
Athanasius, St., 129
Augustine of Hippo, St., 5
Augustine, St., 54, 97, 146, 181, 246, 254, 269
authority, teaching with, 36–37
Avery Cardinal Dulles, 148

Babin, Pierre, 267
baptism: communal bond of, 108–9; faith education responsibility following, 83–87; family's primacy as beginning with, 204; Vatican II as reclaiming radical theology of, 77
Barth, Karl, 267
behavioral decision making, 329, 330
belief: afterlife, 125; apologetics' demand for "unhesitating assent," 146–47; distinguishing between faith and, 26; faith as way of, 116; *lev* ("faculty of knowledge and belief"), 115–16. *See also* Christian values
Benedict, St., 207
Benedict XVI, Pope, 216
Bible: communal nature reflected in the, 64–65; give children and youth easy access to, 192–93; God's revelation recorded in the, 68; God's self-disclosure in, 284–85; Holiness Code of Leviticus 19, 33,

as guiding vision of, 255–56; spirituality of, 251–53; theological anthropology inspiring, 56–75, 239–41. *See also* religious education curriculum

Catholic politics: education inspired by, 250–51; promoting justice for all, 250

Catholic school curriculum: *diakonia* (well-being) aspects of, 258–59; *kerygma* (word/preaching) and *didache* (word/teaching) aspects of, 257; *koinonia* (welcome) aspects of, 257–58; *leitourgia* (worship) aspects of, 258; *marturia* (witness) aspects of, 258; values integrated into, 255–56. *See also* life to Faith to life approach; religious education curriculum

Catholic schools: examining *will there be faith* role of, 232–33; examining the values permeating, 238–39; international statistics on, 233; Pakistan, 231–32; promoting a politics of justice, 250–51; U.S. educational reform and impact on, 235; welcoming non-Catholic students into, 236. *See also* American public education

Catholic sociology: description of, 243–44; education inspired by, 244–45

Catholic spirituality, 251–53. *See also* faith

Catholic universality, 253–55

Catholic Worker Movement, 224

Challenger spacecraft, 160

Chesterton, G. K., 214

children: allowing their voice "at the table," 223; allowing them to respond to discipline, 328; grandparents sharing their faith with, 226–27; helping them to reflect about life issues, 316–17; parents sharing their faith with, 227–28, 322–23; providing access to the Bible, 192–93; students as being both adults and, 76. *See also* families

Christ of faith, 19–20

Christian apologetics: description of, 145–46; history of, 147–49; "new apologetics," 147, 149; of *Roman Catechism,* 146; "unhesitating assent" to beliefs by, 146–47

Christian Church: Body of Christ metaphor of, 108; educational system of Western world through, 97; terminology and meaning of, 17. *See also* Catholic Church

Christian community: baptism as communal bond of, 108–9; *didaskaloi* ("teachers") of first, 86; of disciples, 33–34, 65; family service as part of the, 224; *GDC* on Catechesis responsibility of, 84, 86–87; life to Faith to life participants of teaching/learning, 293–96; religious education paradigm of involving total, 162–67; role in teaching Christian living, 157; teaching for and through, 71–72. *See also* communal personhood; families; parish

Christian community functions: *diakonia* (well-being), 166, 184–88, 206, 222–24, 258–59; *didache* (word/teaching), 166, 193–98; *kerygma* (word/preaching), 166, 188–93, 206, 225–29, 257; *koinonia* (welcome), 165, 167–74, 206, 207–12, 257–58;

76–83; *who* is to do the educating in, 83–87. *See also life to Faith to life* approach; religious education

faith education assumptions: invite people to Christian discipleship lifestyle, 69–70; presume that everyone is responsible, 67–68; provide access to Christian story and vision, 68–69; teach dignity, equality, respect, 70–71; teach people for and through Christian community, 71–72; teach to convince of God's love and mercy, 72–74; teach Christian vision of becoming fully alive, 74–75

"faith-education consciousness," 163

faith education levels: *become* it as, 91, 92; learn *from it* as, 91–92; learning *about* as, 91, 92

faith education strategies: liturgy and worship instruction, 81–82; ongoing education for *habitus* of Christian living, 82–83, 107, 165; teaching how participation in parish or congregation, 82

faith education terminology: education, 94–98; religious and religion, 98–103

faith language: Christian values reflected by, 214–15, 217; using God-talk and, 228–29

false "gods," 100

families: *communio* ("communality") ideal reflected in, 207; community service done as, 224; definition of, 202–3; faith foundation through, 203–4; finances of, 223–24; incarnate transmission of Christian faith through, 205–7; nurturing the nurturers in, 229–30; personal

stories of discouragement told by, 2; primacy of, 201–2, 204; sharing faith stories within, 226–28, 322–23. *See also* children; Christian community; "domestic church"; home

family community functions: *kerygma* and *didache,* 225–29; *koinonia* (welcome), 206, 207–12; *leitourgia* (worship), 206, 218–22; *marturia* (witness), 206, 212–18

family prayer rituals, 219

Finance Council of parish, 171

Finnegans Wake (Joyce), 254

First Baptist Church of Los Angeles, 121

First Vatican Council (1869–70), 97, 116

Focusing Act (FA): definition of, 229, 303; general issues to consider for, 304–9; role of questions during, 337

form, *life to Faith to life* approach to, 12

Fowler, James, 79, 195

Francis of Assisi, St., 151, 172

Francis, Rev. James Allen, 121

Freire, Paulo, 13, 83, 96, 278, 286

Geertz, Clifford, 174, 179

gender inclusivity, 30–31, 217

General Directory for Catechesis (GDC): on Catechesis responsibility of Christian community, 84, 86–87; on Christian community role in Christian living, 157; on contemporary media tools to witness to faith, 176–77; on definitive aim of religious education, 101; on faith education modeled on divine pedagogy, 54; on family catechesis, 204, 205, 206; on

General Directory for Catechesis (GDC) (continued)
Jesus the Teacher, 30; on nature and purpose of Christian faith education, 90; on need for critical thinking, 98; on people as agents of their own knowing, 71; on "permanent catechesis" commitment, 52, 78–79; promoting a pedagogy drawing of people's life experience, 271, 282–83; on purpose of religious education, 105; on starting with praxis to arrive at praxis, 331. *See also* catechesis (*katecheo*)
Generations of Faith program, 170, 196–97
gentle sharing of faith, 85
Gilkey, Langdon, 248
glory of God, 74–75
God: covenant between Israel and, 108; creation myths and, 9, 57–60, 289; *cur Deus homo* ("Why did God become a person?") in Jesus, 127, 128–31; *daat Elohim* ("knowing God"), 118; glory of, 74–75; good news of God's unconditional love of, 3–4; grace of, 15–16, 60–62; greatest commandment is that we love, 285; *imago Dei* ("image of God"), 140; putting Israel on trial, 137–38; religion as centering life around, 99–100; saving Israelites from slavery in Egypt, 133–34, 284–85; *theosis* ("becoming more like God"), 76–77, 129, 131; "therapeutic deism" faith in, 8; *who* are we before, 56–66. *See also* Blessed Trinity; theological anthropology
God's grace: educators as needing to leave the rest to, 75; *gratia sola* ("by

grace alone"), 60; gratitude for God's covenant and, 16; helping us to discern, 285; kindness as instrument of, 73–74; life to Faith to life success through, 338; Paul on abundance of, 122; Protestant Reformation debate over, 60–62
God's jubilee year, 139
God's love: living faith in, 26–27; teaching to convince people of, 72–74; way of trusting in, 114–15
God's mercy: as effective therapy, 123; experiencing, 106; parish life consistent with, 185–86; teaching to convince people of, 72–74
God's reign: Catholic education guided by vision of, 255–56; Christian Story and Vision leading to, 291–92; as focus of Jesus's ministry, 22–23, 37–38; good news of, 3–4, 60, 124; many meanings of, 24; religious education for the, 105–7; as *shalom* ("peace with justice"), 23; as shaping *how* of religious education, 107; as ultimate guideline for curriculum choices, 24–25; work of justice as central to, 33. *See also* Christian Story and Vision
God's will: as being how we should live, 23–24; as fullness of life for all, 23
"golden calf," 72
Good News, 3–4, 60, 124
good Samaritan, 28
Gospels: clues about teaching as Jesus did in, 21–22; disciples as servant leaders, 33–34; on feeding the hungry, 46; on Jesus's inclusion of women, 30–31; Last Supper accounts in the, 42; Mark's Gospel,